Parents Wh KU-743-708 Alcohol

THE NSPCC/WILEY SERIES
in
PROTECTING CHILDREN

The multi-professional approach

Series Editors: Christopher Cloke,
NSPCC, 42 Curtain Road,
London EC2A 3NX

Jan Horwath,
Department of Sociological Studies,
University of Sheffield,
Sheffield S10 2TU

Peter Sidebotham,
Warwick Medical School,
University of Warwick,
Coventry CV4 7AL

This NSPCC/Wiley series explores current issues relating to the prevention of child abuse and the protection of children. The series aims to publish titles that focus on professional practice and policy, and the practical application of research. The books are leading edge and innovative and reflect a multi-disciplinary and inter-agency approach to the prevention of child abuse and the protection of children.

All books have a policy or practice orientation with referenced information from theory and research. The series is essential reading for all professionals and researchers concerned with the prevention of child abuse and the protection of children.

Parents Who Misuse Drugs and Alcohol

Effective Interventions in Social Work and Child Protection

DONALD FORRESTER

Director, Tilda Goldberg Centre, University of Bedfordshire

and

JUDITH HARWIN

Director, Centre for Child and Youth Research, Brunel University

WILEY-BLACKWELL

A John Wiley & Sons, Ltd., Publication

This edition first published 2011
© 2011 John Wiley & Sons, Ltd.

Wiley-Blackwell is an imprint of John Wiley & Sons, formed by the merger of Wiley's global Scientific, Technical, and Medical business with Blackwell Publishing.

Registered Office
John Wiley & Sons Ltd, The Atrium, Southern Gate, Chichester, West Sussex, PO19 8SQ, UK

Editorial Offices
The Atrium, Southern Gate, Chichester, West Sussex, PO19 8SQ, UK
9600 Garsington Road, Oxford, OX4 2DQ, UK
350 Main Street, Malden, MA 02148-5020, USA

For details of our global editorial offices, for customer services, and for information about how to apply for permission to reuse the copyright material in this book please see our website at www.wiley.com/wiley-blackwell.

The right of Donald Forrester and Judith Harwin to be identified as the authors of this work has been asserted in accordance with the UK Copyright, Designs and Patents Act 1988.

Library of Congress Cataloging-in-Publication Data

Forrester, Donald.
  Parents who misuse drugs and alcohol : effective interventions in social work and child protection / Donald Forrester and Judith Harwin.
       p. cm.
  Includes bibliographical references and index.
  ISBN 978-0-470-87150-8 (cloth) – ISBN 978-0-470-87151-5 (pbk.)
  1. Parents–Substance use–Great Britain.   2. Parents–Alcohol use–Great Britain.   3. Child welfare–Great Britain.   4. Children of drug abusers–Services for–Great Britain.   5. Children of alcoholics–Services for–Great Britain.   I. Harwin, Judith.   II. Title.
  HV4999.P37F67 2011
  362.29'13–dc22
                                                                                            2010033359

A catalogue record for this book is available from the British Library.

This book is published in the following electronic formats: eBook 9780470871522; Wiley Online Library 9780470977958

Set in 10 on 12 pt Times Ten by Toppan Best-set Premedia Limited
Printed in Singapore by Ho Printing Singapore Pte Ltd

2 2012

To Mum and Dad, Margaret and Duncan Forrester (D.F.)

To Brian, Tom and Sophie (J.H.)

Contents

About the Authors   ix

Acknowledgements   xi

Part 1   1

   Introduction   3

1   What is 'Substance Misuse'?   9

2   The Impact of Parental Substance Misuse on Child Welfare   29

Part 2   51

3   Parental Substance Misuse and Children's Services   53

4   The Social Worker Assessments   70

5   What Happened to the Children and Their Parents?   93

Part 3   117

6   Assessment   119

7   What Works in Engaging Parents Who Misuse Drugs
   or Alcohol?   143

8   What Works? Substance Misuse Treatment and Evidence-Based
   Social Work   168

9   Motivational Interviewing and Effective Work with Families in which
   Parents Misuse Drugs and/or Alcohol   189

10   Family Interventions with Parental Substance Misuse   201

Conclusion   216

References   229

Index   239

About the Authors

Donald Forrester worked as a child and family social worker in Inner London from 1991 to 1999. During this time he worked with many families in which there was parental substance misuse, and the challenges and opportunities involved in such work have become a central interest since he became an academic. Professor Forrester has published widely in this area. Since 2008 he has been a consultant for the Welsh Assembly Government, helping to develop and implement a radical reform of services towards the use of more evidence-based interventions. Professor Forrester has obtained research grants from a range of national and international funders over the last six years. Most notably in 2008 he led the successful bid by the University of Bedfordshire for a £1.2 million grant to set up the Tilda Goldberg Centre at the University of Bedfordshire. He is currently Director of the Goldberg Centre, which is one of the largest centres for social work research in the United Kingdom with 14 staff focusing on substance misuse issues in social work and social care and developing evidence-based interventions.

Judith Harwin is Director of the Centre for Child and Youth research at Brunel University and professor of social work. She has a deep interest in child protection and the ways in which public policy, service organization, law and practice can promote or constrain opportunities for the most vulnerable children to grow up in stable caring homes and to achieve their potential.

Much of her research has been devoted to the problem of parental substance misuse and the search for effective interventions in social work and related professions. She has recently carried out an evaluation for the Nuffield Foundation of a unique government-funded initiative, a Family Drug and Alcohol Court within care proceedings, and completed an EU 17-country study of children affected by parental alcohol misuse. She has published widely on parental substance misuse and child protection in the UK and international contexts. She has held grants from the UK Government, the Nuffield Foundation, OECD, UNICEF, the EU and World Bank on policy and practice relating to child protection, early intervention, family support and public care.

Acknowledgements

We would like to thank the many social workers, managers and administrative staff without whose cooperation the research at the heart of the book could not have been completed. We really appreciate the time taken out of very busy schedules, and the good humour and persistence shown by administrative staff in following up and identifying files.

The main study described in Chapters 3, 4 and 5 was funded by the Nuffield Foundation. The study benefited enormously from the patience and good sense provided by Sharon Witherspoon throughout the research. Numerous academic collaborators have helped to develop our thinking, but Jim Orford deserves particular mention. His thinking has influenced us profoundly, he contributed throughout the development of the research and he was kind enough to read a version of the first chapter – which was, of course, heavily influenced by his work.

The research described in Chapter 7 was funded by the Alcohol Education Research Council. We would like to thank the social workers who agreed to their interviews being taped. Not every social worker would (or did) agree to make themselves potentially vulnerable in such a way. Particular mention must also go to Laura Hughes and Ayesha Sackey for their assistance. Helen Moss, Sophie Kershaw and Laura were all involved in carrying out and evaluating the research and made a small piece of research most interesting and productive to be involved in.

Of course, there are many others who have helped develop our thinking or supported us in one way or another, including colleagues at Sussex, Brunel, Goldsmiths and Bedfordshire. Our thanks go to all of them.

Finally, we would like to thank our families, who lived with us and supported us throughout. Thank you.

Part 1

Introduction

This is a book about children affected by a parent's drug or alcohol problem. It is written to help professionals to develop best practice, but we hope that the book will also be of interest to policy-makers and researchers with an interest in this area, and to non-professionals affected by misuse of drugs or alcohol by a parent.

Until recently the numbers of children living with parental substance misuse was not clear. Indeed, there was very little British research in this area until the late 1990s and no reliable estimates of the extent of the problem. Based on more recent evidence it seems likely that between 1 in 10 and 1 in 14 children are affected (Advisory Council on the Misuse of Drugs, 2003; Brisby et al., 1997). Looked at another way, in the average classroom two or three children go home to a parent with a drink or drug problem. Recent estimates suggest that the numbers may be even higher. Manning et al. (2009) estimate even higher numbers of children living with parents who binge-drink. This highlights that parental substance misuse is not a small-scale problem that can be left to specialists (Department for Children Schools and Families, 2010); it is a common issue which every professional working with children or their families encounters on a regular basis. It affects every school and every youth club, every hospital and every community centre. Every social worker, health visitor, Children's Centre worker, police officer or other professional working with people comes into contact with families in which there is parental misuse of drugs or alcohol frequently – whether they are aware of it or not. There is also a host of non-professional adults affected by the drug or alcohol problems of parents. This includes non-misusing parents, aunts and uncles, neighbours and grandparents, who often become very involved either in supporting the family or caring for children who can no longer live with the parent with the drug or alcohol problem.

We have learnt far more in recent years about the impact that a mother's or father's drink or drug problem can have on children. Most of these studies have emphasized the serious harm that it can have on children's welfare.

Parents Who Misuse Drugs and Alcohol. Effective Interventions in Social Work and Child Protection, 1st edition.   By Donald Forrester and Judith Harwin.
© 2011 John Wiley & Sons, Ltd.

Children are more likely to be neglected or emotionally, physically and even sexually abused when a parent has a substance misuse problem. They are also at increased risk of a host of negative outcomes, including coming into care, becoming homeless, low educational attainment, emotional difficulties, behavioural problems, involvement in crime and developing an addiction themselves. Yet this is not always so. Many children survive and some thrive despite the adversity they grew up with, and we now have a clearer picture of the factors that make this more likely and the interventions that help children to achieve it. Later in the book we discuss in detail these areas. However, we start by considering the approach we take to the book at a more general level.

The most important general point we would stress is that throughout we attempt to focus on the needs of *both* the child *and* the parent. From the inquiry into the death of Maria Colwell in 1974, through a series of inquiries into tragic deaths through the 1970s, 1980s and 1990s right up to the report into the death of Victoria Climbié in 2000, the danger of being 'family-focused' has been highlighted (Brent, 1985; Department of Health *et al.*, 1991; Greenwich, 1987; Laming, 2003; Secretary of State for Social Services, 1974). Supporting 'families' can lead to the voices of the less powerful individuals within the family, usually children or women experiencing violence, not being heard and to their abuse becoming invisible. From the 1990s onwards this has led many to argue that child welfare professionals, and particularly social workers, should be 'child-centred'. Indeed, this is now the accepted approach within child and family social work.

We believe that for both pragmatic and ethical reasons this is not helpful. Pragmatically, achieving positive change for children generally involves working effectively with parents. This does not and should not mean collusion with parents at the expense of children's needs, or a failure to raise and discuss difficult issues or focus on children's needs. However, it does mean that effective work requires the worker to be aware of the needs of both the child and the adult, and that workers need to be sensitive to the parents' views and needs even when their primary concern is for the child. Reflecting on the findings of research looking at how social workers talk to parents, Forrester *et al.* (2008a) have characterized this as being 'child-focused plus' and suggested that it is an approach most likely to engage parents and thus to achieve positive outcomes for children. We explore further these issues in Chapters 7 and 8.

Yet this is not just the approach that is most likely to work, it is also important for ethical reasons. Working with families in which parents misuse drugs or alcohol involves working with two sets of vulnerable people – the children *and* their parents. Individuals with drug or alcohol problems tend to have serious psychological and social problems, many have experienced abuse themselves and most are deeply unhappy people. In any caring profession, workers have a duty to recognize this and to work sensitively with such individuals. We have a 'duty of care' that extends beyond the legal definition of the term to include a more general professional responsibility in the way we work with vulnerable individuals. While it may be tempting to simplify one's role and focus on just the adult or only the child we believe that this is not only ineffective but that it is against the ethos of all the caring professions. We should be sensitive in working with vulnerable people, because that is the right thing to do. Indeed, we believe that the ability to focus on both parent and child is one of the hallmarks of good quality practice and policy-making.

One of the key implications of this belief is that we spend a considerable proportion of the book discussing parental issues, despite the fact that the book is about children. Thus, the nature of addiction and problem substance use, issues in assessment and methods for intervention all borrow heavily from the literature relating to adults. We see this as an example of being 'child-focused plus' in that we are learning all we can about how to work effectively with these vulnerable parents in order to help not only them but also their children in the most effective way possible. A particular contribution of this book is that we spend much of it considering theoretically and in practice how effective interventions with adults might be adapted to be used by child welfare professionals. With that in mind it seems appropriate to consider the structure and content of the book.

STRUCTURE AND CONTENT

This book reviews the literature on parental substance misuse and presents findings from our own work in this area. In particular it considers a study, funded by the Nuffield Foundation and undertaken by the authors, of 100 families allocated a social worker and follows up what happened to the children over the next two years. Our initial idea for the book was that we would review the existing evidence, present our findings and then draw out their contribution to understanding issues in such families. With the benefit of hindsight we recognize that this approach was naïve. Our research does not provide 'answers'. It describes what happened to the children in these families and identifies some indications of factors associated with 'good' or 'poor' outcomes for children. We present our findings in Chapters 3, 4 and 5. This may be useful for informing assessments and developing policy. However, for us the research posed more questions than answers. In particular the social workers we interviewed were struggling with profoundly difficult dilemmas that they did not know the answer to. The descriptive nature of the research meant that we developed a good idea of the challenges they were working with, but could not state with certainty the best way of dealing with them.

Some examples of issues that emerged repeatedly included:

- When does the worker decide that enough is enough – that the risks to the child are too great to continue in the current way?
- How should professionals talk with and engage parents? In particular, how can they understand and work with the denial and minimization that is so common in these cases? And how can they raise difficult issues around drugs and alcohol in ways that are most effective?
- How can workers assess the impact of the substance misuse on the child? And how can they assess the future pattern of substance misuse? Indeed, how can they move from assessing the current situation to looking at what might happen in the future?

Our research does not provide answers to these questions. Indeed, there may be no 'answer' to some of these dilemmas, and the best we may reasonably aim for is well-informed and wise decision-making. Yet providing professionals and non-professionals involved with such families with the information they need to understand and work effectively with these dilemmas seems crucial. That is in part why we wrote this book.

A further change that arose as we were writing was a realization that many of the challenges that we were describing were structural and therefore required policy-level responses. Thus the book attempts not only to outline the nature of best practice, but also to consider the policies required to nurture and support such practice.

In order to address these areas the book is set out in three parts. In Part 1, we provide an introduction to substance misuse and its impact on children. Specifically, in Chapter 1 we look at what 'misuse' and 'addiction' are, and at the factors that influence the nature of misuse or addiction. This chapter attempts to bring together the many different issues that affect the nature of addictive and problem behaviour into a coherent framework. With this in mind, we structure the discussion around Jim Orford's theory of 'excessive appetites' (Orford, 2001). In Chapter 2, we consider at some length the nature of parental misuse, its impact on children and factors that increase or reduce the harm it may cause. We highlight in both chapters the complexities that researchers struggle with in these areas, for instance in defining terms or unpicking complex and interrelated patterns of causation, as we believe that these are issues that professionals are often struggling with in practice. One of the key issues arising from the literature is that we know very little about the extent or nature of parental substance misuse in the work of Children's Services. For instance, while many studies identify a high proportion of families affected by substance misuse, very few follow up what happens to the children and the interrelationship between the substance misuse and other factors in shaping outcomes for children.

In Part 2 we address this gap through a description of a research study that we undertook. In Chapter 3, we review the limited evidence on the extent and nature of parental substance misuse within child welfare work and then outline the issues in a sample of 100 families affected by parental substance misuse who were allocated a social worker in Children's Services. Chapter 4 presents the views of social workers on the families, with a focus on how they carried out their assessments. Chapter 5 describes what happened to the children two years after their referral to Children's Services, in particular, where they were living and how they were progressing developmentally. At the end of the chapter the key findings from the research, plus the questions and issues arising from them are set out. We are particularly keen to identify the difficulties and dilemmas that social workers and others had in working with these families. These inform the content and structure of Part 3.

With this in mind, Part 3 considers research and theories that might help inform professionals or non-professionals assessing families affected by parent/s who misuse drugs or alcohol. Chapter 6 draws on the literature to consider what is known about assessing the impact of parental substance misuse on children. It builds on the evidence reviewed in Chapter 2. A particular focus of this chapter is the issue of assessing risk of harm in the future. Chapter 7 looks at evidence about what is effective in working with parents who misuse. It presents evidence from recent research by one of the authors (Forrester *et al.*, 2008a) and provides practical suggestions for engaging and working with parents with drink or drug problems. Chapter 8 reviews the evidence about what works in treating problem drinkers or drug-takers. It addresses how research studies produce the positive impacts that they often do and the policy implications for normal services. In particular Motivational Interviewing is identified as a particularly promising approach for use in child welfare settings. Chapter 9 discusses Motivational Interviewing in some depth, including a critical discussion of the challenges and limitations involved in using it in child and family settings. Chapter 10 focuses on the limited number of services focused specifically on parental substance misuse where there are serious concerns about children's welfare.

The book concludes by reviewing the key findings of the preceding chapters. In doing so we consider the wider implications of the findings for practice and policy, and argue that parental substance misuse is essentially synonymous with good practice in the field of child welfare. This is not because parental substance misuse is such a common issue that it is difficult to imagine a competent practitioner not being able to work with it (though this is true). Rather, it is because the issues – of client resistance and child risk, of evidence-based practice and professional discretion, of communication around difficult issues and assessment in an uncertain world – apply to almost all the work that child and family social workers and related professionals undertake. As a result, learning lessons about what works with parents who misuse substances provides the opportunity to improve practice and policy responses across the field of work with vulnerable children and their families. In light of this belief we hope that you find this book to be of help in working with parental substance misuse, but that the lessons from it also apply across the range of work that you may be involved with.

1 What is 'Substance Misuse'?

INTRODUCTION

Even a cursory reading of the literature on misuse of drugs and alcohol reveals a bewildering array of ways of talking about excessive use of substances. Some authors write of 'drug addicts' and 'alcoholics'; others of 'substance misuse' or 'alcohol problems'; a few mention 'use' of substances. Behind these different terminologies lie different views about the nature of excessive use of drugs or alcohol. Understanding these different views is important for two reasons. First, it provides an important introduction to key issues within the field of addiction and problem substance use. Indeed, without an appreciation of the reasons for and significance of these different terminologies it is difficult to understand many studies in this area. Second, the terminologies involve different sets of assumptions, beliefs and values about excessive substance use. They therefore provide an important starting point for considering our own values and assumptions. For instance, a professional who calls someone an 'alcoholic' is – whether they are aware of it or not – making different assumptions from one who says the same individual has an 'alcohol problem'. Informed practice therefore starts with a consideration of the words we use and the models they relate to.

We have noted elsewhere the differences between some of the common words used in this field (Forrester and Harwin, 2004). Some key definitions are:

- *Drug or alcohol use:* This term simply describes use of a substance. It does not imply that drug-taking or drinking is wrong and is therefore useful if one wants to avoid being judgemental. However, it also fails to differentiate between problematic use and non-problematic use, or between use that the individual feels is out of control and use that is occasional and that the individual can control.
- *Drug or alcohol abuse or misuse:* These terms imply that the use is harmful. They refer to use of a substance that is associated with problematic or harmful behaviour, i.e. harm is caused to the user or others, such as

Parents Who Misuse Drugs and Alcohol. Effective Interventions in Social Work and Child Protection, 1st edition. By Donald Forrester and Judith Harwin.
© 2011 John Wiley & Sons, Ltd.

children, as a result of their use. This might range from liver damage to the family having no money for food because it was all spent on alcohol. These terms make a judgement about harm, but they do not imply addiction or dependence.

- *Problem drinking or problem drug-taking:* These terms are similar to 'misuse' or 'abuse'. It is important to note that the problem can come and go over time.
- *Addiction, addict or alcoholic:* These terms imply that the individual cannot easily control their drinking – they feel a sense of compulsion about their substance use. Addiction is a controversial term, with some authors feeling that it should not be used and is unhelpful because it has been associated with approaches that characterize alcohol or drug problems as an illness. This is discussed further below.

In general we refer to parental substance 'misuse' in this book, as the parent's use of substances appears to be contributing to problems for their children – and therefore seems to be more than 'use' – but is not necessarily a physical dependency or psychological addiction, although in this chapter we often talk of 'addiction', as much of the literature relates to this concept. We use 'addict' or 'alcoholic' to refer to individuals who feel that they have difficulty in controlling or abstaining from use of drugs or alcohol. Yet these terms, and the theories underlying them, require further unpacking if we are to have an appreciation of their potential significance in our work with families affected by substance misuse.

WHAT IS ADDICTION?

There are many definitions of 'alcoholism' or similar conditions (such as being addicted to a particular drug or drugs). Historically, the term referred to continued use of alcohol despite it causing the user health or other difficulties. More recently, medical definitions have sometimes referred to alcoholism or addiction as if it were an illness. Thus the American Medical Association defines alcoholism as:

> a primary, chronic disease characterized by impaired control over drinking, pre-occupation with the drug alcohol, use of alcohol despite adverse consequences, and distortions in thinking.
>
> (Morse and Flavin, 1992)

Such definitions should not lull us into believing either that diagnosing 'addiction' is straightforward or that there is widespread agreement about the nature of 'addiction' or 'alcoholism'. 'Addiction' is in fact a hotly contested term, with some academics denying that it is a useful label, while others see it as central to misuse of substances. Indeed, the ICD-10 (a manual defining medical conditions) has no entry for 'alcoholism', but instead defines 'dependence syndrome'. This refers to behavioural, cognitive and physiological phenomena that may develop after repeated substance use. Typically, these include:

- a strong desire to take the drug;
- impaired control over its use;
- persistent use despite its harmful consequences;
- a higher priority given to drug use than to other activities and obligations;
- increased tolerance;
- a physical withdrawal reaction when drug use is discontinued.

In ICD-I0, the diagnosis of dependence syndrome is made if three or more of these have been experienced within a year. The syndrome may relate to a specific substance (e.g. heroin or alcohol), a class of substances (e.g. opioids) or a wider range of pharmacologically different substances (World Health Organization, 2007a and b). However, it is worth noting that even this medical definition does not rely primarily on physical symptoms.

Gifford and Humphrey (2007), in a recent review of the evidence on alcoholism, highlight the contested and uncertain nature of addiction when they contend that: '"Addiction" is a hypothesis, namely that a cluster of correlated phenomena are linked by an underlying process' (p. 352). What do they mean by this? Essentially, that similar behaviours are grouped together and studied as 'addiction', but that we do not currently know that these behaviours are in fact linked. Thus, for instance, one can readily see similarities between the behaviour of people with drug or alcohol problems and individuals who gamble excessively. In all these instances individuals may exhibit many of the characteristics outlined above, such as needing more of the substance, feeling a sense of compulsion, craving when not satisfying the compulsion, and so on. Influential academics have argued that these behaviour patterns can extend for some individuals to a range of other problem behaviours. Orford (2001), for example, argues that sex, internet use, overeating and possibly other behaviours may act as 'rewards' and create 'addiction' for some individuals.

However, Gifford and Humphreys do not just mean that individuals can become addicted to a range of different things. Even for one substance such as alcohol, it has long been recognized that there are different patterns of addiction. Thus, we may describe a man living on the street who drinks constantly as an 'alcoholic'. His history may have included starting to drink very heavily from a young age and he may have had a pattern of heavy drinking for his whole adult life. On the other hand, a woman in her fifties may have always enjoyed drinking socially, but after the death of her husband her drinking might escalate until she feels it is out of control. She may be an 'alcoholic', yet the underlying processes involved in her developing a problem, keeping drinking and how she might best change may be very different from the man drinking heavily and living on the street.

Researchers have spent a lot of time and energy exploring factors involved in different patterns of 'alcoholism'. Some patterns may have more of a genetic link, while others appear to be more about individual and social factors. Fortunately for the practitioner working with a family (and perhaps also for the academics writing a book for them!), it is not necessary to explore this literature in great depth. Instead, we shall briefly review debates around the nature of 'addiction' and its causes and then summarize some key points from Orford's classic book *Excessive Appetites* (2001), which synthesizes different approaches to addiction. We believe that Orford's approach provides a comprehensive framework for thinking about substance misuse problems which is sufficient as an introduction to professionals interested in working effectively with families.

THE HISTORY OF 'ADDICTION'

Until comparatively recently alcohol problems were seen as primarily related to weakness of character – a moral failing, not an illness – and as a consequence the response was a moral one. The 'temperance movement' usually encouraged complete abstinence from the evils of drink (though there were elements that campaigned for controlled or reduced drinking) (Berridge, 2005). It had a strongly Christian basis, particularly in Protestant and Nonconformist traditions. They preached to drinkers and drunks, sometimes from wagons, which they encouraged those ready to change to get on (hence the expressions 'being on the wagon' to describe someone who has given up alcohol and 'falling off the wagon' for a relapse). However, the social elements of the temperance approach are often underestimated. Temperance campaigners saw alcohol as not just an individual but also a *social* evil. They publicized the harmful effect of heavy drinking on women and children, and on society more generally, and identified the brewers and other producers of alcohol as an enemy that needed to be curbed in the interests of society at large. In the United Kingdom, the temperance movement became allied with the progressive Liberal Party, while the Conservatives increasingly represented the interests of brewers (Berridge, 2005). While the language may have changed, elements of the arguments of the temperance movement remain alive in much academic and policy debate around how alcohol use should be managed today.

From the nineteenth century a new discourse emerged which characterized alcohol as an illness. This reached its apotheosis in Jellinek's *The Disease Concept of Addiction* in 1960. Jellinek argued that the most serious alcohol problems are best conceptualized as a disease, with a biochemical basis and an identifiable course through which the disease progresses. Jellinek identified five types of 'alcoholism' and argued that two of these were best characterized as a disease, as they involved a loss of control and inability to abstain.

The concept of alcoholism as an illness has become the dominant conception of alcohol problems over the last 50 years, particularly in the USA and in the public imagination. Thus, there has been considerable research attention directed towards identifying genetic factors associated with alcoholism or 'personality types' linked to alcoholism. Depictions of alcoholism in the popular press and on television also tend to use a disease model of addiction. Perhaps most importantly, the most influential professional group working with addiction – psychiatrists – have tended to accept and promulgate a disease approach to addiction (this is particularly marked in the USA).

The disease model was also embraced and promoted by Alcoholics Anonymous (AA). AA is one of the first, and is perhaps the largest and best known, self-help groups in the world. It is estimated that it has around two million members. It has been paralleled by similar organizations dealing with different problem behaviours. These include Narcotics Anonymous (NA), Gamblers Anonymous (GA) and Workaholics Anonymous (WA). AA grew out of the temperance movement. It was founded by Bill W. and Dr Bob in 1935. The early meetings were comparatively unstructured, but over time the movement has developed a sophisticated set of beliefs and structure. AA combines a belief in problems in controlling alcohol use as an illness with a feeling that the 'cure' for alcoholics requires spiritual conversion. These ideas were set out in detail in 'the book' which outlines the 12 steps of the AA programme.

AA has been enormously successful, and literally millions of alcoholics can testify to the positive difference it has made in their life. It was the first organization in the USA to provide help for alcoholics irrespective of their ability to pay. Help is available in any place and at any time – for instance, when the alcoholic feels at risk of relapse. In its true form it is non-judgemental and accepts that often alcoholics relapse many times before achieving lasting sobriety. Even if one rejects many of the tenets of the approach, there is much that can be learnt from AA about effective intervention in relation to alcohol or drug misuse.

Yet the disease model and the AA approach have been the subject of sustained critique, and in the UK the dominant model of addiction combines social and psychological elements, with the biological approach of the disease model being generally of subsidiary interest. There are a number of criticisms of an overly simplistic application of the disease model to addiction. First, there is evidence that social structures and policies can have a profound impact on levels of 'addiction'. The best known example of this is research which has consistently shown that altering tax levels on alcohol, or changing policies around its availability, has a direct impact on the number of individuals with a serious alcohol problem (Babor *et al.*, 2003).

Second, the pattern of illegal problem drug use suggests important social causal mechanisms. In the UK widespread heroin use emerged as a social phenomenon in the early 1980s. It was strongly focused in areas of high unemployment, which had emerged in part because of Thatcherite social and economic policies. This seems unlikely to have been a coincidence. Pearson (1987a, b), in his classic work *The New Heroin Users*, developed an analysis that highlights the similarities between the social psychology of heroin addiction and the role a job performs for most people. Work provides a reason for getting up in the morning, a structure to the day, colleagues, acquaintances and friends, and a structure of rewards for endeavour and punishments for failure. In a similar way, heroin addicts have to get up to generate money for their addiction, they then have to find and buy some heroin and finally they use it. In this process, they socialize with other heroin users and achieve a position within the group of being respected (or not). Pearson does not argue that high unemployment 'causes' heroin misuse; rather, he suggests that it creates a vacuum in the lives of people that heroin can fill. As he poignantly observes, in many of the estates experiencing severe unemployment the only people walking with any urgency were those with a heroin habit to sustain (Pearson, 1987b).

Pearson's account is particularly important for understanding the importance of the wider social context of drug addiction. This often applies to alcohol problems as well. Giving up alcohol or heroin is difficult for some individuals (though others appear to find it comparatively easy). However, once an individual has stopped using they need to find something to replace it in their lives. Relapse is in part about the issue of craving, but it is also about finding a life to replace the one based on the addiction.

Even more compelling evidence of the social contribution to the development of drug and alcohol problems is provided by research on the experience of American soldiers in Vietnam (Robins, in Royal College of Psychiatrists, 2000). Heroin was widely available and cheap in Vietnam, and many soldiers developed a serious addiction to it. Yet one year after returning to the United States 95% had given up, and most reported doing so with little or no difficulty despite the fact that heroin was readily available on the streets of American cities. The change in the individual's situation, the removal of the terrible stress of participating in a bloody war and the reinstatement of the social networks that existed before service in Vietnam seemed to be enough to reduce the need for heroin for most of these individuals.

These examples point to a social contribution to both the creation and the maintenance of addiction. However, there is also evidence of important individual factors in the development of addiction. Addiction has been shown to be associated with a variety of individual issues. There is some evidence of a genetic predisposition in relation to alcoholism, though the extent and nature of the link are hotly contested. Three types of studies have been undertaken to explore the extent of the genetic link. First, studies looking at adopted children have been used to explore the influence of biological parents compared to adoptive carers. For instance, children born to one or more 'alcoholics' and placed with families in which there is no alcoholic allow the contribution of genetic factors to be explored. However, there are limitations in this approach. The diagnosis of 'alcoholism' in birth parents can prove difficult, collecting accurate information from adoptive carers is also a challenge and the process of adoption may in itself be an environmental influence; being adopted is not the same as being born into a family, and this may influence the likelihood of a child developing an addiction. While care should be taken in interpreting such studies, they do show a genetic link to addiction (e.g. Bohmann *et al.*, 1981; Cloninger *et al.*, 1981, Partanen *et al.*, 1966).

Second, twin studies have been used to look for a genetic link to alcoholism. Twin studies compare identical twins (who are 100% similar genetically) with non-identical twins (who share only 50% of their genes). Broadly speaking these studies rely on assuming that higher rates of shared alcoholism (or other addiction) between identical twins are due to increased genetic similarity. In fact, this may not be true, as non-identical twins may have more different environments than identical twins, and more recent studies have attempted to take this into account. The findings from twin studies also suggest some genetic link for alcoholism (e.g. Kendler *et al.*, 1992; Prescott and Kendler, 1999).

Third, studies have considered family history and relationships. This approach looks at large numbers of individuals related in a variety of ways (full and half-siblings, twins, cousins, etc.) and then calculates the importance of genetic similarity in accounting for the development of alcoholism. Again, such studies tend to find a genetic component in the development of addiction (e.g. Harford *et al.*, 1992).

Taken together, these studies make a compelling case that there is some genetic link that results in an increased likelihood of individuals developing an alcohol problem. However, there are a number of caveats and limitations within the data that need to be taken into account. First, many of the studies that are often cited in this area have serious limitations and problems. For instance, some rely on small numbers, others use rather loose definitions of 'alcoholic' and most have limited information on the actual environments that individuals experience. Second, while the evidence for some sort of genetic link is comparatively strong for very heavy and early-onset drinkers, it is much weaker in relation to other forms of alcohol problem. In fact, individuals with early-onset and heavy drinking comprise only a minority of problem drinkers. Third, overall the genetic component does not generally strongly predict whether an individual will develop an alcohol problem. A fourth issue, which may contribute to this lack of specificity, is that the nature of the genetic link itself is complex; it is not a single gene such as in cystic fibrosis or sickle cell anaemia. It is more likely that there is a large number of predisposing factors that are carried genetically, which work in different ways. For instance, biological children of alcoholics may respond differently to alcohol (e.g. making it more enjoyable for them), they may be more sociable and they may tend to take more risks. Some of these may be genetically linked in a direct way between generations, while others may be broad dispositions that could be inherited.

A crucial fifth issue is that we are only beginning to understand the interaction between genetic predisposition and environmental factors. A couple of studies provide interesting examples of the complexity of this. Jacob *et al.* (2003) looked at the children of adult twins who had histories of alcoholism in their birth fathers (the grandfathers of the children). They found that if the twin had developed an alcohol problem, their children were at increased risk of doing so too. However, the children of twins who had not developed an alcohol problem were at no increased risk of alcoholism. This suggests that environmental factors are important in protecting individuals who may be genetically vulnerable to developing alcohol problems. Buster and Rodgers (2000) looked at family relationships in predicting the development of alcoholism in a large representative sample. They found small to medium genetic components. Differences between households had a similar impact, with most of the reason for individuals developing an alcohol problem not being related to variables within the family structure.

It therefore seems safe to conclude that there is a genetic predisposition for some individuals, but that this is mediated in complex ways through family experiences, environment and the society that the individual grows up in. Furthermore, to date the research on genetic influences has provided very little information to help in assessing or intervening to help individuals with alcohol problems. At present its significance may therefore be largely theoretical.

However, genetic elements are not the only element of individual importance in understanding the development of alcohol problems. Individual circumstances and histories also have a crucial part to play. Individuals with a drink or drug problem are more likely to have had histories of abuse or neglect (Velleman and Orford, 1999). In addition, somebody who develops an addiction of one sort appears more at risk of developing addictions of other sorts. Furthermore, there is some evidence of an inter-generational link between alcoholism in a parent and the development of alcohol problems (Velleman and Orford, 1999). This link is mediated in a variety of ways – there is a genetic element, however learnt behaviour, the influence of parents as role models and the impact of living in often unhappy households seem more important. (The interplay between risk and protective factors in influencing child welfare is discussed further in Chapter 2.) This can be seen as the opposite of the environmental protection provided by a non-alcohol misusing family that was noted above: children brought up in discordant families, particularly if one or more parents misuse drugs or alcohol, are at increased risk of developing such problems themselves.

In an attempt to synthesize these various findings Orford (2001) developed what he terms a social-behavioural-cognitive-moral model of addiction. As this is a rather unwieldy formulation, it is simpler to refer to it as Orford's model of excessive appetites. We think it a useful way of bringing together the wide range of research literature on substance misuse and addiction.

ORFORD'S MODEL OF 'EXCESSIVE APPETITES'

The theory of excessive appetites is useful for two reasons. First, Orford synthesizes a range of different evidence into a coherent theory. This moves us beyond debates about whether there is an 'addictive personality' or whether poverty causes addiction, towards a model that sees a place for both, probably in interaction. Second, Orford, in common with many in the addiction field, helpfully distinguishes between processes involved in defining what an addiction is, starting potentially addictive behaviour, becoming addicted, maintaining addiction and overcoming addiction. Each of these processes is worth considering. Figure 1.1 sets out these processes and some of the factors that influence them in a simplified version of Orford's theory.

First, the 'moral' element of the model is that addiction is to some degree socially defined. Over-indulgence in some behaviours (drugs, alcohol, food or gambling) is subject to social censure. Other behaviours (e.g. working, religious observance or spending time with one's children) rarely receive such disapproval. In addition, societies vary in what they consider acceptable or unacceptable. Thus, in the UK today daily consumption of two bottles of port would be considered to be an indication of probable alcoholism. In the seventeenth century, such consumption was considered perfectly normal (Barr, 1998). This suggests that society has a role to play in defining what is an 'addiction'.

Orford suggests that there is a range of activities which can become:

> so excessive that they spoil the quality of people's lives, seriously affect and give rise to concern among family and friends, are costly to individuals and familiars, attract terms such as 'addiction', 'dependence' and 'disease', and provoke the setting-up of mutual-help and expert-treatment systems.
>
> (2001, p. 341)

These activities include drug use, drinking, gambling, the use of a range of other substances, binge-eating and sex. Orford also suggests that other activities, such as internet use and some forms of criminal behaviour, may be behaviours of this type.

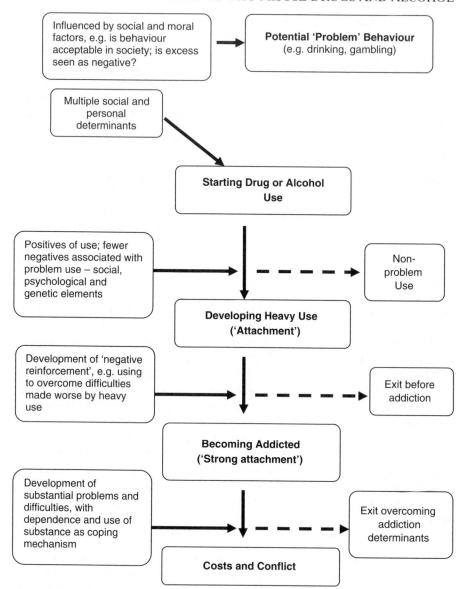

Figure 1.1   A simplified representation of Orford's theory of excessive appetites.

STAGE 1: TRYING OUT ALCOHOL OR DRUGS

A number of individual and social factors interact to shape whether people try these activities. Crucial social factors include whether there are opportunities and social approval for the behaviour. For instance, until recently women have drunk considerably less than men. In large part this was because they were prevented from doing so: it was socially censured and often men controlled the financial resources of the family. This is changing because today we live in a more equal society. Women have therefore claimed the right to the pleasures of alcohol use and their levels of drinking (and also illegal drug taking) are currently rising faster than men's (Alcohol Concern, 2004; European Monitoring Centre for Drugs and Drug Addiction, 2005). Inevitably, a growing minority of women are experiencing the negative side of alcohol and drug use: alcoholism, problem drinking and drug addiction. This is a good example of the way in which social changes can impact on patterns of 'addiction' – and is one of particular relevance for the impact of addiction on children. However, there are many other ways in which social context can shape individuals' exposure to problematic behaviours. Age limits for drinking and making some substances illegal shape availability and perceptions of substances (Babor *et al.*, 2003). Peer groups and older siblings can influence individuals in their attitude to a range of behaviours, including use of illegal drugs (Barnard, 2007).

Andrew Barr's *Drink: A Social History* (1998) provides a fascinating account of the ways in which social and political changes can interact to influence the availability of different substances over time. For instance, the extent of alcohol use in the UK has varied widely over different periods. The lowest levels of alcohol availability were recorded in the middle of the twentieth century, in part due to relative austerity and in part because of government controls put in place during wartime. With increasing affluence and liberalization of society, alcohol use is increasing – and alcohol problems are inevitably also on the rise (Prime Minister's Strategy Unit, 2004). Opium was used predominantly by the upper classes in the eighteenth and nineteenth centuries, but versions of it were widely available, and it was even an ingredient in 'gripe water' – a soothing elixir for babies! It was little used in the early twentieth century until a small number of addicts – generally related to the medical professions – were identified in the 1960s and 1970s. In the 1980s there was a massive increase in heroin use, and instead of being a problem for a comparatively small number of middle-class users addiction was concentrated in areas of high unemployment and associated with a range of other social problems.

Thus social factors profoundly shape the likelihood of an individual trying various substances or other addictive behaviours. How and why does drinking or drug-taking – or other 'appetitive behaviour' – move to becoming a problem?

STAGE 2: DEVELOPING HEAVY USE OF DRUGS OR ALCOHOL

In the move from trying drugs or alcohol to developing heavy use a range of factors interact in complex ways to provide either positive or negative reinforcement for a particular behaviour. Positive reinforcement is the reward that individuals experience from drinking or drug-taking. For most substances – or excessive appetites – there is an obvious reward. Thus, alcohol and drugs produce (generally) pleasant feelings of disinhibition or intoxication; there is the excitement of gambling or the enjoyment of eating 'forbidden' foods, and so on. Sargent comments: 'Few writers appear to have recognized that pleasure is a main motivation for the use of drugs, for they are too busy seeking a deficit in the individual ...' (1992, in Orford, 2001, p. 154). Negative reinforcement is the opposite of positive reinforcement, in that it is the relief or prevention of painful or unpleasant feelings, for instance helping someone to reduce the pain of bereavement or low self-esteem or depression.

However, crucially, individuals' reactions to substances vary markedly. This is easily illustrated in relation to alcohol, where after consuming a few drinks one person will become sociable and relaxed, another may become sleepy, while a third may be aggressive or act irresponsibly. The focus of much research by those supporting the 'medical model' of addiction has been to try to identify the differences between individuals in their response to substances and thus their likelihood of becoming addicted. In truth, even at this level there are important social elements that mediate individuals' reactions to substances. For instance, research has identified that in some cultures drinking alcohol is associated with relaxed socializing, in others it is more likely to be linked to aggressive or confrontational behaviour, while in some drinking is linked to religious rites. In these different contexts, individuals exhibit different behaviours related to similar doses of alcohol, indicating the role of social expectations in mediating the link between consumption and behaviour. Furthermore, in Western contexts individuals who are given a placebo (i.e. a drink that they believe to be alcoholic but that actually has no alcohol in it) generally behave in much the same way as those given genuine alcohol (see Hammersley *et al.*, 1992 for a discussion). This suggests that the socially created expectations of individuals and the situations in which substances are imbued have an important influence on behaviour.

Yet, while these social expectations are important, there are also significant variations between individuals in their response to any given substance (or other potential excessive behaviour). For a variety of reasons, related in part to the medicalization of theorizing and in part to the nature of funding for addiction research, individual aspects of addiction have been the focus of far more research than social and cultural factors. Gifford and Humphreys (2007) found 50 times as many articles relating to the keywords 'alcoholic' and 'personality' compared to articles with 'alcoholic' and 'poverty' as the keywords. Orford (2001) suggests that those likely to develop an 'excessive appetite' experience the behaviour in question, such as taking drugs, as more positive and causing fewer problems than individuals who are unlikely to develop an addiction.

The positive enjoyment associated with using drugs or alcohol was discussed above. However, substance use may help individuals to cope with negative emotions. Some individuals may have unhappy feelings that the substance temporarily mitigates or masks (there is a strong association between a history of abuse and substance misuse problems (Deren, 1986), and a probable link for some people with recent difficult experiences such as bereavement). On the other hand, individuals may experience fewer disincentives or restraints on use. This also operates on multiple levels. Socially, individuals may have less to lose through excessive consumption. Thus, people with happy families for whom they have responsibilities and challenging jobs that they enjoy are less likely to develop alcoholism: they have more to lose from excessive consumption. Some individuals find the negative side of drinking or drug-taking – such as the risks of being caught with illegal drugs, the hangovers or the 'down' after taking a stimulant – to be more important.

One way of conceptualizing this is that substance use and other forms of excessive behaviour provide individuals with a way of regulating their emotions. Thus, drinking and smoking, and some other addictive behaviours, may help individuals to reduce their stress levels; they may help as a form of 'self-medication' for painful or troubling emotions; they may help individuals to overcome low self-esteem, shyness or other social difficulties. In general, use of any substance tends to be associated with positive desired effects (related to pleasure) and to avoiding negative effects (for instance, coping with difficult emotions). It remains true that to date the best way of predicting the potential for individuals to start using a substance excessively is to ask them how much they enjoy using it (Orford, 2001).

Orford (2001) places little weight on genetic factors in the development of addiction. Indeed, genetic links do not appear in his book. Yet proponents of the medical model tend to emphasize individual differences at the biological or genetic level and, as discussed above, there is some evidence that they may contribute to the development of alcohol dependency. It seems likely therefore that some individuals have a genetically predetermined tendency to find alcohol more rewarding and/or to experience fewer negative effects from alcohol use. This plays a role in both individuals starting to drink heavily and in the development of an 'addiction', though only as one factor in a complicated series of processes.

STAGE 3: THE DEVELOPMENT OF 'ADDICTION'

Thus far we have considered processes that frame excessive behaviour, such as its social and moral context, and reviewed issues linked to developing excessive behaviour, such as heavy drinking or using illegal drugs regularly. Many of the parents whose misuse harms their children may simply be heavy or periodic binge users. However, for most there is a sense of compulsion and consequent difficulty in giving up, a feeling that is best captured by the concept of 'addiction'. What is the nature of the move from heavy use to 'addiction'? And what factors are associated with the move?

In most cases the development of addiction is a gradual process. It is something that needs to be worked at. This is not the general perception of addiction – particularly in relation to illegal drugs, but also for alcohol. In both the earlier drug education literature and popular culture there has been a tendency to portray use of illegal substances such as heroin, cocaine or crack cocaine as having the potential to lead swiftly to addiction. A wonderful – and ludicrous – example of this can be found in a notorious episode of the 1970s TV show *Starsky and Hutch*, in which Hutch is kidnapped by baddies who want to find out where his girlfriend is. The kidnappers hold Hutch and inject him with heroin over the course of a week. By the end of the week he is hopelessly addicted, indeed, he has been transformed into a stereotypical 'junkie', from the overwhelming desire for heroin to a pallid and unhealthy complexion. This episode was not screened in the UK until 1999 because of its drug-related content, however a more valid reason for not broadcasting it would have been its absurd depiction of drug addiction. The complex social and individual dynamics of addiction were ignored, and addiction was seen as something created by exposure to an addictive substance over a comparatively brief period. Central to the misunderstanding about the nature of addiction was the idea that withdrawal symptoms were synonymous with addiction. In fact, they are only one element of 'addiction'. Other, equally important elements include a reduction in other behaviours (such as non-drug-related socializing), which is linked to a prioritization of use of the substance over other interests, a more focused use of drink or drugs (to get a desired effect) and a feeling of craving when not using.

In stark contrast to the image of addiction suggested in *Starsky and Hutch*, Geoff Pearson describes the process of addiction to heroin as a slow and insidious one. He suggest that 'Heroin's advance is not like some sudden cavalry charge; more like the slow trudge of a foot army' (1987a, p. 63). Or to put it another way, addiction tends to creep up on individuals rather than coming at them head on. Each step on the path to addiction seems innocuous, yet the end-point is a sense of being trapped with behaviour that one feels one cannot control.

This development of addiction includes some important behavioural changes. First, it involves prioritization of use of the substance over other activities. This might start with individuals no longer engaging in other hobbies or activities and can end up with them neglecting their children and themselves in favour of their addiction. Second, the pattern of use tends to become the same every time – a change in behaviour called 'narrowing of the drinking repertoire' in relation to alcohol misuse. Thus, where an individual may have started by experimenting by drinking various alcoholic drinks in different ways, and may have then started to drink more heavily in certain situations, for alcoholics the pattern of drinking tends to become rather similar. An alcoholic will often be drinking to achieve a particular state – whether that is a certain level of alcohol in the blood that allows them to function as they wish to or achieving oblivion by drinking until losing consciousness. For instance, during the 1930s, Winston Churchill would drink whisky throughout the day and considerable quantities of wine at mealtimes. He then spent the evenings writing a series of books that won him a Nobel prize for literature, and campaigned tirelessly against appeasement of Germany.

The development of physical dependence is also part of the 'slow trudge' of addiction. It has two elements: the first is tolerance (more of the substance is required to achieve the desired effect) and the second is withdrawal (a characteristic set of symptoms associated with ceasing to use a substance). Jellinek (1960) identified the disease of 'alcoholism' as only being present when these characteristics were identified, and thus saw them as central to the nature of addiction. In particular, the development of tolerance leads to greater consumption, while the experience or possibility of withdrawal symptoms provide potentially powerful reinforcers for maintaining substance misuse. In effect, one is rewarded for continuing to drink or take drugs, while stopping provides the punishment of withdrawal.

However, dependence should not be seen solely – or even perhaps primarily – as a physical condition. Dependence is as much about the psychological belief that one needs a substance (or behaviour). Thus, many of the symptoms associated with 'dependence' can be found in those with gambling problems and other problem behaviours not associated with physical dependence.

The centrality of dependence to addiction is crucial to the conception of addiction as an illness. As such it has been hotly contested. Orford (2001) argues that dependence does not explain how individuals develop an addiction and thus become physically dependent, that for many overcoming withdrawal is not particularly difficult and that a focus on physical dependence does not explain why people so often relapse after having overcome their initial withdrawal symptoms. Indeed, in general overcoming initial withdrawal is considerably less hard than sustaining abstinence or controlled use. Indeed, this pattern of lapse (use after abstinence) or relapse (returned to previous patterns of behaviour) is a consistent feature of addiction, with many individuals having to overcome withdrawal a number of times before they are able to maintain abstinence or controlled use. In addition, there are substances or behaviours that clearly appear 'addictive' but that do not have a strong physiological dependence. One example is gambling; another is cocaine. Cessation of cocaine – and in particular crack cocaine – use has all the hallmarks of an addictive behaviour. However, there is not the gross physiological dependency that is associated with alcohol or heroin. This poses difficulties for models of addiction that place physical dependence as central.

In truth, the situation will vary from individual to individual. However, it is worth considering further the situation of those who consider themselves to be addicted. By this stage they will generally be making considerable sacrifices to sustain their alcohol or drug problem. They may have problems in their work or family; their children and relationships are likely to be suffering; their physical health may be affected; they may be experiencing legal problems; and they are likely to have done things they are ashamed of. This is not always the case – the example of Churchill was provided earlier, and he indicates that some alcoholics appear able to sustain high levels of dependent drinking with comparatively few problems. However, this is unusual. It is much more common for those on the outside to see the severe damage that the individual is doing to himself and to others. In such circumstances, it can be almost impossible to understand why they do not do something about the problem.

CONFLICT AND AMBIVALENCE

This leads us to a central psychological element of 'addiction', what Orford characterizes as 'conflict' and Miller and Rollnick (2002) describe as 'ambivalence'. Addicted individuals are likely to be acutely aware of all the negative effects that substance misuse is having for them and those they care about. However, they also have powerful reasons for continuing with the problem behaviour. This may be in the form of the rewards of their addiction or the challenges and difficulties of changing.

A useful way of conceptualizing this when working with an individual can be to use the 'decisional matrix'. This is a simple box with four sections. The top row is divided into the pros and cons of continuing as at present; the second row is for the pros and cons of changing (for instance giving up). In Figure 1.2 we have completed a box for someone addicted to heroin. The box is not meant to be a realistic illustration of how such a matrix is usually completed, but demonstrates the complex and conflicting feelings and thoughts that an addict may be going through.

In section 1 it can be seen that the individual is well aware of the problems that their heroin use is causing them and others. They list the loss of respect, sense of chaos, worry about the future and about current health, the impact on their children and the possibility of the children being removed into care. Yet they also see important positives about their heroin use. Their friends, contacts and indeed their whole life are structured around heroin use. Most importantly, using heroin makes the problems go away (even if this is a temporary effect). The quickest and easiest 'solution' to the problems in section 1 is to use heroin; yet this is precisely the behaviour that creates the very problems it is being used to 'resolve'. This paradox is at the heart of addiction.

For Laura, a 31-year-old White woman now six months pregnant. Laura is a heavy user of heroin and also smokes cannabis and takes crack cocaine. She has two other children, both of whom were taken into care.

1 Good things about using heroin	2 Bad things about using heroin
Helps me sleep.	The effect on the baby inside me.
Helps me cope with feeling anxious about the baby being taken away.	Might lose baby.
It is a world I know.	I can't look after my baby properly.
	Need money – so I shoplift and end up in prison.
	Live in fear due to debts to dealers.
	Move house a lot.
	Feel I am doing nothing with my life.
	Health problems.
3 Good things about giving up	**4 Bad things about giving up**
It would allow me to look after the baby properly and do something with my life.	Going through withdrawal.
Avoid all the bad things about using.	Is giving up best for the baby?
I could return to college.	Even if I give up will I keep off?
	Will social workers understand how difficult I am finding it?
	How will I spend my time? Who will I spend time with?
	How will I cope with bad feelings about my childhood?

Figure 1.2 Decisional matrix.

In sections 3 and 4 it can be seen that 'giving up' is not a straightforwardly positive option. In section 3, the removal of the problems identified in section 1 is supplemented by additional positives such as the possibility of returning to college and becoming the sort of mother that their child can respect. Yet in section 4 can be seen the very great problems associated with trying to

change. Withdrawal and subsequent cravings, a feeling that one cannot overcome the addiction and a fear of how one will cope emotionally and in structuring one's life are identified as issues.

The feelings of ambivalence and associated conflict at the heart of 'addiction' are central to understanding and working with people with a drink or
drug problem. From the outside (as seen by professionals or family members)
it can seem quite obvious what the person should do. The harm that drinking
or drug-taking is creating is clear, and the improvement in the person's life
that would result from stopping seem so self-evident that it is very hard to
understand why the individual does not change. This can be even more pronounced when the addict is a parent. Yet the addict is the expert on their own
addiction and they will know all the arguments for changing (or not changing).
However, the conflict they cannot resolve – the central ambivalence – is that
for the individual there are positives about their substance misuse, or negatives about changing, that make abstaining or controlling their use very
difficult.

One way of developing some understanding of this conflict is to think about
a behaviour that you know you should change, but have not changed. This
might include what you eat or the amount of exercise you do; it could be a
bad habit that you would like to stop or a new behaviour you would like to
start and stick to. Take a moment to complete a 'decisional matrix' for your
own behaviour.

The chances are that an outsider would not see why you do not simply
change. You should go to the gym/eat more healthily/stop biting your nails
or smoking or whatever change you need to make. But from your perspective
it is likely to be more complicated. You will have reasons why you do not
change, relating both to the positives about your current behaviour and the
difficulties and downside of changing. So, while you know you should perhaps
go to the gym or start jogging regularly, it may be difficult to fit it into your
busy life, you are tired when you come home, perhaps you have family responsibilities – and after all, the hour you spend watching TV is the only time you
have to yourself all day. And perhaps you think, 'I'm not that unfit. And
anyway, I have tried to go to the gym regularly and it never lasts more than
a week.' And so on.

These types of conflicts and confusions are more pronounced for an addict,
but they are not that dissimilar from dilemmas and ambivalences we all experience about making changes that we 'should' make but find difficult to. In
Chapter 8 we discuss at length ways of helping individuals to explore and, if
possible, resolve such conflicts. For now, the key point is that this type of
conflict is at the heart of addiction and it is not completely alien from the
challenges we all experience in changing 'problem' behaviours. Crucially, it
means that the individual with an addiction is an expert on their own situation,
for only they fully understand the pros and cons of continuing as they are or
changing.

This leads us to the final stage in understanding 'addiction' – how individual overcomes it. This issue is discussed in Chapters 8 and 9, which consider effective interventions and treatments for drug or alcohol problems.

CONCLUSIONS

This chapter has reviewed approaches to substance misuse and addiction. The differences between use, misuse, problem use and addiction were discussed, and issues relating to medical and social approaches to understanding misuse or addiction outlined. An attempt was made to consider the contribution of both individual and social factors to substance misuse and addiction. This was done through a discussion of elements of Orford's approach to the development of 'excessive appetites'. In particular, an attempt was made to differentiate between factors associated with starting the use of a substance, those linked to moving from use to heavy use and those related to becoming addicted.

Four issues stand out as being particularly important. The first is that the terminology used in relation to substance misuse problems reflects important conceptual differences in approaches to the issue. As discussed, there is a big difference between talking about someone having an alcohol problem and someone being an alcoholic, though the two may be related.

Second, it is useful to differentiate the process of developing excessive use into four stages: initial use, heavy use, addiction and stopping after addiction. Each of these stages is influenced by different factors. Crucially, factors that may have been important in moving from use to heavy use, for instance, may not be relevant for stopping or controlling use.

Third, an attempt has been made to highlight the importance of social factors in understanding addiction and problem use. There is a tendency to see addiction as an individual illness. Instead, we have argued that an interplay of individual and social factors is the key to understanding addiction. It is therefore more appropriate to see problem use or addiction as a psycho-social problem than as an individual issue requiring psychiatric or psychological treatment.

Finally, we have indicated the complexity of substance misuse. The development and maintenance of 'addiction' take place through a variety of stages, and at each stage an apparently bewildering array of factors may interact. Furthermore, for each individual the constellation of causal factors and the types of help likely to be effective are different. This may leave the professional or non-professional with a view to helping a parent with a drug or alcohol problem feeling confused. We hope that in later chapters we can provide useful suggestions for effective ways of working with parents who misuse substances. However, a sense of the sheer complexity of substance misuse may not be a bad thing. Understanding the difficult and interrelated nature of the issues when people misuse substances is a good first step towards being able to assess and intervene effectively. It provides a solid grounding in humility from which the professional can engage with the person who is most expert in their particular circumstances: the individual with the drug or alcohol problem.

In Chapter 2, the focus shifts to how the parent's misuse of drugs or alcohol can impact on their children and the factors that exacerbate or reduce the potential harm that it can cause.

2 The Impact of Parental Substan... Misuse on Child Welfare

In Chapter 1 the focus was on the parent and their drug or alcohol problem. In this chapter we move on to look at the impact that misuse of drugs or alcohol can have on children. It is obvious to anyone who has had contact with families in which parents have serious drug or alcohol problems that substance misuse can have a very harmful effect on children. This can take many forms. Genuine examples taken from the practice experience of the authors, with names and details changed to ensure anonymity, are described in Box 2.1. We use them to illustrate some of the ways in which substance misuse may impact on children and some of the complexities involved in unpacking the 'impact' of substance misuse. We shall refer to them at various points in this chapter in order to relate the theoretical issues discussed to the realities of actual children and their families.

Looking at the children described in Box 2.1 it seems obvious that substance misuse can harm children. Amy is directly affected by her mother's use of drugs during pregnancy and would be at risk of neglect if left in her parents' care. Jez is having physical, educational and possibly emotional needs not met, and we do not know what other risks he is being exposed to. Jenny is less obviously at risk (something we discuss below), however we do not know what the emotional impact of her mother's drinking has been on her. Yet, despite the apparent obviousness of the harm that substance misuse by parents can have on children, the research evidence for the link is less straightforward than might be expected. There is certainly a correlation between parents misusing alcohol or drugs and a range of negative outcomes for children. Thus, studies looking at prison, psychiatric or homeless populations find a high proportion had parents who misused alcohol or drugs (Velleman and Orford, 1999). Population samples suggest that children are at higher risk of neglect or physical abuse if a parent has a diagnosed 'addiction' (Chaffin et al., 1996; Kelleher et al., 1994). Children of alcoholics seem to do poorly at school and are more likely to have emotional and behavioural problems than other children (Velleman and Orford, 1999). The evidence is less strong in

Parents Who Misuse Drugs and Alcohol. Effective Interventions in Social Work and Child Protection, 1st edition. By Donald Forrester and Judith Harwin.
© 2011 John Wiley & Sons, Ltd.

Box 2.1

Amy is one week old and was born addicted to heroin due to her mother's drug problems. She was born four weeks premature and is very small. She is being cared for in a Special Care Unit at the hospital. Her mother and father have only visited her twice. When they did, staff believed that they were under the influence of drugs as they were swaying and appeared not to be fully aware of what people were saying to them. Staff on the unit believe that Amy is of mixed parentage, though her mother and putative father are both White. Social workers are applying to court for an interim care order.

Jez is a big, friendly 9-year-old, but his teachers are very worried about him. His school attendance is poor and when he does attend he is often late. Jez is not naturally strong academically, and his poor attendance and a perceived lack of support from home are contributing to him doing extremely poorly. Jez is White British of Irish origin and lives at home with his mother. She is part of an extended family with many relatives living in the area. His grandparents came from Ireland, but Jez's mother has always lived in inner London. Social workers have been involved with the family for some time. Often when they visit Jez's mother has appeared drunk and sometimes does not know where Jez is. There have been reports of him wandering round the estate begging for food. Social workers are becoming extremely worried and considering care proceedings.

Jenny is now 16. She comes from an affluent White British family and attends private school. She is doing well academically and has many friends at school. Jenny's father and mother divorced when Jenny was 11 and initially Jenny lived with her mother. Following the divorce, Jenny's mother started to drink heavily: she would drink until she lost consciousness most evenings. The family decided that Jenny would be better off attending school as a boarder. During school holidays Jenny lives with her father who pays for a nanny to do much of the care and she visits her mother at weekends.

---

relation to parental misuse of illegal drugs, in part because we have not been studying the issue for as long a period of time, but the indications are that some of these harmful effects may be even more marked (Advisory Council on the Misuse of Drugs, 2002; Barnard, 2007). There is also a strong link between a parent misusing drugs or alcohol and children being involved in criminal behaviour (Advisory Council on the Misuse of Drugs, 2002; Velleman and Orford, 1999), and there is a well-established relationship between a parent being an alcoholic and children later developing an addiction to alcohol or drugs (Prescott and Kendler, 1999).

These research findings highlight the likelihood that parental substance misuse is harmful for children. Yet the story is not as straightforward as it might seem to be. Deren (1986) makes the point that drug or alcohol addiction tends to be strongly related to a host of other factors and it cannot be assumed that it is the use of the drug that is causing the problems identified in children. Thus, at the social level drug addiction is strongly linked to poverty and deprivation, whilst at the psychological level individuals who misuse drugs or alcohol are more likely to have been abused, to have low self-esteem and to be depressed (Deren, 1986; Gifford and Humphreys, 2007). Even at the genetic level it is possible that some of the dispositions that led the parent to develop a drug problem may be contributing to their child having other types of difficulty. For instance, a propensity to require excitement and being involved in criminal behaviour may have a genetic element. It is therefore possible that it is these factors individually or in interaction, rather than the substance misuse itself, which are causing the problems. At the very least, the substance misuse is rarely an isolated issue, and disentangling its particular contribution can be virtually impossible.

This can be illustrated even in relation to one of the most obvious and direct forms of impact that drug or alcohol misuse may have on a child: the effect on a newborn child of a mother ingesting substances during pregnancy. Here we have direct exposure to potentially harmful substances via the placenta; it is hard to imagine a more obvious and direct link between substance misuse and potential harm to a child. One can see from the impact on Amy (Box 2.1) that her mother's use of drugs appears to have harmed Amy directly. Yet even in this situation the relationship between drug use and harm to the foetus is not straightforward. Drug addicts often eat poorly, they tend to smoke cigarettes and they often live in poor or inadequate housing. Women are more likely to be exposed to violence and some are involved in activities, such as prostitution, that may be harmful to their health and that of their child. Some studies have suggested that poor diet and smoking cigarettes rather then ingestion of illegal drugs are responsible for most of the harm to newborn babies (Hepburn, 2007). It is thus possible that even though Amy being born addicted is the result of her mother's heroin use, her prematurity and low birthweight, which are more strongly associated with long-term harm, were due to her mother smoking or not looking after herself, or because did not have a consistent supply of good quality heroin and therefore used it in an unpredictable and varied way (which increases the risks to the foetus). Alternatively, prematurity and low birthweight may have been the result of a completely different factor: some children are born early and at low weight from healthy mothers who have looked after themselves throughout pregnancy. Thus, even in the comparatively obvious and direct case of a newborn baby affected by maternal substance misuse during pregnancy, the relationship between the misuse and the child's welfare is more complex than it appears to be.

If it is difficult to demonstrate the link between taking substances during pregnancy and harm to children, how much more difficult is it to show the links when the relationship between the substance use and harm to the child is not direct. A parent drinking or taking drugs does not hurt the child. It is the fact that the individual becomes violent when drunk; they tend to leave the child home alone when they need to 'score'; they prioritize money for drink over decent furniture; they are emotionally and/or physically unavailable or unpredictable as a result of their substance misuse; or it is a host of other behaviours linked to their use of a substance that is potentially harmful to the child. Indeed, some commentators have picked up on elements of this complexity to suggest that there is little link between substance misuse and child welfare. Parton (1985), Parton *et al.* (1997) and Thorpe (1994) have gone on to argue that social workers are making moral judgements rather than considering risks to child welfare when they focus on parental alcohol problems.

However, to argue this is to ignore the wealth of evidence for a link between parental alcohol and drug problems and problems for children. Yet the fact that some academics are able to do so points to the fact that the relationship is not straightforward. This complexity is the biggest challenge in understanding the link between parental substance misuse and child welfare. Substance misuse is part of a complex psycho-social picture – what we have termed a 'web of disadvantage' (Forrester and Harwin, 2006). It is thus difficult to disentangle what the impact of the substance misuse is, as opposed to other factors that may be linked to both the harm to the child and the drinking or drug-taking. And, like a web, it is almost impossible to pick out a single strand. To make matters worse, the strands may reinforce one another, capturing the individual, who finds they drink or take drugs as a way of 'coping' with difficulties, but that in the long term the substance misuse exacerbates the very problems that it is used to cope with in the short term, leading the person to drink more or take more drugs. In such a situation, substance misuse is only one aspect of a family situation that may be harming a child. To focus solely on the substance misuse may be simplistic and runs the risk of failing to appreciate wider individual and social processes that may be important. Nevertheless, not to consider the substance misuse would be to fail to appreciate its crucial importance within the family being worked with, and the ways in which it can act to reinforce already existing disadvantage. An approach that can wrestle with the sheer complexity of the relationships appears to be needed, and the aim of this chapter is to begin to explore what the essential elements of such an approach might be.

HOW DOES PARENTAL SUBSTANCE MISUSE IMPACT ON CHILDREN'S WELFARE?

As a first step, it is worth analysing the ways in which misuse of substance/s by a parent may impact on children. In practice, *how* does substance misuse harm the child? We think that that it is useful to distinguish between two types of effects:

1. *Direct effects of the parent's misuse on the child*, i.e. things that happen when the parent is intoxicated or recovering from intoxication.
2. *Indirect effects related to the parent's prioritization of drinking or drug-taking* over the child's needs.

This division has a number of advantages. First, it helps to unpack the impact of different patterns of substance misuse. For instance, how do binges compare to steady but heavy consumption? How does the impact of heroin compare to that of alcohol? This provides a starting point for assessing the effect of parental substance misuse on children. Second, it provides a way of beginning to differentiate between the impact of different substances and the impact of 'addiction'. There is widespread variability in whether academics and policy-makers focus on different substances or whether the focus is on substance misuse regardless of substance. Thus there are separate government policies on drugs and on alcohol (Prime Minister's Strategy Unit, 2004), yet within the Assessment Framework drugs and alcohol are treated under the rubric 'substance misuse' or lumped together as 'drug or alcohol misuse' (Department for Education and Skills, 2006). Similarly, some studies focus solely on alcohol or on drugs, while others look at 'substance misuse' across substances. We feel that there are similarities *and* differences between substances in the ways in which they impact on children. The similarities generally relate to the prioritization of substance use over child welfare. This happens across a range of different substances and its impact on children has similarities irrespective of the substance. The differences in impact on children are related to factors that are substance-specific; for these the most important differences are linked to the pharmacology and social context for the use of different substances, i.e. what using a particular substance tends to do to the individual.

It is worth noting that the impact of both direct and indirect effects of substance misuse are mediated by social factors. Parental substance misuse is a psycho-social phenomenon. Both the factors that cause it and the ways in which it impacts on children are mediated by the social context within which it takes place. The role of social factors in creating a substance misuse problem was considered in Chapter 1. Towards the end of this chapter we discuss the ways in which the impact of parental substance misuse on children's welfare may be mediated by risk and resilience factors. The social context of misuse is crucial in approaching this issue. The discussion of risk and resilience factors also provides a crucial context for understanding the research discussed in the next three chapters, as well as a foundation for the approach to assessment outlined in Chapter 6. However, before considering the ways in which potential harm may be avoided – or conversely, made more likely – it is necessary to describe the ways in which misuse of drugs or alcohol may impact on children.

DIRECT HARM FROM SUBSTANCE MISUSE

Harm to a child as a direct result of parental drinking or drug-taking includes harm to a newborn baby as a result of substance misuse by the mother during pregnancy and harm to children as a result of the impact of the substance use on the parent's behaviour, including the after-effects of substance use. It is worth considering each of these in turn, using research and the examples in Box 2.1 to consider some of the issues in each area. We return to these areas in Chapter 6 on assessment.

HARM *IN UTERO*

As noted above, disentangling the direct impact of substances on a foetus from other related influences is difficult. Nonetheless, three types of direct impact of substance misuse can be identified. First, foetuses exposed to heroin or methadone on a regular basis are liable to be born experiencing 'neonatal abstinence syndrome', as Amy did in our example. Watching a newborn baby mewling or crying through the pain of withdrawal is emotionally draining. However, provided it is treated medically, withdrawal alone does not seem to have any long-term consequences that we are currently aware of. Second, babies born exposed regularly to crack cocaine *in utero* do not experience withdrawal symptoms, however they do tend to exhibit similar symptoms because the process of the cocaine leaving their system can be painful. The treatment is also similar: children are given a reducing dose of painkilling drugs to help them to cope with the problems. Third, exposure to alcohol *in utero* can cause children profound long-term harm. This can range from full-blown Foetal Alcohol Syndrome (FAS), through to elements of the syndrome (Foetal Alcohol Tendency).

FAS is comparatively rare in the UK, though it seems much more common in the USA. Some of this may be due to a failure to identify FAS in the UK, but it is likely that other factors are also important. These may include different patterns of drinking, lower levels of poverty and different social structures (including the National Health Service) in the UK. The behavioural challenges and learning difficulties experienced by these children are severe and permanent. They make these children particularly challenging to care for, and they require long-term help and support.

There is a range of other harmful effects on unborn or newborn babies that are associated with maternal substance misuse. Mothers who misuse illegal drugs are more likely to be miscarry, their children are at increased risk of premature birth and they are more likely to be small at birth (Hepburn, 2007). However, as noted above, it is difficult to disentangle the impact of substance misuse from other important influences that are known to be harmful to children. First, the vast majority of these mothers smoke heavily.

Smoking is very harmful to babies, and it may account for a substantial proportion of the problems noted above. Second, in general, women with serious drug and alcohol problems do not look after themselves. Perhaps most importantly for the unborn child, they may not be eating adequately and this can result in babies not receiving sufficient nutrition. There is some evidence that supportive services that provide vitamins and minerals may succeed in avoiding some of the harmful effects associated with maternal drug misuse during pregnancy (Hepburn, 2007). Third, there is a strong association between maternal drug or alcohol misuse during pregnancy and severe poverty. Poverty is known to be linked to a range of problems for children from birth onwards, including lower birthweight. It may be the poverty in which these families are living that creates the problems for the children. Fourth, women who misuse drugs and alcohol are often exposed to a range of other problems. These may include poor or temporary housing, involvement with the police or criminal justice system or working as prostitutes to earn money. Perhaps most importantly, they are likely to be at increased risk of violence from men. Research indicates a strong link between misuse of substances and violence towards women (see Galvani, 2006). Such violence tends to increase during pregnancy. This may also therefore be contributing to some of the risks that the unborn child and mother face.

Finally, it can be difficult to disentangle the impact of the substance directly on the foetus and the contribution of the home environment after birth to problems that the child develops. Children who live with parents with drug or alcohol problems tend to be exposed to the potential risks we discuss below, and it is therefore hard to be sure how much exposure during pregnancy produces lasting harm and how much it is the later environment that creates difficulties. There has in fact been considerable research in relation to this with children born affected by maternal crack misuse – so-called 'crack babies'. In the USA research studies suggested that crack babies exhibited serious behavioural problems as toddlers (Arendt et al., 1996). These were hypothesized to be related to the impact of direct exposure of the developing brain to crack cocaine during pregnancy. The findings resulted in considerable press attention and concern that a generation of babies would exhibit permanent and long-term harm as a result of such exposure. Further studies tried to unpick the contribution of direct exposure and that of the environment by looking at babies adopted or placed elsewhere. In general, these studies found no impact of being born affected by crack cocaine on babies removed at birth. Yet there were clear problems for the children who remained with parents with drug problems. This finding suggests alarm about the direct pharmacological impact of crack cocaine on children was exaggerated. However, it highlights the potential damage that children can experience from being brought up in families where there are serious drug problems.

HARM AS A RESULT OF THE IMPACT OF THE SUBSTANCE ON PARENT'S BEHAVIOUR

A common assumption is that the primary impact of substance misuse on children is through its pharmacological effect on parents. Thus, a father's drinking may 'cause' him to become disinhibited and therefore violent, or a mother's taking of heroin may lead to her being 'out of it' and unable to care for her child. A challenge here for both the researcher and the practitioner is to understand the exact effect of substance misuse on an individual. As a result of the UK's long relationship and ongoing intimacy with alcohol use, most of us have an awareness of the different impacts that alcohol can have on individuals, or even on the same individual at different occasions. Thus, some people tend to feel drowsy after a few drinks, while others feel gregarious. That impact may be mediated by the context in which drinking takes place. Consumption of 5 units over a Christmas lunch may make an individual feel like taking a nap; the same person drinking the same quantity of alcohol in the pub with friends on a Friday night may become lively and sociable. Some of these variations hold for other drugs. Thus, heroin can result in individuals being completely 'out of it', but used in smaller quantities it can promote a sense of well-being and sociability, while for those with an addiction it can sometimes be difficult to tell whether they have been using. For these individuals, the use of heroin is linked to functioning as normal and the avoidance of withdrawal, more than getting 'out of it'.

This variation in the impact of drugs means it is important to gather information on the specific individual and not make assumptions. It is made even more complicated by the fact that individuals often combine substances, and this can alter their impact. Nonetheless, there are some broad associations between use of certain substances and particular behaviours that may be harmful to children. We summarize some general information in relation to this in Box 2.2. These include the potential negative impact both of substance use and its after-effects such as hangovers or the 'come down' after the high of drug use.

The link between taking a substance and behaviour is complicated. Individuals respond to substances in different ways and, as noted in Chapter 1, cultural expectations shape the way in which people behave when they are intoxicated. However, some general points can be made in relation to the impact of different substances. Some seem to have a comparatively direct link to behaviours of concern. Thus, alcohol and cocaine (particularly crack cocaine) make some people more likely to be violent. Most mood-altering substances, when taken in excess, reduce the user's awareness of their child's needs. Some, such as alcohol or heroin, may lead individuals to have very low levels of awareness to what is happening, and may also lead the individual to lose consciousness. It is therefore important to obtain a picture not just of

---

Box 2.2   Types of drug and their common effects.

A wide range of drugs are used – sometimes in combination with some of the substances below. These include cannabis (in a variety of forms), LSD, ecstasy, hallucinogenic mushrooms, Khat and a range of prescribed medications that can be misused. Even common household substances, such as glue and nutmeg, have been misused. However, the bulk of parental substance misuse concerns alcohol, heroin and crack cocaine (with some areas having amphetamine misuse issues) and therefore we confine our discussion to those substances.

Combinations of drugs can produce complex and unpredictable effects. Illegal drugs often vary in their strength and can be mixed with other substances. Effects vary by individual and the situation they are in. The following are therefore broad types of effect. The categorization is based on information from the Drugscope website (2009) and Kroll and Taylor (2003).

Opiates (includes, heroin, methadone and morphine)

Heroin can be smoked or injected. Methadone is generally prescribed as a heroin replacement in liquid or pill form. Morphine is used medically as a painkiller.

Heroin initially produces feelings of pleasure and well-being and detachment from pain, anxiety or difficult emotions. Frequent users tend to report fewer of the positive effects from use. It can lead to individuals being unaware of their surroundings or losing consciousness. Used regularly all the opiates can be psychologically and physically addictive, though some people use regularly without becoming dependent. Methadone prevents the feelings associated with withdrawal but used as prescribed does not produce the positive feelings associated with heroin.

Withdrawal from opiates can include physical symptoms such as vomiting, sleeplessness, cramps and acute flu-like symptoms. Intense cravings for the drug may be as or more difficult to cope with. Physical symptoms usually peak within three days but can last longer, with anxiety and insomnia being particularly likely. Cravings can persist for far longer and can appear acutely months or years after the individual has stopped using.

Stimulants

Amphetamine, cocaine and 'crack' (a derivative of cocaine) produce feelings of euphoria, confidence, sociability, extreme happiness and energy. They can reduce inhibitions, and individuals can become very talkative and feel confident, though their behaviour can also be unpredictable and their mood can be volatile. For some individuals this can be linked to an increased likelihood of violence. Stimulants tend to be taken for over one or more days (rather than constantly like heroin), and this tends to be followed by a 'down' with low energy and sometimes feelings of depression. Some individuals try to get over these feelings by using again, and this can lead to heavy patterns of use. Heavy use of stimulants can also lead to feelings of paranoia and even delusions. Stopping heavy stimulant use is often associated with severe feelings of hopelessness and depression and with cravings to use. As the impact of stimulants reduces with regular use and is not long-lasting, regular heavy use requires large amounts of money.

Depressants

Alcohol, tranquillizers and sedatives all depress the central nervous system. Light use can appear to have the opposite effect, for instance, light drinking may reduce anxiety and inhibitions. Heavier drinking negatively affects physical and mental functioning, and can produce vomiting, unconsciousness and even, on occasion, death. It is also linked to erratic and disinhibited behaviour (including violence). Long-term heavy use has a variety of health-related problems, particularly liver damage. Alcohol can cross the placenta and produce serious damage to babies (Foetal Alcohol Syndrome and Foetal Alcohol Tendencies). Alcohol withdrawal effects can range from a hangover through to serious medical complications.

Tranquillizers produce feelings of calm and reduce or remove negative feelings and anxiety. They are highly addictive and, when combined with alcohol, can be particularly dangerous.

consumption, but of what that consumption means in terms of parental behaviour and family functioning.

A crucial issue here is often what the pattern of consumption is. What is used? How much is used? When is it used? The frequency and quantity of use of substances are particularly important for understanding the potential health implications for the individual. It is also useful in considering the sacrifices that the parent may have to make in order to obtain their substance. Knowing how much an individual consumes and when also provides an indication of the likelihood of the person having dependent use. Individuals who take substances in significant quantities every day are likely to have at least psychological dependence, and may well be physically dependent, on the substance that they are using. This has implications for how they approach changing their substance use.

An even more important issue in relation to child care concerns is whether the use is regular and comparatively predictable or episodic and unpredictable. The word 'binge' has come to mean drinking to become intoxicated or drinking until intoxicated. However, until recently it was used for drinking until unconscious or at least extremely inebriated, usually over a period of more than one day. Similarly, a crack cocaine 'binge' is smoking crack repeatedly over hours or days. In general, when we refer to 'binge' use this is the type of behaviour we are referring to. Such patterns of use can be particularly difficult for children.

Often individuals progress from trying out a substance to a pattern of excessive 'bingeing'. Some give up or moderate their use, but others move to steady, excessive use. For instance, they may drink heavily or take heroin or methadone on a regular basis. In general terms, it is when individuals are misusing in 'binges' or with unpredictable patterns that the risks to the child (and the parent) are the greatest. However, it is possible for individuals to use heavily in a steady way and periodically 'binge'. It is also possible for the daily quantity of alcohol or drugs used to be so high that parents are effectively bingeing every day.

HARM AS A RESULT OF THE PRIORITIZATION OF SUBSTANCE USE OVER THE CHILD'S NEEDS

The impact of substance misuse is not confined to the direct effects associated with taking particular substances. There are more general harms that are related to parents' prioritizing the substance over the child. These can include direct neglect or emotional abuse. It can also include risks associated with the broader drink and/or drug-taking culture in which the family becomes involved. In both instances, children are at greater risk of disrupted care, including exposure to risks from individuals outside the family. In broad terms, these types of risk occur across different substances, as they are less the product of the use of a particular substance and more related to the parent's addiction and consequent prioritization of their need for the substance. However, an important mediating factor is whether the substance is legal or illegal. Illegal substance use by parents tends to carry additional dangers for children, as discussed below.

The form that prioritization of drink or drugs takes varies between families, but its impact has a common and central element: the child's needs take second place for their parent. This can result in neglect of important elements of children's care. Children may not have adequate furniture, bedding, clothing and even food. Their need to be taken to school on time or picked up from school or supported in developing their talents may not be met. And myriad other forms of neglect may form part of the picture, including failure to meet medical needs, identity needs, social needs – almost any need a child has (Brisby et al., 1997). Crucially, as a child gets older they begin to realize that they are not the most important relationship that their parent has: that their mother or father puts their own need for drugs or alcohol first. As one child in a study by Barnard (2007, p. 88) put it:

When my mum is using drugs it just makes me feel as if I am here myself – not got anyone else here.

Jenny, aged 15

This understanding of the relationship with the substance coming first appears to be a common issue across substances. It is important that we do not idealize the reality of parenting. All parents can and should sometimes put their own needs first, and children need to learn that their wants and needs do not dominate over everything. Yet, for the children of alcoholics and drug addicts all too often the experience is one of always coming second; and some children do not even come second. A feeling that their parents are not able to put their interests first can contribute to serious emotional and behavioural problems in the child (see Kroll and Taylor, 2003).

A failure to prioritize the child's needs is also related to a more general risk associated with substance misuse by parents, namely that the substance misuse may influence the family's broader lifestyle. This may take a number of forms. Children can become involved in illegal activities, such as accompanying parents on shoplifting expeditions to fund drug misuse. They can be exposed to inappropriate situations and potentially dangerous individuals, for instance when their home is used on a regular basis by individuals with drug or alcohol problems. They can also be affected indirectly but profoundly by the consequences of prioritization of drug or alcohol use over the needs of even the parent. Thus it is common for families with substance misuse problems to have multiple changes of address and they are far more likely to experience poverty if a substantial proportion of the household income is spent on drugs or alcohol. The parent may also experience ill-health as a result of their substance misuse. The children of parents with drug and alcohol problems often talk about the emotional scars of finding their parents unconscious or overdosed and having to call emergency services.

It was Christmas morning and I was getting up to go to the toilet and I couldn't get in the door because he [uncle] was against the door and from then I realized something had happened to him ... and I ran down the stair and I got my big brother and the two of us went up and we eventually got the door opened and he was lying, his face pure chalk white ... his lips were ... bluish with blood and sick around his nose and his needle lying beside him.

Kylie, aged 14 (in Barnard, 2007, p. 96)

FACTORS THAT INFLUENCE OUTCOMES FOR CHILDREN

Thus far, this chapter has painted a deeply concerning picture of the impact that parental substance misuse can have on children. Children are at increased risk of physical, sexual or emotional abuse or neglect, and this is associated with a range of poor long-term outcomes. Furthermore, the picture is complicated by the multitude of ways in which substance misuse can have an impact on children and the complex way that substance use interacts with other factors within families. It is important to move from an awareness of this complexity towards being able to analyse the factors that make outcomes for children more or less likely to be negative.

A crucial fact in starting this process is that most children who have a parent with an alcohol problem – and presumably many with a parent with a drug problem – enter adulthood without apparent difficulties (Advisory Council on the Misuse of Drugs, 2002; Velleman and Orford, 1999). Indeed, some research suggests that the children of alcoholics are not only at greater risk of negative outcomes, they are also more likely to be high achievers. Children of alcoholics in Iceland, for instance, are more likely to require treatment for alcohol problems than their peers, but they are also more likely to appear in *Who's Who* (a book identifying high achievers in Iceland) (see Orford, 2001). A look at the family background of recent US presidents also identifies two (Ronald Reagan and Bill Clinton) from families in which there were serious alcohol problems. Of course, one can be a high achiever and be unhappy, but these examples do indicate that having a parent who misuses drugs or alcohol does not condemn a child to a lifetime of individual and social problems. And quite apart from the level of achievement, there is ample evidence that many children of alcoholics go on to live happy and fulfilled lives.

THE NATURE OF 'WELFARE OUTCOMES'

The possibility that an apparently successful individual may be unhappy highlights the complexity of knowing what a 'good' outcome is. Therefore, before turning to consider the ways in which outcomes for children are influenced for good or ill it is worth analysing briefly what is meant by an 'outcome' and some of the difficulty involved in measuring it. Human beings are enormously complex and our thriving – or failure to thrive – is multifaceted. Thus, human welfare can be related in research to our emotions, behaviour, relationships, achievements, health or even earning power, yet none of these captures the whole of welfare. Furthermore, it is rare for anybody to achieve 'success' or 'failure' in every dimension. This alone makes the consideration of welfare outcomes extremely challenging, for research studies have to have a focus, and this rarely allows a rounded view of human needs or flourishing to be reflected.

In addition, the impact of parental drinking or drug-taking may sometimes be hidden. A child may appear to be doing well at school and to be happy, but this may conceal deeper unhappiness and issues such as poor self-image. It is even possible that for some children doing well academically (in particular) may be because the child finds school a refuge from the difficult emotions and experiences that they have at home. In this case, welfare outcomes may be particularly difficult to unpack where parents misuse drugs or alcohol because of the pervasive secrecy that surrounds this issue (Kroll and Taylor, 2003).

As if these considerations did not sufficiently illustrate the difficulty in looking at welfare outcomes, in reality the situation is even more complicated. Our welfare changes over time. Consider the hypothetical example of a young person whose mother misused heroin. Let's call him Sam. Sam did not exhibit particular difficulties at his primary school – perhaps because it offered a safe and nurturing environment for him, or possibly because his grandmother was offering a lot of support. At this stage, Sam's welfare appeared to be 'good'. However, at 11 he moved to a large secondary school and at 12 his grandmother died. By 14 Sam was exhibiting serious behavioural difficulties and rarely attended school. At this stage there were serious concerns about his welfare. These escalated as he became involved in using heroin and committed a number of crimes, which resulted in him spending several periods in prison or on the street homeless between the age of 16 and 19. During this period his welfare seemed 'poor'. Yet at the age of 21 Sam entered residential treatment and his life turned around. He stopped using heroin, started studying, met and eventually married a woman who was very supportive. By this stage the 'outcome' for Sam appeared very positive, and as if to confirm this at the age of 26 Sam started to train as a social worker. What more positive outcome could there be? The future looks positive for Sam, but it is not possible to certain that this is so. Sam may go on to have a fulfilling career and a satisfying home life, and he may make a positive contribution to society and be happy in himself. But what if his wife dies? This may precipitate a return to heroin use and a host of associated problems, even an overdose and early death. Or perhaps Sam will develop a problem with alcohol – often individuals replace one addiction with another – and this will have a negative effect on his health and happiness. Sam's life-story illustrates a further layer of complexity in considering welfare outcomes. People's lives are complex and almost all of us experience both good times and difficult times. In this context, how can we measure welfare 'outcomes'? Is it not like trying to freeze a moving picture and thus likely to produce a distortion of reality?

Of course, the answer to this is yes. Research cannot realistically capture the complexity of even one individual's life-history. So how can researchers and practitioners approach the issue of outcomes in general? Considerations such as those we have outlined should lead us to be circumspect when considering the literature on outcomes. Often the research evidence is fragmentary (for instance, relating to one dimension of welfare) and it is rare for individuals to be followed up in the long term. Furthermore, the evidence is often complex and sometimes even contradictory. As a result it is important to be aware that research provides us with an indication of broad patterns and possible relationships, but that we should exercise considerable caution in applying it to particular children or their families. This is not to say it is not useful to have an understanding of the research literature. Quite the opposite. Research provides us with the best evidence we have on the ways in which substance misuse impacts on children and the nature of the factors that may mediate such impacts. However, an informed humility about the limits of such knowledge is probably a good place to start when working with families in which parents misuse drugs or alcohol.

Having taken these important challenges in interpreting the literature into account, it is worth turning to consider the research evidence in relation to parental substance misuse and children's welfare. In particular, it is important to understand the ways in which a drink or drug problem in a parent may be mediated, either to reduce the potential harm it may cause or to make it likely to be more harmful. An awareness of such issues is crucial both for assessing risk and need and for designing effective interventions.

RISK AND RESILIENCE FACTORS

A classic study in this area was carried out by Vellemen and Orford (1999). A particularly useful contribution from their study was the distinction made between some of the stages that a child with a parent with a drug or alcohol problem experiences and the eventual impact in their adulthood. Velleman and Orford highlight the central importance of family disruption (a composite measure that includes arguments and failing to respond to the child's needs) and the significant impact of protective and resilience factors. Based both on their data and on a comprehensive review of the broader literature, they suggest that there is a relationship between a parent having a drink problem and the family experiencing disruption; that family disruption is related to children having problems; and that children who have problems are more likely to have difficulties as adults. Yet at each stage many children or families avoid progressing to the next stage. Thus, some families in which a parent has an alcohol problem do not experience serious disruption; some children in disrupted families do not experience difficulties; some individuals with problems in childhood do not go on to exhibit difficulties in adulthood. Understanding what factors mediate the impact of substance misuse at each of these stages is useful for developing a more nuanced appreciation of the complexities involved, as well as for developing effective interventions to reduce harm to children in the long term. A simplified diagram outlining these relationships, based loosely on the work of Velleman and Orford (1999) but incorporating findings from other relevant research, is set out in Figure 1.1.

Another way of looking at this is to differentiate between protective factors, resilience factors and recovery factors. Protective factors act to reduce or even negate the impact of a potential risk factor. Thus a parent's drug problem might place a child at risk, but if the child goes to live with grandparents and is happy there, this would protect the child from potential risk. Most protective factors are not as clear-cut as this; they often reduce the risk a particular type of adversity poses for a child rather than removing it. Resilience factors are those within a child or their social situation that help the child to 'bounce back' despite experiencing a risky environment. Finally, recovery factors are those that help children who have experienced harm to overcome it as they mature and become adults. Less is known about recovery factors, but they are an important part of understanding the process by which some children survive and even thrive after a difficult childhood. Taken together, an understanding of risk, protective, resilience and recovery factors are important in undertaking evidence-informed assessments and developing appropriate interventions.

SUBSTANCE MISUSE AND FAMILY DISRUPTION: PROTECTIVE FACTORS

Identifying the impact of drinking or drug-taking on family functioning is central to understanding the likely impact of misuse on any particular child. Velleman and Orford (1999) found that where a parent's alcohol problem was not associated with family disruption children experienced no measurable harm. This is a crucially important finding and one that has had a profound impact on our understanding of the impact that problem drinking or drug-taking has on children. It highlights that it is not the drug or the drinking itself that harms children, it is its impact on their experience of family life. What does this mean?

Velleman and Orford found a strong correlation between having a parent with a drink problem and a host of family problems. The most important of these, and the one that appeared to have the most negative impact on children, was where there was violence between parents linked to the drinking. However, drink problems also made it more likely that family life would be unpredictable, that children would spend a lot of time worrying about their parents, that they would experience less positive feedback and more criticism, and that they would see less of the parent with the drink problem. This is a familiar picture. The types of issues discussed thus far in this chapter are very much of this type, and some examples of the ways in which these issues may impact negatively on children can be seen in Box 2.1.

Yet this picture of the misery that problem drinking can cause was not universal. In some families problem drinking was not associated with violence or arguments, parents did find time for their children and the anxiety or failure to meet the needs of children that so often accompanies heavy drinking was not found. Unfortunately, Velleman and Orford do not analyse in great depth these families in which heavy drinking was not associated with family disruption. We also know little from other research or practice experience, as most studies and the bulk of our professional experiences focus on families in which alcohol or drug misuse is causing serious problems. This is a clear gap in the literature: how do some families manage to cope with problem drinking without it causing serious family disruption?

While the evidence is not strong, we can speculate about key features of such families. One feature that is surprising in its failure to act as a 'protective' factor is the presence of a non-misusing parent. One might assume – and indeed elsewhere we have assumed (Forrester and Harwin, 2006) – that a non-misusing parent might 'shield' a child from much of the negative impact of the drinking of the other parent, but Velleman and Orford did not find this. Furthermore, on reflection this is perhaps a naïve view. It relies on an implicit assumption that the non-misusing partner does not get embroiled in the problem drinking and its associated difficulties and that they are able to protect the child from them through their mere presence: that they are a selfless protection for the child. In truth, the non-misusing parent's ability to care for the child is in large part determined by the nature of the misusing partner's substance misuse.

In this respect a key issue in understanding the relationship between heavy drinking and family disruption is the presence or absence of violence associated with the drinking. Families in which a parent – particularly but not only a father – drinks heavily are at far greater risk of domestic violence. Yet, despite this strong and important association, this is not always the case. Furthermore, the testimony of children provides suggestive evidence that the nature of parent's behaviour when drunk may be crucial. There is now a rich body of evidence giving voice to the experiences of children and young people living with a parent with an alcohol problem (e.g. Bancroft *et al.*, 2004; Barnard, 2007), and a developing body of researchers who have interviewed children whose parent/s have a drug problem (Barnard, 2007). In general, these studies make grim reading and highlight the disruptive and damaging impact of parent's substance misuse on children's lives. However, this is not always the case. There are children who do not experience the parent's drinking as problematic, or who at least can identify positives as well as negatives. These include the parent being warm and emotional when drunk – as well as being more likely to give extra pocket money!

These exceptions point to the complexity of understanding the impact of a drug or alcohol problem. As noted above, and highlighted throughout this book, it is not the drinking or the drug-taking itself that should be focus of assessment or of intervention. It is the impact that the drinking or drug-taking has on the family's functioning and the child that is crucial. In this respect, the behaviour associated with the substance misuse is central.

Thus the behaviours that are associated with a parent's drinking or drug-taking and the social context in which it occurs are important influences on the likelihood of the behaviour resulting in family disruption. However, even where there is family disruption this does not always result in children exhibiting difficulties. Instead, a variety of factors mediate the impact of family difficulties, with many allowing children to prosper despite the adverse environment they find themselves in and some making it more likely that such an environment will result in the child having difficulties. To understand the nature and processes involved in children not developing problems in the face of an adversity such as parental drinking or drug-taking it is worth considering not just the literature in this area, but the more general literature on the topic of resilience in the face of adversity.

CHILD RESILIENCE FACTORS IN THE FACE OF FAMILY DISRUPTION

A feature of a number of studies of children exposed to adverse circumstances – by which is meant experiences such as institutional care, living with a parent with a mental illness or being cared for by a parent with an alcohol or drug problem – is that many of the children, indeed perhaps most of them, have few problems in adult life (Velleman and Orford, 1999). To understand this a more complex conception of the pathways that children take to adulthood has been developed over the last 20 years. This emphasizes the interplay of factors that increase or reduce risk (see Luthar, 2003). In addition, the choices children themselves make and their role in shaping their own destiny have come to the fore.

A number of factors stand out that promote resilience for some children in the face of adversity. These can be broken down into factors within the child and those within their social situation. The factors within the child that are most strongly linked to children doing well in the face of adversity are positive attributes such as intelligence and attractiveness (Rutter, 2003). Children with these attributes are more likely to overcome difficulties for two reasons. First, they are more likely to have positive experiences elsewhere. A clever child with problems at home may find school a sanctuary – indeed, this may explain the relationship between high achievement and parental alcoholism. In contrast, a less able child with problems at home may find that school reinforces their sense of failure and low self-esteem. Similarly, physically attractive children tend to be sought out by peers as friends and are treated more favourably by adults (Dion and Berscheid, 1974) – facts that shed a rather depressing light on the superficiality of human beings from a young age! Again, less attractive children may find social life and the response of other adults do nothing to ameliorate the difficulties that they have at home.

An awareness of the importance of such positive factors in the child is important if we are to understand the likelihood of resilience in the face of adversity, however it is important to move beyond a reified vision of these resilience factors as 'things' that cannot be changed. It is likely that it is through the increased propensity to achieve positive experiences in areas outside the home that these factors work to allow resilience to be achieved, and we do not therefore need to see these as attributes that cannot be changed through intervention. For instance, less academic children may have skills and talents that give them positive experiences to overcome adversity. They may be talented at music, sport or art or enjoy social activities such as Girl Guides or Scouts or Woodcraft Folk. Furthermore, school does not need to be a negative experience for less academic children – recognizing and celebrating other forms of achievement may help such children overcome difficulties that they are experiencing at home.

The second reason why intelligence in particular is likely to be associated with children overcoming adversity is likely to be that clever children are more likely to develop effective strategies that help them to cope with difficulties experienced at home. This might include avoiding getting into arguments, spending time away from home or seeking out supportive individuals within the neighbourhood and/or wider family. The hypothesis is that more intelligent children plan their way through difficulties more effectively. It is also possible that such children interpret what is happening in a more sophisticated way and in particular that they (correctly) attribute the problems as being due to their parent's drinking or drug-taking and not their own fault. Certainly, attributing difficulties as being due to external sources, while remaining prepared to take the credit for those things that one does have control over (internal attribution of positives) seems strongly related to positive emotional well-being in both children and adults (Rutter, 2003; Velleman and Orford, 1999). Intelligent children may be more likely to do this.

Again, this should not be seen as a concrete and fixed attribute associated with intelligent children. Planning through difficulties and correctly identifying problems as not being one's responsibility are both things that can be taught. Indeed, interventions with the partners of heavy drinkers have done just this and found a positive effect from a comparatively brief intervention (Copello *et al.*, 2008). There is no reason to think such an approach would not be effective with children too.

SOCIAL SITUATIONS THAT PROMOTE RESILIENCE

There is a tendency to focus on the immediate family as the primary agent that raises children – at least in the West. This has a large measure of truth to it, but the family is far from the only important influence on children's welfare. Children spend a large percentage of the day in school. They have significant relationships with other adults, including members of the wider family, neighbours and professionals who have an ongoing input into their lives. Many participate in activities outside home that can have an important influence on their welfare and sense of self-worth. These factors can act as powerful barriers against harm when things are not going well at home and be promoters of positive welfare outcomes.

In this respect two things appear to have a particularly strong relationship with resilience in the face of adversity: children experiencing success outside the home and children having an ongoing positive relationship with one or more adults not in the immediate family. Either or both of these tend to provide children with a sense of worth and success, positive relationships and pro-social values such as the importance of hard work to achieve success. Thus, creating the opportunity to experience some of these positives may be a crucial issue in developing resilience for children affected by substance misuse.

However, these resilience factors are not distributed evenly across society. In particular, it is influenced profoundly by the resources available to a family and the community in which they live. There is not a clear and straightforward relationship between a parent's problem drinking, socio-economic circumstances and the outcomes for the child. Indeed, Vellemen and Orford found class had comparatively little impact, and in some areas it seemed to be linked to worse outcomes for the child. Nonetheless, it seems likely that where substance misuse takes place in a context of extreme poverty its impact on children is often far more negative. For instance, problem heroin use is strongly concentrated in areas with very high levels of social deprivation. As noted above, deprivation is likely to contribute to the high levels of problem drug use in these areas; indeed, it is probably the most important single factor in understanding why problem heroin or crack use takes place. However, it is also easy to see ways in which it interacts with a parent's drug problem to make outcomes for children worse. The resources available to poor families in which parents misuse drugs are severely limited. There is therefore little to buffer children against the harmful effects of their parent's substance misuse. In addition, the tendency for poor schools to be found in poor areas and for cultures of crime and delinquency to be more common among young people in such neighbourhoods immediately removes some of the key processes that might create resilience in a child.

In contrast, children in more affluent homes may have multiple buffers against the negative impact of a parent's drinking. The example of Jenny in Box 2.1 illustrates this well. Jenny was, in fact, very upset by her mother's drinking and this may have caused her long-term harm. However, her family's financial resources have allowed them to buy alternative care that has harnessed some of Jenny's innate strengths and limited her exposure to her mother's difficulties. Thus, in comparatively affluent families in which there is a problem there are often resources that allow drink or drug problems to be 'buffered' and that offer the child some protection from its impact. In contrast, for families living in poverty, not only is there a lack of resources to protect children from the negative impact of parental drinking or drug-taking, but often the opposite is the case and children are exposed to environments and experiences that exacerbate the risks of a negative outcome. In other words, these children are often exposed to greater risk of negative outcomes at home, in their neighbourhood and at school. Achieving positive outcomes in such circumstances can be exceptionally difficult; however, it is not impossible. Some children benefit from crucial relationships with members of the wider family or become involved with local churches, sports clubs or other organizations that help to provide for their needs. This is simply more difficult for children brought up experiencing both social and familial adversity.

FACTORS THAT PREVENT CHILDHOOD DIFFICULTIES BECOMING ADULTHOOD DIFFICULTIES

As noted above, not all children who experience difficulties in childhood go on to have problems as adults. If we are interested in promoting positive outcomes for children in the long term, understanding how this happens is important. This is not to say that it is only outcomes in adulthood that are important: children's experiences and difficulties are important in their own right and not just because they influence their welfare as adults. Yet there is no contradiction between agreeing with this and emphasizing the importance of knowing how some children appear to overcome difficulties as they move into adulthood.

Factors that allow children to overcome identified difficulties – what we have termed recovery factors – are generally less well studied than the other factors that we have discussed. Nonetheless, there are some clear indications from the literature of the types of issues that help individuals overcome difficulties in childhood. What is less clear is how these can best be promoted in children with such difficulties.

A seminal discussion of recovery factors is provided by Quinton and Rutter (1985). Based on their research, which followed up girls who had entered institutional care in the 1960s, Quinton and Rutter identified the fact that even among the girls who had demonstrated behavioural and self-esteem problems in childhood many went on to live apparently happy and fulfilled lives. Quinton and Rutter suggested that a caring husband without a history of anti-social behaviour and a sense of planning into adulthood appeared important in overcoming childhood difficulties. Velleman and Orford (1999) came to a similar conclusion in relation to children whose parents had an alcohol problem. They identified the following factors as being associated with over-coming childhood difficulties:

- A consistent and caring primary relationship into adulthood;
- A rewarding and enjoyable job or career;
- A supportive group of friends.

A problem with this finding is that it is difficult to disentangle the outcome and the reasons for it. Individuals who overcome difficulties tend to have better relationships and enjoy their work more, but is this the cause of their success or a symptom of it? A satisfying relationship and work and good friendships are not things that simply happen; they are achievements that we work at. So how do some children with behavioural and emotional difficulties achieve such outcomes while others do not?

Both Quinton and Rutter and Velleman and Orford point to the potential importance of an element of planning within young people during the crucial years in which they make the transition into adulthood. Thus, there was quali-tative evidence that some young people ended up in relationships that they had not deliberately chosen (which often made them unhappy or ended), some young women had unplanned pregnancies and some individuals did not plan for a job they wanted. In contrast, young people who consciously planned their career (and presumably made the sacrifices and deferral of immediate rewards that most careers require) and who chose their partner (rather than falling into relationships) were more likely to overcome difficulties. However, the evidence in this area is in general far weaker than for protective and resilience factors. We know that many children with difficulties as a result of their parent's drug or alcohol problems overcome them, but our understand-ing of how and why this is so is much more limited. The insights of Rutter, Velleman and Orford are a helpful starting point, but they do not provide robust evidence, and in particular, there is a lack of prospective research (i.e. studies that look at factors that predict children successfully overcoming difficulties before this happens). It is all too easy to look back and interpret a successful outcome as being planned; it is less clear that it would be possible to identify a positive approach to planning one's life before changes for the better happen. Furthermore, while young people's agency (i.e. their ability to make decisions about their lives) is important, we do not currently know much about social factors that may influence this. As Karl Marx noted: 'Men make their own history but ... they do not make it under circumstances of their choosing.' Thus, some children are likely to have more material resources and emotional support to help them overcome difficulties; but for other children, their family and individual problems are likely to be exacerbated by the circumstances they find themselves in. We do not currently know enough about factors associated with children overcoming difficulties to be sure about the ways in which individual decisions and social circumstances interact to shape outcomes in adulthood.

CONCLUSIONS

This chapter has outlined the potential negative impact of parental substance misuse on children and then explored the complexity of this relationship. A model has been suggested that tries to account for the interplay of risk and resilience, protective and recovery factors in shaping the welfare of individuals over time. Three recurring themes that relate to all of these factors and to understanding the ways in which negative circumstances influence children's welfare are worth highlighting:

- Children are active agents not passive victims, and many find ways of coping with difficulties such as parental substance misuse or overcoming the problems it causes for them.
- Substance misuse occurs within a social context and has a major influence on the resources that tend to be available to children and their families to help them overcome family difficulties.
- Activities and relationships outside the immediate family can provide crucial help for children who are experiencing problems at home related to parental misuse of drugs or alcohol.

However, these findings relate to parental substance misuse in the general population. The families that come to the attention of Children's Services are likely to be different in profile (one would expect them to tend to have comparatively serious problems) and therefore the challenges in understanding and working with them may be different. In the next chapter we review the limited evidence on parental substance misuse in child welfare services in the UK context and then turn to present the first stage of the research that we undertook.

Part 2

3 Parental Substance Misuse and Children's Services

In Chapter 2 we explored the complex ways in which substance misuse by one or more parents interacts with other factors to impact on the welfare of children. It was argued that parental substance misuse increases the risk of negative outcomes, but that this impact is mediated by a range of factors. Some of these (e.g. an association between substance misuse and violence) make poor outcomes more likely; others (e.g. positive experiences outside the home) can help to reduce the risk of a poor outcome. These findings are important for understanding the nature of parental substance misuse in the general population and the ways in which it interacts with other factors.

However, it is unlikely that the children known to Children's Services or other professionals will be typical of all children affected by parental substance misuse; the fact that they have been referred means they are likely to have more serious issues than most children whose parents have a drink or drug problem. To go beyond referral to allocation is likely to mean that the children are affected by comparatively serious drink or drug problems. Given the non-representative nature of this group of children it is important to consider the literature in relation to parental substance misuse and Children's Services, as the profile of presenting problems, types of interventions and outcomes are likely to have both similarities and differences to those available for all children affected by parental substance misuse.

So what is known about parental substance misuse in the work of Children's Services? The answer is, surprisingly little. In their seminal book on child abuse Kempe and Kempe (1978) identified parental addiction as one of a number of factors related to their proposed 'battered baby syndrome', however it was not given a prominent place in their discussion. This sense that parental misuse of alcohol or drugs was a comparatively common issue but one that was rarely highlighted or studied in its own right can be found in much of the literature from the 1970s, 1980s and 1990s. Thus, in their studies of inquiries into child deaths Reder et al. (1993) found that in 20% a parent

Parents Who Misuse Drugs and Alcohol. Effective Interventions in Social Work and Child Protection, 1st edition.   By Donald Forrester and Judith Harwin.
© 2011 John Wiley & Sons, Ltd.

had a drug or alcohol problem, but they said little more about this; instead, their account concentrated in relationship issues. Interestingly, in their next analysis of child death reports (Reder and Duncan, 1999) they found the same proportion involved drug or alcohol problems, but they discussed this at length. At the same time key textbooks had virtually nothing to say about parental misuse of alcohol or drug misuse (see e.g. Stainton Rogers *et al.*, 1989). As an issue it is generally noted either as present in many families or as a 'risk factor' for abuse or neglect, and then not discussed further.

During the 1990s this began to change. A series of studies looking at families coming to the attention of services because of child protection concerns identified that 25%–40% of the families in their samples were affected by parental substance misuse (see Cleaver *et al.*, 1999). Indeed, in broad terms the more serious the level of official concern the higher the proportion of families in which parental substance misuse featured. Around a quarter of child in need, 40% of children on the child protection register and up to 60% of those subject to care proceedings appear to be affected by parental substance misuse (Forrester, 2001).

The first academic responses to these high proportions of cases involving alcohol or drug misuse tended to be critical of social work processes. Thus, Parton (1985) argued that there was little or no evidence that alcohol misuse was associated with long-term harm to children and that therefore when social workers focused on alcohol misuse they were actually making moral judgements about parental behaviour rather than reasonable estimates of risk to child welfare. In effect, the social worker identification of concern around parental drinking was a manifestation of their role as agents of social control. Thorpe (1994) provides an important study in this area. His research was undertaken in Australia and used file studies of 325 families. He found a very high proportion of the cases involved concerns about parental alcohol misuse, with a particularly strong relationship between alcohol misuse and Aboriginal families, and that social workers often struggled to engage and work with the parents in these families. Thorpe went on to look at what happened to the children. Of particular interest was the category he terms 'becomes care', i.e. children who were admitted to care after a period of social services involvement. In general, these children were admitted at a later point because something had gone wrong, such as a serious incident of abuse or neglect. Thorpe therefore considers them to be an important category in understanding the effectiveness of the child protection system.

Overall, Thorpe found that while a high proportion of the cases referred with child protection concerns involved alcohol misuse, this did not appear to be associated with children entering care after a period of time. He concludes:

> Alcohol and drug misuse are good predictors for children appearing in child protection statistics. They are *not* however good predictors for further harm or injury to children.

> (1994, p. 141)

Thorpe goes on to argue, as Parton did and they do together in a later pub-lication (Parton *et al.*, 1997), that child protection work is in large part about policing parenting patterns that might be conceptualized as 'deviant'. Thus, 'that which does not conform to standard middle-class patriarchal child rearing norms is represented as 'at risk' of abuse, neglect or abuse' (Thorpe, 1994, p. 202).

This argument needs to be taken seriously, not just because it is put forward by two of Britain's best known social work academics, but also because it points to the complexity of assessing families in relation to child welfare con-cerns. We return to it in Chapter 6, when the role of personal values and assumptions in an assessment is discussed. However, the key issue for the current discussion is whether this seems a reasonable formulation of profes-sional interest in parental drug or alcohol misuse. In this respect, there are a number of problems with Parton and Thorpe's critique. First, it seems clear from research on general community samples and on samples known to social services that parental alcohol misuse is associated with increased risk of abuse or neglect. It is reasonable to assume that the same is true for drug misuse. As we saw in Chapter 2, whilst the picture is complex, the poor outcomes for some children whose parents misuse drugs or alcohol appear clear. Second, Thorpe's conclusion is based solely on file study information and provides no independent view of the welfare of the children. Indeed, the research did not even systematically attempt to make a judgement of child welfare from the files. It is thus not possible to conclude that the children exposed to parental heavy drinking did not suffer harm; it is only true to say that social services did not subsequently take children into care in such cases. This is an important limitation in his study.

Third, and perhaps most important, is the question of whether the analysis by Parton and Thorpe is a credible explanation for the behaviour of social workers and other professionals. Underlying their formulation is an argument that social workers are not assessing child welfare and future risks, but rather that they are judging the moral worth of parents. This may be true, but it relies on characterizing the beliefs of the workers concerned and most of the published literature as a form of mass 'false consciousness'. Social workers, social work academics and policy-makers write and talk about assessing chil-dren's needs and evaluating risks; social work degrees and post-qualifying courses provide training on such issues; the Government issues policies pur-porting to focus on such areas. Yet Parton and Thorpe argue that *in fact* what is primarily happening is that social workers are judging the moral worth of parents.

This might be true, but the evidence which they use to make such a claim is limited to file studies interpreted with an unspecified methodology (Parton *et al.*, 1997) which produced results broadly in line with the pre-existing theoretical beliefs of the researchers. This is certainly not sufficient evidence to support such a claim. An alternative interpretation, which we would favour, would appear to be that social workers recognize the damage that parental alcohol (or drug) misuse can pose to children and thus have a legitimate interest in drug or alcohol misuse in parents. It is possible that they misunderstand the nature of this risk and it is likely that their own values affect the way in which they understand families, but such considerations are very different from arguing that the identification of alcohol misuse is purely or primarily a moral judgement about parenting behaviour. The evidence for the harm it can cause children is too strong to support such a conclusion.

Nonetheless, the work of Thorpe and Parton is useful for two reasons. First, it underlines the complexity of decision-making in all child welfare cases, and in particular those in which drugs or alcohol are an issue. Issues around values and assessing risk are considered further in Chapter 6. Second, they highlight both the high proportion of families in which substance misuse was an issue and the lack of preparation that social workers tend to receive for such work.

This lack of training is perhaps linked to the lack of research attention given to parental substance misuse. Practitioners tend to be very interested in drug and alcohol misuse issues as they wrestle with them every day, yet academics have tended to pay little attention to them. Where they have identified them, they have often tended to play them down in relation to the issue that they consider more important. Thus, Thorpe found high proportions of families involved alcohol problems, but felt that poverty and broader issues for Aboriginal families were the real causes of difficulties. Reder *et al.* (1993) found a high proportion of families affected by substance misuse, but their analysis concentrates on relationship issues within a systemic framework. Little is said about alcohol or drug misuse. Researchers interested in domestic violence consistently find high levels of drug or alcohol problems, but see these as subsidiary to the violence issues. Indeed, some see a focus on substance misuse as potentially allowing perpetrators and victims to excuse the violence (see Galvani, 2006).

This highlights one of the key features of substance misuse, which we have tried to emphasize throughout this book, namely the fact that substance misuse rarely happens in isolation. As Shakespeare said:

When sorrows come they come not single spies,
But in battalions.

(*Hamlet*, IV, 5)

Thus, substance misuse is linked to a host of other difficulties – from poverty to violence; depression to a history of having been abused. However, an unfortunate effect of this is that most social work research has tended to consider substance misuse as a subsidiary issue. This seems to misunderstand the complex interplay of substance misuse issues and other problems.

Recent years have witnessed the beginnings of a focus on substance misuse specifically. The main reason for this appears to be a recognition of the sheer number of families affected by substance misuse, particularly at the 'heavy end' of children on the child protection register or subject to care proceedings (Cleaver *et al.*, 1999; Forrester, 2001). This in turn may be in part a result of a higher proportion of women of parenting age misusing drugs and using larger amounts of alcohol (see Chapter 1). There are thus a small number of studies that have focused specifically on substance misuse in the work of children's social services in an attempt to outline the scale and nature of the problem.

RECENT RESEARCH ON SOCIAL WORK AND PARENTAL SUBSTANCE MISUSE

Forrester (2000) and Hayden (2004) carried out small-scale, 'snapshot' studies in particular areas, and both found that a high proportion of families involved parental substance misuse issues and that social workers struggled to work with the issues involved in such cases. More recently, reviews by Kearney *et al.* (2003) and Statham *et al.* (2002) have supported these findings, emphasizing that a very high proportion of cases involve parental substance misuse, that social workers are poorly prepared for working with such issues and that increasing incidence of maternal drug and alcohol problems may be contributing to the rise in the number of care proceedings from 1994 to 2004.

One of the earliest recognitions of the extent and impact of parental difficulties such as substance misuse, mental illness and domestic violence was Cleaver *et al.*'s (1999) review of the literature in this area. Cleaver *et al.* suggested that such difficulties can have a profound effect on children, and that in general they are worse when combined than individually. Cleaver *et al.* also identified evidence from a range of studies that such issues were common in the work of Children's Services.

Cleaver *et al.* (2007) followed up their key work in identifying these issues with a study looking at policies and practices relating to domestic violence, substance misuse and child care concerns in six contrasting local authorities using a variety of methods. The research included consideration of key policy documents, reviews of files for 357 referrals received by Children's Services in which substance misuse and/or domestic violence were identified, questionnaires sent to 78 managers and interviews with parents and social workers in 18 families. In broad terms the research concluded that a high proportion of the work of social services involved such issues, but that policy, training and practice were often not well geared to addressing such issues. An interesting element of Cleaver *et al.*'s study is the finding that policy and training in relation to domestic violence appeared to have a higher profile than substance misuse.

Despite these exceptions, it remains true that remarkably little research has been undertaken specifically focusing on parental substance misuse within Children's Services. As such, a number of crucial questions remain unanswered. These include:

- What proportion of children allocated a social worker in Children's Services involve parental substance misuse?
- What are the features of such families?
- What are the similarities and differences between families in which there is drug misuse compared to alcohol misuse?
- How do social workers assess and work with such families?
- How do Children's Services work with other agencies, particularly specialist substance misuse workers?

And perhaps most importantly,

- What happens to the children?
- What factors appear to be associated with better – or worse – outcomes for children?

In the following sections we outline the research we undertook and the data about the sample we collected. Chapter 4 provides information on interviews with social workers and Chapter 5 looks at the outcomes for children two years after they were referred to social services.

THE NATURE OF THE RESEARCH

In presenting research there is a balance to be struck between making the research accessible and ensuring that all the relevant details, including potential limitations in the research, are set out clearly. In order to deal with these issues we have tried to explain the research in as straightforward and clear a way as possible. Fuller details can be found in the research articles referred to. For instance, the quantitative method and basic descriptive data in this chapter were presented in a different form in a previous publication (Forrester and Harwin, 2006).

BACKGROUND TO THE STUDY

The first aim of the study was to obtain an idea of the extent and nature of parental substance misuse in social work caseloads. In many studies to date the definition of parental substance misuse was not made clear, and in some instances parental substance misuse was not differentiated from mental illness. It is also rare to have information presented in relation to different drugs or comparing drugs or alcohol.

To address this, the research gathered information on *all* cases allocated a social worker in four local authorities. Overall, while the time periods varied, this was approximately equivalent to collecting information on all allocated cases in four authorities over one year. All four local authorities were in London. It is possible that different patterns of drug and alcohol misuse would be found in local authorities in other parts of the country, but it was not feasible within the scale of the study to obtain a representative sample. An attempt was made to choose contrasting local authorities, resulting in the selection of two inner London authorities and two outer London authorities.

Families were identified shortly after they were allocated a social worker for long-term work. Although the definition of 'long-term' varied between families, in general it was equivalent to allocation after a core assessment under the Assessment Framework.

The file studies gathered information using a pro-forma that had been developing during a pilot study for the project. Because we were interested in exploring social workers' decision-making and understanding their views, data from the file studies were supplemented by interviews with social workers. These were carried out with 59 social workers for 89 of the families at Stage 1. Our original intention was to interview the parents in families identified as involving parental substance misuse. However, despite extensive efforts this did not prove possible. As a result the study relies in large part on information from social work case records (particularly in this chapter and Chapter 5). These vary in the quantity and quality of information provided.

Files studies were carried out on all allocated cases. Cases entered the parental substance misuse sub-sample if the file included information from any professional expressing a concern about the parental misuse of drugs or alcohol (this is sometimes referred to as the parental substance misuse sample when compared to all other allocated cases). This criterion is a deliberately broad definition of 'parental substance misuse' and includes false accusations and families in which parental substance misuse was not the primary concern. This was because we wished to describe the full range of families in which parental substance misuse appeared to be an issue and explore outcomes for children and parents. These families were then compared with cases allocated to a social worker for long-term work that did not involve parental substance misuse.

This methodology enabled us to generate a picture of every case in the four authorities that was newly allocated for long-term work over a one-year period (on average), whether or not they involved parental substance misuse. It provided a valuable picture of overall case numbers, the characteristics of the parents and their children and the reasons for initial referral and for long-term work. What were the results? These are discussed in relation to each of the research questions identified above.

RESULTS

WHAT PROPORTION OF FAMILIES ALLOCATED A SOCIAL WORKER IN CHILDREN'S SERVICES INVOLVE PARENTAL SUBSTANCE MISUSE?

A total of 534 children in 290 families were allocated for long-term social work intervention during the sample collection period/s in the participating local authorities. There were 412 adults living in these families. Within this total number of allocations, 100 families (34%) with 186 children entered the substance misuse (or parental substance misuse) sample because of actual or alleged parental substance misuse (139 adults lived in these households).

An unexpected finding was that, despite the very different profiles of the four authorities, broadly similar proportions of cases involved parental substance misuse. Substance misuse was identified for:

- 35% of families in authority A;
- 30% in authority B;
- 42% in authority C;
- 41% in authority D.

There was a higher incidence of drug misuse cases in inner London authorities (authorities A and D). However, the outer London local authorities contained a higher proportion of families in which alcohol misuse was an issue. As a result, the proportion of families involving substance misuse overall was relatively similar for inner and outer London authorities – 36% and 32% respectively.

WHAT ARE THE FEATURES OF PARENTAL SUBSTANCE MISUSE FAMILIES COMPARED TO OTHER FAMILIES ALLOCATED A SOCIAL WORKER?

Similarities

Overall, the profile of all the families allocated a social worker was one of considerable individual and social adversity. Thus, all allocated families had very high levels of unemployment, most were one-parent families and many had housing difficulties. A high proportion of the parents had had experience of being in care themselves, many had identified mental health difficulties and there was a lot of domestic violence in the sample overall. A reflection of the level of difficulties was that most of the children were either on the child protection register or were subject to care proceedings.

In important respects the children in the parental substance misuse sample were similar to other children allocated a social worker. Thus, for the following there was no statistical difference between parental substance misuse and non-parental substance misuse children:

- Household composition: 59% of parental substance misuse children came from one-parent families; 53% of other allocated families;
- size of sibling group;
- the age and gender of the adults was very similar in the two groups.

Children in each group were also equally likely to have one or more parent who had:

- Learning difficulties;
- A diagnosed mental illness;
- Physical illness.

In terms of race and ethnicity there were broad similarities, but also some important differences. For most ethnic groups around one third of the children were in the substance misuse sample. In contrast, Black African children were under-represented in the parental substance misuse sample: they accounted for 11% of all children but none was in the substance misuse sample. White European, White Irish and Black children of mixed parentage were somewhat over-represented in the substance misuse sample. Roughly half the children in each of these groups were in the substance misuse sample.

However, the more striking difference was not related to race *per se*, but was about whether the family were first-generation immigrants (i.e. the parents had moved to the UK having been born elsewhere). While a high proportion of immigrant families were Black or ethnic minority, many were not: a quarter were White (particularly Irish or from Eastern Europe). Adults in the non-substance misuse sample were twice as likely to be first-generation immigrants as those in the substance misuse sample (39% compared to 18.5%).

The reason for this appears to be partly that immigrant families were much more likely to be referred to Children's Services for complex social problems, often linked to mental health difficulties. This was particularly true for families from Africa and the Indian subcontinent, who were often experiencing acute social deprivation, lack of social support and other problems. However, it was also in part because Black families with parents who had entered the country relatively recently tended *not* to have substance misuse problems. This helps explain both the under-representation of Black African children and the over-representation of children with one or more White parents.

The comparison shows that the parental substance misuse and non-parental substance misuse groups had broadly similar profiles. But whenever a difference emerged, it suggested that the children in the parental substance misuse group might be more vulnerable. These differences are considered next.

Differences: social and environmental factors

As noted above, a picture of severe social disadvantage emerged in all cases. Yet difficulties in the substance misuse sample always exceeded those in the comparison group. Substance misuse families were almost twice as likely to be without a working parent (82% compared to 65%); they were twice as likely to be living in temporary accommodation (23% compared to 12%); and three times as likely to have identified housing concerns (26% compared to 8%).

This picture of severely disadvantaged families held in all the local authorities, but there was a striking difference between the parental substance misuse and non-parental substance misuse families in the distribution of disadvantage and problems. Non-parental substance misuse cases in the outer London authorities involved considerably less social disadvantage. By contrast, the parental substance misuse cases tended to have severe social difficulties even in relatively affluent areas. Whether these social difficulties contributed to or were caused by parental misuse of substances, they nonetheless form part of a picture of families with complex and interrelated difficulties.

Differences: parental factors

It was noted earlier that one of the aims of the study was to chart the full picture of parental difficulties and their relationship to parental substance misuse. To this end, the incidence of other parental difficulties based on file information was also coded. The 'parental difficulties' considered were: learning difficulties, mental illness, experiencing violence, ill-health or disability, criminal convictions, having been in care as a child, having been known to social services as a child, or being a first-generation immigrant. In the following analysis, any parental difficulty is included if it is either proven or suspected. The adults in the substance misuse sample had particularly complex problems. Indeed, none of the potential difficulties that parents might experience were notably *less* likely if a parent misused substances. For some issues the rates of identification were broadly similar. However, substance misuse was significantly associated with three areas:

- a history of being in care or known to social services as a child;
- criminal convictions; and
- experiencing domestic violence.

Criminal convictions were far more common in the substance misusing cases. This might have been expected among those who misused illegal drugs, but the proportion among those misusing alcohol was also very high. This is interesting because in previous work a criminal record of any sort has been identified as a risk factor for child abuse (Taylor, 1989). Given that the identification of a criminal record and parental substance misuse are virtually synonymous in the social work files in this study it is possible that having a criminal record has inadvertently been a marker for parents with a substance misuse problem.

Another striking result was the very strong relationship between substance misuse and violence in the home. Almost two-thirds (64%) of those experiencing violence were in the substance misuse sample. Alcohol was more strongly linked to violence than were drugs. Where drugs and violence were found together, crack misuse was much commoner than heroin misuse. The victims of violence were predominantly women (91%). Adults experiencing violence were also considerably more likely to have a range of other personal difficulties – they were twice as likely to be experiencing mental illness (usually depression), to misuse substances themselves or to have been in care or known to social services as children.

Differences: child factors

The children whose parents misused substances were significantly younger than other children allocated a social worker (5 years 6 months compared to 8 years 3 months). Thus 45% of all children aged 5 or under, 33% of children aged 6–10 but only 20% of children over 11 were in the substance misuse sample. While both drug and alcohol-affected families had younger children on average than non-parental substance misuse cases, drug misuse was particularly strongly linked to newborn babies.

Differences in statutory basis for allocation

By the time cases were allocated, substance misuse was strongly associated with 'heavy-end' allocations. At the point of allocation 62% of children subject to care proceedings and 40% of those placed on the child protection register (CPR) were in the substance misuse sample. Conversely, relatively few (25%) of the children allocated as 'children in need' were in the substance misuse sample. Only 2% (i.e. one child) of children accommodated had parental substance misuse identified. The reasons for this last finding are unclear.

Important differences also emerged within the substance misuse sample depending on whether alcohol or drugs were misused. Drug misuse was associated with care proceedings (41% of *all* children subject to care proceedings at allocation involved drugs compared to 21% that involved only alcohol). By contrast, alcohol misuse was associated with placement on the CPR (31% of all registrations involved alcohol misuse while 9% involved drug misuse alone).

At allocation 60% of all the children in the parental substance misuse sample were judged by the researchers to have experienced significant harm. Neglect was the commonest concern, affecting 46% of the children. This included neglect of medical needs, education, health and parental supervision. Significant emotional abuse was also present at substantial rates (22%) but only 7% of the children experienced significant physical abuse and just one child had been sexually abused. The children also commonly experienced problems in their health and well-being. Educational difficulties affected 41% of all the parental substance misuse children with 30% each experiencing problems relating to health and emotional well-being.

Summary

As might be expected, families allocated a social worker have complex and interrelated social and individual problems. However, those involving parental substance misuse tend to have more serious difficulties: they have significantly higher levels of social difficulties such as unemployment and poor housing, as well as being linked to problems such as violence within the home and a history of having been in care. There do not seem to be any difficulties that are more common in families in which there is no parental substance misuse. This high level of complex problems appears to be reflected in the strong association between the more serious statutory basis for allocation and substance misuse by parents.

WHAT WAS THE PATTERN OF SUBSTANCE MISUSE IN THE PARENTAL SUBSTANCE MISUSE SAMPLE?

What substances were misused?

The most commonly misused substance was alcohol (65% of children). An unexpected finding was that the next most common was crack cocaine (36%) with heroin third (27%). 'Other' drugs, including unspecified allegations, were noted for 30% of children; however, these were almost always drugs that were used in addition to the primary drug of concern. The most common 'other' drug was cannabis, though many other substances were used.

The high proportion of cases involving crack cocaine was an interesting and potentially important finding. It has not been found in previous British research (Kroll and Taylor, 2003) Nor was it found in earlier research in an inner London authority (Forrester, 2000) or in the pilot study in 1999. It therefore seems likely that this may reflect an increase in crack cocaine misuse in London from the late 1990s. In contrast, very little amphetamine use was identified, and when it was mentioned it was always as a subsidiary drug. This reflects the high level of geographical variability in drug use.

There was a very high-level use of multiple substances. For a quarter of children where parents misused alcohol they also used heroin or crack. The overlap was even more pronounced for crack and heroin. Exactly half of crack cases (and two-thirds of heroin cases) involved use of both heroin and crack.

Who misused substances?

For 84% of families the main carer was misusing substances. As the majority were one-parent families, it meant that most of the children lacked access to a potentially 'protective adult'. However, children living in two-parent families were also very vulnerable, with almost half living in households where both parents misused substances. Indeed, only 27 families had an adult in the household who did not misuse substances.

With mothers most frequently the main carer, the focus of concern largely centred on maternal misuse of substances. In 62 of the 100 families there was only concern about maternal substance misuse, in 21 there was concern about both parents and in only 17 families was there only concern about the father's substance misuse.

The picture of who misused was broadly similar across substances; however, a higher proportion of the heroin cases involved two resident parents (41%) than was found for crack (18%) or alcohol (13%). This was because the heroin cases were particularly likely to be newborn babies and both parents were more likely to be together at this early stage in a child's life. On the other hand, where a parent misused heroin the child was unlikely to have a non-misusing parent in the household (16%) compared to crack (27%) or alcohol (35%).

Similarities and differences between parental misuse of substances

As noted above, there were substantial overlaps in the use of different substances, particularly in relation to illegal drugs. This makes it difficult to identify the impact of specific substances. Nonetheless, given the lack of research on this topic, it is worth highlighting the similarities and differences between families affected by different substances.

Overall the similarities in parental profiles and difficulties identified in social work files outweigh the differences when parental substance misuse parents were compared by type of drug misuse. Parental substance misuse on its own without other parental difficulties was the exception whether crack, alcohol or heroin was misused. Irrespective of the drug type, rates of co-occurring mental illness were similar and so were experiences of violence. A parental history of having been in care as a child or known to social services occurred at virtually identical rates whatever the drug type. Finally, the parental substance misuse parents were nearly all unemployed and on benefits: the drug type again was unimportant. The only important difference was that parents who misused crack or heroin were more likely to have housing problems. This was because twice as many parents who used illegal drugs were either homeless or living in temporary accommodation compared to parents who misused alcohol (50% compared to 24%).

Despite similarities in the social and parental difficulties across substances, differences emerged in the incidence of types of maltreatment. Most notably, more children affected by parental alcohol misuse had experienced significant harm (67%) compared to crack (44%) or heroin (32%). One reason was that the alcohol sample contained fewer babies at potential risk, a group who in general had not experienced maltreatment. Only 15% in the alcohol group were babies at risk, compared to 33% of the crack and 41% of heroin samples. However, the difference remained even when babies at risk were excluded because in cases involving crack only, referrals were also made about concerns that had not resulted in significant harm. In contrast where parents misused alcohol, children were more likely to have already experienced significant harm.

There were also differences in the types of difficulties that children exhibited. Children affected by alcohol misuse were more likely to be showing evidence of educational problems (45% compared to 31% of both heroin and crack cases) and emotional or behavioural problems (32% compared to 27% for crack and 12% for heroin). Children affected by illegal drug misuse were less likely to already have identified difficulties.

Similarities and differences between crack and heroin cases at the point of allocation

As noted above, there was considerable overlap between the use of crack and that of heroin. One would therefore expect to find broad similarities between the groups, and indeed this was often the case. In both groups a high proportion of referrals related to babies at risk of harm, similar proportions of children experienced significant harm and educational difficulties. However, some differences emerged between the crack and heroin samples. First, they had different ethnic profiles. Only 32% of the children in the crack sample were White compared to 57% of the heroin sub-sample (65% of the children affected by alcohol misuse were White). Children in the crack group were particularly likely to be of mixed Black parentage (29% to 16%) and Asian (12% to 2%). They also had twice the rates of emotional and behavioural problems, possibly because more of them were teenagers: 18% were aged 13–16 compared to just 2% in the heroin sample. By contrast, children exposed to parental heroin misuse were more likely to be significantly neglected and to have health difficulties.

Parental misuse of both heroin and crack cocaine affected many of the children (n = 33). However, its influence at allocation did not follow any clear-cut pattern. There were two exceptions though. More of these families were in rather chaotic situations and nearly half had a baby expected or just born at the time of the referral.

HOW DO CHILDREN'S SERVICES WORK WITH OTHER AGENCIES?

As this chapter is reporting primarily on information in social work files, the information it can provide about the inter-agency framework is limited. Nonetheless, it can shed light on two elements of inter-agency working. First, who made referrals? Second, what was the involvement of substance misuse specialists?

Overall the similarities in sources of referrals between parental substance misuse and non-parental substance misuse families were greater than the differences. Nevertheless there were some important differences in patterns of referral. Interestingly, substance misuse cases were more likely to be referred by non-professionals, particularly neighbours or relatives (11.5% of children compared to 5% of non-parental substance misuse cases). Hospitals were also more likely to refer children in the parental substance misuse sample (17.5% of parental substance misuse children compared to 11.5%). The vast majority of these referrals concerned babies where there were worries about parental drug misuse. Referrals generally came from multidisciplinary teams monitoring babies who might be at risk, which sometimes included substance misuse professionals. The only group that was notably less likely to refer parental substance misuse children was the 'other' category. This covered a wide range of professionals working in the community, such as youth workers, counsellors, childminders and others. This diverse group tended to refer families for other issues – particularly concerns around families needing social support or allegations of possible sexual abuse.

The most surprising feature of the referrals in the parental substance misuse group is the almost complete absence of referrals from substance misuse professionals – only *one* referral for a child in the substance misuse sample (as an interesting point of comparison, the same number of referrals was received from pub managers). None came from GPs. This is, on the face of it, a cause for concern. However, it is a difficult finding to interpret without further information. One possibility is that substance misuse workers do not identify child care concerns or do not trust children's social services and that these issues lead them to not make referrals. However, a second explanation is that while parents are in contact with substance misuse services they tend to be doing comparatively well. This points to the importance of substance misuse services having ways to identify when parents *stop* attending. It may be that at this point it is crucial to identify children who may be at risk.

Given the crucial importance of substance misuse professionals in cases in which parents misuse drugs or alcohol, we looked more closely at their involvement in families. It has often been hypothesized that there would be difficulties in relationships between child care social workers and substance misuse professionals arising from differences in approach, conflicting ethical views, confidentiality issues and having different clients within the family (LGDF, 1999). We were therefore surprised to find a positive picture of the working relationship between social workers and substance misuse agencies. There were occasional instances of particular problems – especially around confidentiality – but these were generally relatively easily resolved.

The above picture of constructive co-working omits one important fact: by the point of allocation most cases did not have a substance misuse professional involved – in 71% of cases there was little or no involvement from substance misuse professionals by the file study.

Two factors influenced the likelihood of a substance misuse professional being involved. The first was that more serious cases were more likely to involve substance misuse professionals: substance misuse workers played a part in 23% of children in need cases but this rose to 30% of child protection cases and 44% of care proceedings. Second, substance misuse professionals were involved for only a quarter of children where alcohol or crack cocaine was an issue, but were involved in 40% of those where heroin was an issue. The most important reason for this appeared to be that many drug users were involved with agencies providing substitute prescriptions. These provided an important point of contact and source of information for social workers. The biggest factor associated with the non-involvement of substance misuse professionals was parents saying that they did not need or want specialist help.

CONCLUSION AND DISCUSSION

The research confirms that parental misuse by parents is a very important issue in the work of Children's Services. Indeed, it was the single most common parental difficulty. Moreover, the children exposed to parental substance misuse were particularly likely to be the most vulnerable and at high risk. While all families allocated a worker tended to have a range of individual and social problems, they were always more likely to be more severe when substance misuse was involved. The parents were more likely to be unemployed or to have housing difficulties, they were more likely to have been in care or to have a criminal record, and there was a strong association between substance misuse and domestic violence (particularly for alcohol). It is also noteworthy that other issues that might be considered to be separate reasons for social work involvement, such as parental mental illness, were as common in the substance misuse as they were in the non-substance misuse samples. In addition, the children involved were younger. Their vulnerability was reflected in a greater likelihood of more serious types of allocation, such as being placed on the child protection register or being made subject to care proceedings. Despite the fact that a deliberately low threshold had been chosen for entry into the parental substance misuse sample to capture a wide spectrum (any professional expresses a concern about parental drug or alcohol misuse) cases were mainly at the heavy end.

The pattern was broadly similar for the main types of substance – alcohol, heroin or crack cocaine. However, illegal drugs were associated with a greater likelihood of referral before a child had experienced harm, with a significant minority involving concerns about potential harm to a child. By contrast, the children whose parents misused alcohol tended to be older and more likely to have experienced significant harm. These findings suggest that it is important to consider the influence of the drug type so that patterns of similarity and difference can be explored.

Finally, the children in the parental substance misuse sample showed evidence of serious concerns in a range of areas, with most having been placed at risk of significant harm and substantial minorities demonstrating substantial deficits in areas such as educational, behavioural or health development.

The overall picture the study provides points to the importance of parental substance misuse within the work of Children's Services. The frequency of parental substance misuse, its severity and impacts on child well-being suggest that it poses a major challenge to Children's Services in direct work with parents and children, in management and in service planning. In the next chapter we explore how social workers tackled the cases when parental substance misuse was an issue, the difficulties they encountered and their solutions. Chapter 5 concludes the discussion of this study and focuses on a key question – what happened to the children two years after they were referred to Children's Services?

4 The Social Worker Assessments

The overriding message from Chapter 3 was that children and families allo-cated a social worker had extremely complex difficulties and a wide range of problems. Acute financial difficulties, the risk or experience of eviction, mental health and learning difficulties, crime, debt, physical and emotional abuse, and especially child neglect were common features of these families. In this chapter we turn our attention to the social workers and look at how they assessed parental substance misuse and the risks it posed to the children. We draw extensively on the social workers' own accounts to help explain the decision-making processes, the difficulties they faced and their solutions. Their accounts are used to help identify best practice and to explore dilemmas and problems.

The chapter starts with a brief overview of the social worker sample. We then describe our research method. However, the bulk of the chapter is a description of the key issues the social workers identified, including the chal-lenges they faced and how they attempted to overcome them, and a discussion of the implications for practice and policy.

THE INTERVIEWS: AIMS AND METHOD

In all, 59 social workers were interviewed in relation to 89 cases. The inter-views generally took place shortly after allocation, though in some instances this was not possible and there was a delay of some months. The interviews varied in length from 45 minutes to 1½ hours. They were semi-structured and covered a number a key themes. The workers were asked to provide a brief pen picture of the case, the presenting concerns, the assessment aims and processes, and how these informed the interventions. All the social workers were asked to comment particularly on the substance misuse aspects of the case. All interviews were tape-recorded and transcribed. The analysis was carried out by both researchers to increase the reliability and validity of the findings.

Parents Who Misuse Drugs and Alcohol. Effective Interventions in Social Work and Child Protection, 1st edition. By Donald Forrester and Judith Harwin.
© 2011 John Wiley & Sons, Ltd.

The interviews were analysed in order to identify key themes. We identified themes that emerged from the interview material. We then clustered the key concepts and categories into subgroups and organized our analysis around these themes. Once the theme had been identified and the data were only confirming the picture, we moved on to a new theme, having first looked carefully for examples that ran counter to the interpretations which we had put on the data.

Our initial intention had been to interview the children and parents, however this proved unfeasible. Numerous attempts were made to interview the first 12 families in the study but it ultimately proved possible to inter-view just one parent. This was because at the time of the study families were going through very difficult times, often including the initiation of care pro-ceedings (and the meetings with multiple professionals that this entailed) and multiple moves of accommodation. There were therefore practical and ethical issues about conducting the interviews, and it was reluctantly decided that it would not be possible to carry out that aspect of the study. Of the information presented all data are anonymized, and where names are given they are fictional.

The social workers interviewed varied widely in experience levels. There was a high proportion of relatively newly qualified workers: 41 (71%) had been qualified for five years or less; and 22 (37%) of those had qualified within the last year. The staff group reflected problems endemic within London, including a high proportion of agency staff, newly qualified workers and a significant number of workers employed short-term. Almost two-thirds (63%) of workers had been in their current job for one year or less. A high propor-tion of those interviewed were agency staff.

ASSESSMENT OF CHILD WELFARE

The social workers were faced with a wide array of situations in which they had to assess child care concerns, risk and protective factors in the family situ-ation and the possibility of the need for out-of-home care, with or without legal intervention. The cases varied from concerns over babies who had never been harmed through to children with serious medical conditions such as heart problems, cystic fibrosis and, less frequently, children as young as 10 years old who themselves were misusing and selling drugs. In other cases, children were living in homes where they were caught in the crossfire of parental violence, or, even at the age of 5 or 6, were already taking on parental caring roles, cooking for themselves and looking after younger siblings. Less commonly concerns involved teenagers who had dropped out of school, had become involved in violence or had attempted suicide. In one case a young person died in an accident linked to their own risk-taking behaviour.

What were the social workers looking for when carrying out the assessments of child welfare? The first consideration was usually to establish whether the child's most basic needs were being met. As one social worker commented:

> It doesn't matter if the parents have problems, as long as they can provide adequate care for the child. Can the parent feed the child? Do they take them to school? Do they keep them clean and tidy? Is the home clean? Is the child safe?

These questions formed the bread and butter of the assessments and would be used to establish or discount the presence of neglect or abuse and whether or not the child should be placed or remain on the child protection register or whether care proceedings should be instigated. The social workers were confident of the kinds of information that they needed to collect. The assessments were made through their own observations – for example, comments on the appearance of the child included 'boils due to poor hygiene' and 'grubby and wore dirty clothes', and of the house, 'full of human and animal excrement' – which were collected first hand to support a judgement of child neglect posing a risk to safety and health. There was also liaison with other professionals.

It was very rare for social workers to use a theoretical model. However, there was a pragmatic hierarchy of concern moving from the assessment of children's basic needs through to establishing a picture of other, less immediate aspects of child development – the children's emotional and behavioural well-being, their language development and intellectual abilities. A mass of information was collected on concerns about children's emotional needs, far more than on their language and intellectual development, play, motor skills, interests and special gifts and abilities. These examples capture some of these:

> Hyperactive: very aggressive ... foul-mouthed ... very busy and difficult to engage with.

> Simon's concentration is poor and he is unable to obey adult instructions.

> Heather starting to wet herself and her brother to poo himself.

> [Children] confident and not subdued.

> Were not stuck in a chair, you could see the freedom they had, the autonomy.

> [The child] sat there like she was really spaced out, she was in her own little world.

Some of this information was collected first hand by direct observation but often it came from other agencies, most frequently the school, but health visitors were also sources of information with regular liaison to monitor progress. Paediatricians and speech therapists contributed rarely but more commonly than GPs. It was also rare for reports on delays in language or intellectual development to be supported by reports from psychologists unless the problem was so severe that it triggered a statement of special needs. The social workers' own observations formed the core of the assessment and were very rarely backed up with other types of evidence such as standardized instruments, questionnaires or reports from specialists, and few of the workers thought this was necessary. The main source of information was observation and discussion in the interviews with clients.

Establishing a profile of the child's emotional and behavioural development went hand in hand with an assessment of the child's family and social relationships. In all the interviews this latter aspect was given great importance. The workers considered themselves to be experts in this area and undertook the assessments themselves, relying largely on unstructured observation within the family home and conversations with parents, but only rarely on conversations with the child. Their observations were informed particularly by literature on bonding, attachment and attachment disorders. To this end they would look for evidence of warmth, responsiveness to the child's needs and signs of subtle or overt rejection and its impact on the child's emotional wellbeing and for quality of sibling interactions. These examples are typical:

> When the child, was distressed, he would turn for comfort to his mother.

> [Child would also] cuddle her father ... did not appear frightened of him.

> [Frequent sibling fights linked to stepfather's ambivalence to his stepson] 'this boy is hurting my daughter'.

> [Dad has a] very high regard for her ... gives her lots of attention.

They also assessed the kinds of responsibilities placed on the children, whether they were age-appropriate and if they took account of the special vulnerability of any child within the family. Assessment of developmental milestones was far more evident in relation to very young children than it was for older ones. Core assessments frequently produced information on this:

> [John (aged 6) does] everything for himself, including baths, apart from preparing meals.

> [Stacey (aged 7)] routinely prepared all her own meals.

The focus was both on the extent to which the practical aspects of self-care were age-appropriate and on the emotional repercussions. 'Quite an adult child' was the observation for one 8 year old whose mother had misused drugs from the child's early childhood; 'very mature' for a 5 year old; and a comment about the damaging burden of responsibility placed on an 8 year old who was the confidante of his drug-misusing and prostitute mother.

A prime focus of the assessment was to identify the links between the child care concerns and the parenting. When it came to exploring the substance misuse issues, this proved to be the most challenging and difficult aspect of the assessment. It is to this question, which forms the main focus of the chapter that we now turn.

HOW DID THE SOCIAL WORKERS ASSESS PARENTAL SUBSTANCE MISUSE?

It might have been expected that the social workers would routinely carry out an assessment of the parental substance misuse themselves. This did not prove to be the case and there was a variety of reasons for this. In some cases the assessment had already been done by a drugs and alcohol worker or, more unusually, by another professional. In other cases, the presenting assessment task did not explicitly include examination of the role of the substance misuse. In several cases the assessment task was to consider the suitability of out-of-home placement or to assess the impact of domestic violence on the children. Sometimes the substance misuse had only recently come into focus: an assessment was planned but had not yet been carried out. Finally, and most importantly, assessments were sometimes not carried out because of the difficulties of doing so. We discuss this shortly.

Assessments that had been carried out by a substance misuse specialist were always highly valued because this specialist provided the social worker with information needed to establish the role of parental substance misuse in the case. They were also viewed as better able to commission specialist tests, such as a liver function test or other blood tests, and thereby keep usage under regular review on the basis of 'hard evidence'. But there was another less obvious benefit: the social workers also said that specialist input helped facilitate conversations between them and the parent on substance misuse and improved the parent–worker relationship.

> It was discussed because of, I think, the good rapport I had with Tony who is a drug worker and any information I needed I felt that, I did have a lot of information and what signs to look for in case I thought the couple were relapsing or – so I felt that I had a good rapport, good working relationship with the drug worker, and there was regular sharing of information.

Very unusually, other professionals would carry out the substance misuse assessment. Again, this was valued for the factual information that it generated and because it opened the door for the social worker to talk about substance misuse and other aspects of parenting. In one case the GP did the assessment and bluntly told the father he would die if he did not stop drinking. The social worker commented that, as a result of the GP's intervention, the father began to open up and it led to helpful discussion about his drinking and associated problems with the father and his children.

The benefits of relying on a substance misuse specialist to carry out the assessment were consistently reported by the social workers. But it was a limited strategy because specialists were involved in only 29% of the cases and they were particularly uncommon in alcohol misuse. For the most part, social workers relied on their own resources. How did they go about the assessment in these situations? We identified two main approaches which have called full and limited assessments. In *full* assessments the social worker would undertake the following tasks:

- Assess the amount, types, pattern and duration of substance misuse with the parent suspected of it.
- Discuss reasons for misuse, including short-term triggers.
- Assess parent's level of commitment to tackling the misuse and previous efforts to give up or cut down.
- Talk to the children separately about the misuse and its impacts on them.
- Assess the relationship between the child care concerns and the parental substance misuse.
- Assess the link between the substance misuse and other parental problems.

Full assessments were undertaken in only a handful of cases, but when they were done, they provide excellent examples of best practice (see Box 4.1). For example, instead of just asking children about their activities to build rapport, the worker would also discuss with the child whether they had anyone to turn to when they were upset about the parental substance misuse – a far more focused approach, which could then lead to concrete action. They would try to establish how far the parent was committed to giving up their use of drugs or alcohol, what kinds of treatment had been tried with what results, and what could be made available. But what really marked out the full assessments was the clear focus on the interrelationship between the drug misuse profile and child's well-being, based on an up-to-date picture of the extent and pattern of misuse.

LIMITED ASSESSMENTS

By contrast, in the far more common *limited* assessments the social workers would carry out some but not all of the above tasks, and their information on the substance misuse aspects tended to be very partial. But why were these the norm? The social workers provided us with detailed examples of the multiple and interconnected obstacles that beset them when attempting to assess parental substance misuse. It is important to consider these in some depth in order to understand both the challenges that social workers encountered in this work and some of the ways in which they attempted to resolve such challenges.

CLIENT MINIMIZATION AND DENIAL

Client minimization and denial emerged as the most common obstacle to conducting an effective assessment. They were also associated with some of the most serious problems in carrying out the assessment. Minimization took

Box 4.1   A full assessment.

nown to social services for many years and had
... to London. They were currently living in a cramped
... there were four children, one with serious health problems. Mr
Lang misused illegal drugs and the mother had longstanding mental health
problems. The referring authority also drew attention to the fact that the
children were not attending school and were missing health appointments
and the family lacked any social supports.

Features of the social worker assessment

A starting point to effective assessment is clarity around the aims and purpose. The quotation below demonstrates clearly how the social worker's
primary objective in the Lang case was to establish the interrelationship
between substance misuse, parenting and impacts on child well-being.

> We had to assess risk because of Mr Lang's drug use which was really impor-
> tant because we had to assess how much heroin he was taking ... We had to
> assess whether it was safe for the children being in the hostel – where did he
> leave the drugs, how often he takes them? – so we had to assess that. We had
> to assess the parents' ability to care for the children as well – whether their
> parenting was good enough. I think they were basically the main things that
> we had to look at.

This went hand in hand with a detailed set of questions to build up a picture
of the substance misuse that focused on immediate safety considerations,
readiness for treatment and consideration of the longer term:

> Well basically I would go into the home ... and then I would ask Mr Lang
> about his drug use, so I would ask questions like 'How often are you taking
> the heroin? How much are you taking? Are you taking any other drugs?
> Where do you leave your drugs? What are his expectations, does he think that
> he's going to be taking this for the next year, five years? Is he prepared to get
> any help? Has he thought about the impact that it has on the children?' That's
> the sort of questions I would ask in my assessment. And also part of my assess-
> ment would be to get in contact with other agencies, so I would speak to the
> health visitor, I'd speak to the GP, I'd speak to drug units, so that would be
> all part of my assessment.

With this information, the social worker could start to develop a concrete
action plan around the substance misuse, but only after talking to Mrs Lang
and to each child separately. Talking to the children separately was very
unusual. Note here how the social worker wanted to explore the children's
attitudes to the father but also specifically to identify whether they had a

confidant to whom they could turn for support. Here he was using research evidence on the importance of protective adults to build resilience and the answer would tell him whether he needed to identify someone to take on this role.

> I found out from the children that they really thought of Mr Lang as a father, they really felt so much for him because they spoke so highly of him. We tried to find out what was going on for them, you know, were they happy? What did they do in their spare time? Did they have friends at school? Did they have somebody they could speak to if they had problems? What did they like? What don't they like? Things like that.

Once the social worker had accrued this information he began to prioritize interventions. As a first step, he and the parents agreed where the drugs would be kept so that they were out of reach of the children. As Mr Lang had shown commitment to tackling his substance misuse, a place in a detox programme was arranged. The questions around substance misuse, which on the face of it might seem intrusive, started to provide the foundation to develop a purposive relationship with the social worker and, as seen below, were important in the way in which the case unfolded subsequently.

The assessment with the parents, which looked at the causes and repercussions of Mrs Lang's depression, was used to develop ground rules to ensure the children got to school and kept health appointments. A whole array of practical supports was put in place to help the family in the short and long term. These included a family assistant, advice on benefits and rehousing, after-school activities and referral for child development support. Work was intensive and goal-directed. Parents could see that Children's Social Care was trying to help: as well as motivating the parents, it provided the social worker with evidence of progress.

Close contact with the inter-agency network was another important component of the assessment in this case, but this was not easy as different ideologies and practices created barriers that needed to be overcome. For example, confidentiality issues prevented the social worker from obtaining updates of father's progress in the detox. Through negotiation it was agreed that if father failed to attend, the social worker would be informed. This proved vital. There were other difficulties. The child development centre was unwilling to take on the family until it had addressed its other problems. This was one of the reasons for putting in place so quickly the family assistant and out-of-school activities to act as a safety net. Finally, there were attitudinal barriers. Some of the agencies were very sceptical as to whether Mr Lang could change in time for his children. These differences in perception were important because they helped reinforce the importance of the social worker constantly monitoring and verifying his information. While the whole case strategy was based on giving the parents a chance, with a clear set of goals and timescales, when things started to go wrong the 'rule of optimism' was kept in check. The social worker acted swiftly. He visited the father and had the knowledge to judge what was going on:

> ... because of his glazed eyes, his slow speech. So when we went round to the home again, I think it was quite soon after when I saw him and I said to him, 'Look, you have to be honest with me, have you taken any?' And he said to me 'Yes', and they were quite open and honest as well, so he said to me, 'Yes, I have been taking some but I'm not taking as much'. So that's how we knew, I could tell by his presentation.

His experience had also taught him about relapse and that relapse can be part of the process of change. A new plan had to be developed but with tighter timescales.

many forms. Clients would be reported to be prepared to admit to a problem in the past, but not in the present. They would acknowledge that they 'might have a beer once a month' or simply refuse to discuss the topic:

> Every time you delved into that ... you would literally see the iron gates just come and that would be it.

> Accepting responsibility, minimizing the actual abuse, especially, like I said, if there are small children. The adult in the home usually says, 'Oh well, they were here, they were in another room, they were sleeping, they don't know what's going on. What's the problem, you know, maybe I only drink at night and you know – whatever'. So it's these sorts of things.

The problem for the social worker was that this response ran counter to information they had received from schools, police and health visitors, reporting that a parent had arrived drunk at the nursery or picked up the child high on drugs. Minimization and denial also often contradicted the information given from partners, extended family and even the children, as we shall explore later. Even when the social worker was astute enough to make it easier for the parent to admit misuse by acknowledging that, from the parental view, denial may be a rational strategy, this did not necessarily end the deadlock. In the following example the social worker states that they had articulated one of the most widely acknowledged parental fears in these cases, but this had not led to admission of substance misuse problems:

> *Social Worker*: I don't think she tells me everything. I've asked her on almost every visit – well not on every visit, but quite frequently, 'Rachel, are you on drugs because if you're on drugs we can get you help'. I do believe that some clients feel that if they admit to being on drugs, the children will be taken away and it will go against them but I've said to her – in this instance I said, 'Look, if

you need help, we can get it for you because if you are on drugs it might be even more difficult for you to meet these, you know.'

Interviewer: And she's just denied it?

Social Worker: She's just denied it. I've given her a lot of opportunities to tell me.

This created huge problems for the social workers and left them feeling stuck and uncertain how to proceed:

It's a difficult thing to do because you feel that people deny that they have a problem.

It's difficult when they're just in a denial. You find that you are stagnant and you can't do nothing. Because until they admit it, you could be pushing against all the surfaces you can push. It doesn't mean that it's going to work.

INTIMIDATION

Feeling stuck was exacerbated by some clients deliberately intimidating the social worker. In one case the social worker admitted that she sometimes needed to end the interview prematurely with a verbally aggressive mother because she could 'sense some sort of violence' waiting to explode. In another case, the father had made threats to 'cut up' the previous worker, while in a third all interviews had to be carried out in the presence of a security guard following an incident in which the worker had been assaulted. The same client had thrown a brick through the window of the social worker's office. These examples demonstrate powerfully the very difficult circumstances in which the interviews were sometimes conducted. The workers were understandably worried about their safety and were reluctant to pursue what they knew could be an explosive line of inquiry.

In reality, assault was far less common than fear of it. But the consequences were similar. Fear and anxiety structured the intervention and led to outright avoidance of the topic and/or delay. In these situations, problems could escalate, thereby increasing anxiety and pressure on the social worker. It was a vicious circle.

SOCIAL WORKER ROLES AND KNOWLEDGE

Even in far less frightening circumstances, social workers found many other reasons that made it difficult for them to undertake a parental substance misuse assessment. A particularly interesting dilemma occurred when social workers asserted that that their role did not entitle them to carry out an assessment of substance misuse, arguing that this was the role of the drug and alcohol specialists and that it would impede focus on the child protection concerns. This kind of barrier was unusual but it was important because it was not feasible to rely on substance misuse experts and because it deprived the worker of potentially vital evidence.

Lack of confidence in conducting assessments was a much commoner theme in the social work interviews. Frequently, the social workers noted that they had not been trained to recognize the signs and symptoms of misuse, to understand the pharmacological effects of different types of drugs and to know what comprised safe levels of use. As a result, they were unable to recognize whether a client was high on illegal drugs or alcohol during an interview or to make sense of the information that they were being given on consumption patterns.

A lack of basic knowledge on drug misuse and its effects was widespread and had a profound influence on case management. It helps explain why so few cases included clear information on the drug problem itself and instead why the picture was often sketchy and often based on opinion rather than facts.

> No, I haven't actually. I just relied on her telling me and I rang up other people. I just feel looking around the house and her presentation seems to point to drug abuse but without having the proof there wasn't anything I could do.

Knowledge of what information was needed was a prerequisite to a useful assessment but it was not necessarily sufficient to move the case forward. Some social workers doubted the value of undertaking an assessment if the parent was in denial. What was the point of asking the questions if the answers would be evasive or downright dishonest? These dilemmas are clearly articulated in the following example:

> Maybe that's an area I should get into, I don't know … but it's one of those areas that maybe in supervision one could talk about, how you approach this. Because … you want to be able to do it in a way that she would feel able to answer. But you see that's the trouble, you know that someone's not going to tell you, 'Look last night I couldn't put the kids to bed because I was totally out of it', they won't tell you that, will they?

As a result social workers became ambivalent about investigating the substance misuse and that made them indecisive and uncertain. It also made them pessimistic. Here are two social workers speaking and illustrating how they vacillated on whether or not to confront the suspected misuse:

> It's a difficult thing because you feel that people deny that [they have a drinking problem, so I'm] expecting it not to be a very useful discussion.

> Always at the back of my mind, I've got to be aware that some people admit to a certain amount of things to conceal the rest. So I've got that at the back of my mind, she says she's drinking too much, but is she just saying that so that I think 'Oh, she's honest, that's good'?

Being unsure of the basic facts around substance misuse blocked off other potentially linked important lines of inquiry. In one case, the social worker was fairly sure a mother had a serious drug problem but had not been able to collect factual information to support her suspicion. As a result, she was unable to explore the likely impact of misuse on the children. These were the major questions in the social worker's mind that remained unanswered:

> Had the children seen her injecting? Had they seen her at night-time 'totally out of it'? I feel she may be aware and keep things in control for the children but I just don't know.

The problems arising from lack of information on the substance misuse were particularly common when workers wanted to build a picture of a client's finances. Sometimes the workers suspected that parents had far more money available to them than would be expected from their benefit profile, due to prostitution or dealing. In other cases the opposite applied. The client denied misusing, yet there was no money for food, housing and heating. The social workers were left guessing, suspicious and frustrated. 'All alcoholics are liars' one worker remarked and, when coupled with a view that 'very few people kick the habit', it created pessimism about the value of assessment.

THE SOCIAL WORKER–CLIENT RELATIONSHIP: HONESTY AND PARTNERSHIP

Pursuit of discrepancies in information, client minimization and denial was always problematic because it ran counter to what many social workers saw as the basic principles of social work – that the relationship needed to be open, honest and conducted in partnership with the client. There were countless examples of this conflict which either stopped social workers from undertaking an assessment of misuse with the client or made them suspicious about the truth of their answers:

> But it's in the child protection arena. And that must have an impact in families in terms of how they view you. And I would have thought it was better for him [father] to have somebody outside of that who doesn't feel I might be looking at all, 'Oh that's a bit dicey, we're going to register those kids again' or something. That he feels free who he can talk to and there's going to be no one judging him unless he was saying 'I'm going to kill my kids' – the council won't have to tell us, but it's, you know what I mean, he needs somebody neutral, you know.

It could have further repercussions because it also inhibited their willingness to talk to other professionals, so the case could become starved of reliable information from different sources. Here is a social worker wishing to explore treatment possibilities but feeling unable to do so for fear of damaging the relationship:

It [how rehab went] is something that I need to find out ... but I want to talk to him first about doing that. I just feel really conscious about – people think that social workers are really sly and we go behind people's backs and we gain all this information, and I want to talk to him about getting that info before I go off and do it ...

In another case, the social worker wanted to let the client know that he was planning to get information about his drinking from other professionals, but the client rarely turned up for appointments. At its most extreme, a need to demonstrate commitment to the ethos of partnership could lead to serious distortion of the facts. The following case example, in which the social worker singled out working with the family as the key difficulty, speaks for itself:

... kind of taking over the case and knowing there's been lots of intimidation and hostility but at the same time having to go to court and say 'yes, we were working in partnership with this family', and then being frustrated when you can't. It's just what you do.

Far more commonly, however, it was simple things, such as the client's lack of reliability in keeping appointments and general unpredictability, that damaged the prospects of an assessment being carried out in a spirit of partnership based on honesty.

It might be asked why the social workers strove so hard to build partnerships in such unpromising circumstances. Indeed, its absence could surely be used as an argument of lack of parental cooperation and be perceived as a parenting risk factor in its own right. Where social workers were confident of their capacity to investigate parental substance misuse, this was precisely how client denial, minimization and hostility were treated. These behaviours and attitudes were perceived to be part of the assessment evidence. But when social workers doubted their experience and expertise in substance misuse, they were more likely to blame themselves and keep trying to broach the subject. Keeping the relationship friendly became an end in itself and it led to delay in making inquiries into the misuse.

BEING OPEN-MINDED ABOUT HARM FROM SUBSTANCE MISUSE

Honesty and openness were highly prized by the social workers as the best way of working and the most likely approach to develop trusting relationships in which clients would be able to discuss their problems and, with social worker support, become good enough parents for their children. As we have seen, this was principally a value position that ran the risk of excluding collecting accurate information. Another equally important value was the determination not to judge parents because they misuse.

I think there was one message that came over to me [from an article the social worker had recently read] that just because somebody has a drug or alcohol problem ... it does not necessitate not being able to parent and love and be committed to their children.

The problem for the social worker was how to move beyond the value position to test it empirically on the basis of the case evidence. This was yet another reason for assessment difficulties.

CHILDREN'S EVIDENCE AND THE CONSEQUENCES OF ASSESSMENT DIFFICULTIES

Assessment difficulties had important repercussions on the relationships the social workers established with the children. First, it could make the social workers mistrustful and reluctant to believe the children's evidence. In one case, the social worker noted that 6-year-old Natalie 'doesn't like it when her mother gets drunk, it frightens her'. But she was reluctant to use this information in her discussions with the mother because she felt she needed to see and hear things for herself and not rely on what she characterized as mere 'hearsay'. Yet in other cases, it was the child who silenced the social worker. The following heartrending example makes the point far more vividly than any adult commentary:

> Please, oh please, don't tell my mum because my mum will scream and shout at me and I don't want her to.

Of course, in these situations, it was not really the child silencing the social worker but the parent who struck terror in the child by threatening that they would be taken into care if they talked.

In other cases the young age of the child was cited as a barrier to talking to them about parental substance misuse. As a result, the worker might approach the topic obliquely, hoping that it would provide an *entrée* to the subject. As a strategy this had very variable chances of success as the following example demonstrates:

> *Interviewer:* Have you had chance to talk to the children about their parents?
>
> *Social Worker:* They're too young really. Wayne's coming up to being five and I think it was too young. What I've said is, 'Where do you normally go with your mum?'
>
> *Interviewer:* And what does he say?
>
> *Social Worker:* He says, 'I go to the collect the giro'. I haven't built up that much of a relationship because I haven't seen them really to do some direct work with the children. I haven't seen them that regularly.

But even with older children, efforts to broach the subject directly could lead to the same evasive answers that social workers encountered so frequently with parents, as illustrated below in a case involving 13-year-old Stacey, which the social worker had held for over a year. The social worker explained that he had unsuccessfully tried to discuss substance misuse with the father and wanted to talk to the teenager who was living in foster care.

> It [was] something I wanted to ask Stacey at the time but it wasn't appropriate to ask because I said to her 'What does he drink?' and she said 'Cans'.

In these cases the social worker was faced with a dilemma because it was considered essential to keep open the relationship with the child or young person and to be seen to be an ally. This was a common theme.

> I want to be on their side I want the best for them.

So instead the social worker focused on what was happening in Stacey's life (school, boyfriends, music, fashion, etc.). A fear of upsetting the child was a closely related reason for avoiding talking about substance misuse, particularly in the case of young children. Mirroring the approaches seen with the parents, social workers would avoid or deliberately delay broaching the subject with children in the hope that a good moment would eventually arise. It kept open the relationship but it meant that sometimes the important questions were not asked.

Finally, there were more practical reasons why children's evidence was not collected on substance misuse. In many of the cases, children were only seen by the social worker with their parents or they were seen so irregularly on their own that it was not possible to ask what were always seen as 'difficult questions'. All these reasons – the practical, knowledge, values and skills-based difficulties – were interrelated. The consequences were that they could leave children unsupported and unprotected.

STRATEGIES TO DEAL WITH ASSESSMENT CHALLENGES

The multiple and interconnected factors outlined above help explain why limited assessments predominated. They also forcefully demonstrate the complexity of the tasks facing the social workers. So how did staff try to deal with being stuck? There appeared to be five main strategies:

1. Collecting further information.
2. Confrontation.
3. Concentrating on other tasks to develop trust.
4. Monitoring.
5. Getting advice from their supervisor.

Gathering further information was an obvious and common strategy and included liaison with colleagues who had originally held the case, with other agencies and the non-misusing parent. Although a conversation with the non-misusing parent might have been viewed as problematic because it was 'hearsay' and possibly unreliable, it was usually valued.

A less expected strategy was confrontation. This tended to be mentioned more by social workers who felt confident about dealing with substance misuse. In some cases the social worker decided to challenge the parent and 'up the ante' to force the issue to a head. In others, the social worker wanted to cut through dishonesty. In both of these situations, the social worker was attempting to set the agenda and take control. But in some cases, it was not the social worker who initiated the challenge: instead, the confrontation was a response to the actions of external agencies. For example, in one case, the NSPCC argued that care proceedings had to be initiated without further delay. Finally, confrontation was likely to be used to counter client intimidation and again as a way of asserting control. The following examples illustrate these different reasons for confrontation.

> I'm a bit stuck at the moment because I haven't talked to her about any of this yet and I have been open and friendly and there has been no confrontation whatsoever so far, except 'come and work with me and I can try and support you in trying to get your kids back'. I think she needs a shock, so I think I need to up the ante ... She needs to be shocked into doing something.

Another ploy was to resort to different types of case monitoring. These included unannounced visits to the family home and the use of written agreements to set out a very explicit list of expectations on the parent. As the following examples show, these written agreements were not forged in the spirit of partnership: they were a strategy to try to control the situation and delineate the repercussions of non-compliance:

> Yes, there's a list of things that they're supposed to do. The more they avoid us the more is added to the list, you know, things that they have to do. They were given a list and were given a deadline.

> It was a nightmare. Just like five sentences 'You will, you will' nothing about involvement ... local authority's responsibility, how we will support, how we will befriend and why we are moving tasks forward and what would happen if these tasks weren't met.

A fairly common strategy, and one linked to the pessimism discussed earlier, was that social workers adopted a passive stance and just waited for things to get worse:

> I'm concerned about those things and I'm concerned about mum because I'm concerned about how much longer it will take for things to get worse and about the conditions of the home. So there are a number of issues.

> The problem with that is that in some of these child protection cases you are almost waiting for something dreadful to happen before you can move in and say 'Aha!' ...

Sometimes a critical incident was seen as the only way forward; the slow accumulation of risk over time was far less likely to be seen as constituting the kind of evidence that could move the case ahead.

The final approach was to get advice from their supervisor. There was a very mixed picture in relation to how helpful workers found this. In light of the many difficulties in these cases, the quality of supervision played a key role. To use the parlance of risk assessments, good supervision appeared to protect social workers from potential difficulties associated with working with complex cases even when the workers had the 'risk factors' of little previous experience or training in relation to substance misuse. Conversely, poor supervision could lead to even highly qualified workers feeling unprotected and 'lost' in their work with families. One newly qualified worker dealing with a complex case responded to whether supervision was useful by saying:

> [It is regular] and very useful ... it's kind of nice, because I get frustrated and I just want to say 'What are we going to do?' Anything comes out and she goes 'OK, that is this' you know, to put me straight on where we are, where we're at, what our role is, what our position is, what we need to wait for before we can then do this and do that, and it's like, 'OK, OK, I'm with you now. I'll get this in place, yes'.

However, while most workers broadly reported positively about supervision, a substantial minority had considerable reservations. Most common were that they simply did not receive much supervision – for instance, one experienced social worker replied to the question 'Did you discuss the assessment process in supervision?' by saying, 'What's supervision! Not at all' – and an even more common complaint was that supervision tended to concentrate on a list of tasks rather than discussing cases in depth. One worker commented:

> I think part of the problems with supervision is it feels a bit like going through a checklist to inform your supervisor what you have been doing rather than evaluating stuff. I do think sometimes we are very good at collecting information but not very good at knowing what to do with it.

This was quite a common complaint and was sometimes explicitly linked to wider developments within child care social work. For instance, supervision might concentrate on whether forms had been filled in rather than discussing the process and content of assessments. Similarly, some workers felt that drives by local authorities to improve on certain indicators or to prepare files for inspection had led to a form of supervision focused on task completion rather than on more thorough consideration of cases.

HOW DID THE SOCIAL WORKERS USE THE INFORMATION FROM THEIR ASSESSMENTS?

Once the social workers had identified the child care concerns and assessed the parenting difficulties, the next major task was to link these two components in order to be able to draw up a plan. Much of the literature emphasizes the importance of undertaking this kind of analysis because it provides the evidence base for the care plan. It is also seen to be important because it enables the social worker to set and prioritize goals, formulate contingency plans, take account of the risks and decide when a change of tack is needed. Finally and less frequently mentioned in the literature, it is important because it enables the social worker to share with parents the strategy and its rationale.

This type of synthesis and case formulation was identified as one of the most challenging aspects of case planning. It required the social workers to move beyond description to analysis and in particular to make judgements about present risks, protective factors and parental capacity to change in time for the children. The difficulty of this task was explained clearly by one of the social workers:

> I think my problem is that within social work the word assessment is banded around quite a lot, and I think actually there's not many people are very clear about what assessment means ... so we assess [the] child's needs, assess [the] parent's ability to meet [the] child's needs and ... I think there's a lot of detail is sort of got but ... it's only ever in the care proceedings you actually get to the analysis bit... and I don't think we do that very well ... It's the same within looked after children stuff, we have the assessment and action records, we do them and then we don't really extrapolate the information from them very effectively ... And I think that that perhaps is the same for assessing parents, that we ... gather all the information but we don't connect it very well ...

So how did the social workers move beyond description to make these connections and what helped them in doing so?

THE USE OF THEORY, ACTUARIAL MODELS AND GOVERNMENT ASSESSMENT FRAMEWORKS

The social workers did not appear to find any of the research-based, theoretical or practical guides particularly helpful. Although they regularly acknowledged that the Child Assessment Framework usefully specified the types of information needed for an assessment, none said it helped with synthesizing the information and establishing how to weigh up the relative importance of different factors. As one worker memorably remarked, 'it's the *Orange Book* as a triangle'. Nor were actuarial models or checklists mentioned often as guides to balance risks against strengths and theories too were not seen to provide much assistance. The following comment captures a common view:

> To be honest with you, when I was at [college], there were so many theories that I went through that I forget them all. The theories that I now use are my gut feeling and my life experience and ... how the person reacts to me.

As a result, the social workers tended to rely heavily on intuition and life experience to make these difficult judgements to establish what was risky, how risky and how far the risks were offset by protective factors. The most widely used yardstick to answer these questions was to consider the impact of the specific factor on the child. As noted earlier, substance misuse was not automatically a risk factor unless the evidence highlighted risk or actual harm to the child. The same was true of mental health and learning difficulties. For example, in one case a young mother with learning difficulties was considered to place her baby at risk because she did not understand how the violence she experienced from her husband placed their baby at risk.

Apart from the yardstick of child impact, it was difficult to identify a systematic set of principles that underpinned how risks and protective factors were assessed. The commonest approach was to generate a simple list of risks and strengths. With regard to risks, parental substance misuse was mentioned most frequently and five times as often as domestic violence, mental health or learning difficulties. On the strengths side, three sets of factors were mentioned regularly:

- the support of the extended family;
- the strength of parental attachment and child's bonding;
- good communication and engagement with social services.

Other strengths that were mentioned less frequently were:

- parent wanting to or having the capacity to change;
- maternal ability to prevent abusive partner having access to the child;
- strong cultural identity;
- child being clean, tidy and well-dressed;
- child having a good relationship with the carer;
- child doing well at school;
- parent being open about their substance misuse;
- permanent housing;
- good access to day care.

This list has been reproduced in full because it makes a number of points. Unexpectedly, structural factors and resource issues such as housing and day care were not given much emphasis, but as in many other studies, cooperation with social services emerged as a key factor. The shopping list approach tended to emphasize the presence or absence of a factor rather than assessing the degree of risk it posed or how strong the counterbalancing strengths were. These finer-grained judgements were uncommon. Finally, it was unusual to organize individual factors into clusters, but occasionally the social workers explained how important it was to establish a pattern of risk. The following example illustrates the interrelationship between factors and their significance over time:

Interviewer: When you say a pattern of risk, what do you mean?

Social Worker: Well exactly that cycle that we go along, and everything is fine …
and then something will happen. So I suppose it is trying to find the pattern and

the risk is when mum gets drunk she may bring back people to the house who she doesn't really know to have sex with. She may fall asleep and leave the children unattended. She may leave the house entirely and leave the children unattended. And she had her money stolen, she got mugged herself. I don't know if she was physically attacked, but she certainly had her bag stolen with her money in it. And we have got the longer-term effects of all this ...

More often the separate 'clues' were individually recognized by the social workers but without an analysis to bring them together, to consider the pattern of concerns over time and to offset risks against strengths. This offsetting exercise was always particularly challenging and raised a number of dilemmas around knowledge, values and the prediction of outcome.

Strengths, Risks and Predictions

The social workers' accounts did not readily demonstrate how they resolved the kinds of dilemmas outlined above. Yet it is a crucial piece of the jigsaw. For this reason, some new questions were added to later interviews in which the social workers were asked to make a prediction of the likely outcome two years post-referral. A few social workers had not done this kind of analysis before and were flummoxed by it. But far more had an implicit framework for forecasting the future of the cases and the predictions questions were helpful in revealing the influences on decision-making.

CASE PREDICTIONS – EXPECTATIONS OF OUTCOME TWO YEARS AFTER REFERRAL

The predictions varied considerably from very full multifaceted accounts to the briefest of pictures. The most complete dealt with all aspects of the case and covered all the categories specified above. In addition, the social workers would review the child's needs and the likelihood of seeing improvement where there were current problems, as well as outlining timescales for making critical decisions. Some, but not many, would discuss the picture for each child individually. Finally, they would discuss in some detail the role of the social services in helping achieve or undermine the prediction. At the other end of the continuum, the prediction would deal with all the family members *en bloc* and not discuss the child's welfare at all. The two biggest clusters of answers focused on the likelihood of the case being open or closed and whether parents would be able to care for their children at home. It was more common for the social workers to have views on the likely basis of case allocation than on how far the child's problems would be resolved. It was rare for the prediction to begin with a statement of the child's need. Typically, an outline of the parental situation led the prediction.

The predictions fell into four main types:

- hopes and fears;
- hopes only;
- fears only;
- unable/unwilling to make a prediction.

By far the largest cluster fell into what we have called the 'hopes and fears' approach. In this category, social workers would present two contrasting scenarios for the future outcome of the case. They followed a common pattern. First, the social workers would outline what they hoped would happen in the case and this picture would be followed by a very different scenario describing what they 'expected' would happen. Often the latter picture would be described as 'more realistic' or speaking with the 'head', but the important point is that both possibilities were presented.

> I'm hoping that you'll find they are with their grandparents and ... Jon is thriving and that ... mum has admitted she has a drink problem and is dealing with it. But my head says 'we'll get the court, we'll go to court'. I've got a feeling that the children are going to stay in care ...

> As to whether they will be together – normally I would say 'together' and that's what is ideal I think. However, I'm going to really have to listen to James and his attachment to his current family, and I don't want to prejudge and pre-empt that decision. And I think we'll find that – I would hope that mum has stopped drinking, maybe even reduced her drinking, but from what I can tell the problem is, the prognosis is pretty poor for mum.

> Mum will have had treatment for alcohol but cut down to safe levels and not be harming the children. They will be living in a new house with the children at school. But she was very drunk at the last visit and if things don't improve, we will consider care proceedings.

> What I would like and I think what will happen are two different things. What I would like is for Leanne to be a good mum to Kenny and for her to have the support of the family, but also in the ensuing year support really from professionals ... And the optimistic side of me would really like to see that work. But I think in terms of the proof of the pudding or whatever on the history of what's happening recently to Leanne but also what has happened to Leanne over the last three and four years and the quality of parenting she has had, I think the odds are stacked against her to be honest.

A second approach was for social workers to voice only one aspect of the fears/hope dichotomy, portraying exclusively either the optimistic picture or the pessimistic one. There were more examples of the 'hopes only' scenarios than the 'fears only' accounts.

> *Social Worker*: Hopefully, they will have moved and we will have started to address the early years with mum ... hopefully, won't need her psychiatrist appoint-

ments any more and then we can start to address her past. And hopefully, people will be assessing them as a family. It's hope because at the end of the day it's resources … of allocating a social worker, resources of finding a home.

Interviewer: And of this, what is possible?

Social Worker: Hopefully, all of them.

I would hope that we would have one mother who has acknowledged an alcohol kind of misuse or dependency and hopefully working at addressing that … hopefully we won't have any more babies! … hopefully we would be able to say that they are possibly living together and that's an OK situation and he is looking at his alcohol use.

What was particularly interesting about the pessimistic judgements was that the social worker was likely to apologize for being negative. 'It sounds awful' said a worker in one case after predicting that one year later the mum would be abusing drugs. 'I think all of them will [go into care] because … she can't look after the children, she's struggling to look after the children'. In two other cases, a similar apologetic note can be detected. Having described how a mother had been misusing drugs over the long term, the worker then prefaced her prediction by remarking:

We don't want to write her off, but I haven't seen anything to prove to me that she can do it.

And in another case:

I think that, going on previous experience, we will find that mum has gone into detox and rehab and not really done it, so it's awful to say it, but I think she will fail at any detox or rehab.

These examples suggest that social workers found it difficult to predict failure. By contrast, it was notable that none of the workers expressing the 'hopes only' picture ever commented that the picture might be too 'rosy'.

As already noted, the fourth group was reluctant to make a prediction, usually because the social worker considered the case could go in any number of directions. In the final cluster, social workers simply bypassed the prediction and outlined with considerable precision the expected outcomes. These cases were typically at an advanced stage in planning, frequently in care proceedings with a care plan in place that addressed the main components of the predictions task.

The hopes/fears framework used by the social workers to think about the cases over the longer term was unexpected. At first sight it seems to put the social workers in an untenable position as the two case scenarios they outlined for each case were often so very divergent. For example, in one case the social worker predicted that 'Either all will be fine or Jason will be on register with possible removal being envisaged' and in another: 'I think you'll probably find that it will be closed to the department ... or you'll find that the child will be back on the register again, or they're using crack'. So how could planning proceed on this basis? We think that there are several ways in which the social worker approach can be understood to be more logical and coherent than at first sight. First, social work's value base is predicated on a belief about capacity to change and human dignity, and yet simultaneously legislation and the experience of child deaths point to the importance of assessing risks to children. Keeping in mind a range of outcomes may be seen as a way of trying to cope with the conflicting imperatives of the system that social workers find themselves in. Second, it is possible that in doing so social workers actually have a more nuanced approach to assessment than is generally considered in research or policy relating to assessments. For a key issue at the heart of risk assessment is that it involves predicting the future – and yet the future is never entirely predictable. We return to these issues at length in Chapter 6, in which the hopes/fears dichotomy is used as a way of dealing with major practical and conceptual challenges in carrying out risk assessments.

CONCLUSION

The interviews underlined the evidence presented in Chapter 2 which described the complex and challenging issues that social workers were grappling with. In this context workers were all too often ill-prepared and had received little training or guidance. They were often left wrestling with difficult issues such as parental non-cooperation with limited support. Two issues stood out as particularly difficult. One was how to make an assessment with often limited information and at best partial cooperation from parents. The second was how to engage and work with parents whose interactions were often actively or passively non-cooperative. How can workers build partnerships when the context of the relationship creates such strong incentives for a lack of honesty and active resistance – including violence and the threat of violence – from parents? And in this often hostile situation, how can the needs of vulnerable children be understood and met? These issues are the key focus of Chapters 6, 7, 8 and 9, and they also inform Chapter 10 and the conclusion which look at policies to support good practice.

However, before looking at what the literature and research can tell us about good practice in this area it is necessary to explore what happened to the children and parents in the two years after the referral to Children's Services. This is the focus of Chapter 5.

5 What Happened to the Children and Their Parents?

What happened to the children and their parents two years after referral to Children's Services? This is probably the most important question that our study addressed. Every social worker comes into the profession to make a difference and to ensure that children for whom they have responsibility are safe, have stable living arrangements and face better futures than would have otherwise been possible. But we have seen in the previous chapter that social workers found these futures difficult to predict and it is well known that many factors influence children's prospects. We now find out what actually happened to the children and their parents.

The chapter is divided into two main sections. The first considers the quantitative data on where children were living, how they were doing and what factors influenced these issues. The second explores in greater depth the nature of the findings. We tease out the patterns that emerged from our quantitative analysis and draw extensively on our qualitative data, illustrating the themes with case examples.

OUR APPROACH TO THE ANALYSIS

The key findings from the quantitative analysis were set out in an article published elsewhere (Forrester and Harwin, 2008). This chapter summarizes the key findings before discussing them at length in the context of data from the file studies. We begin by examining five main questions:

1. Where were children living two years after the referral to social services?
2. What factors were associated with children remaining at home or moving to alternative care?
3. What differences in children's welfare were there in the two years after the referral?

Parents Who Misuse Drugs and Alcohol. Effective Interventions in Social Work and Child Protection, 1st edition.   By Donald Forrester and Judith Harwin.
© 2011 John Wiley & Sons, Ltd.

4. What factors statistically predicted welfare outcome?
5. What other factors appeared important in understanding patterns of welfare outcome?

To explore the factors associated with outcomes, such as where children were living or their welfare at follow-up, it is important to carry out a multivariate analysis. To do this we use regression analysis. This is a powerful way of identifying key relationships, because it allows for interrelationships between variables. For example, there is a strong correlation between being in bed and dying. However, this does not mean that going to bed is dangerous (Calder, 2007). A regression analysis allows the relationship between several variables to be analysed. In the example of the correlation between being in bed and dying it would (presumably) discover that having a serious illness made it more likely that someone was in bed, and that if one allowed for that, then no relationship between being in bed and dying would be found (or even that bed is one of the safest places for healthy people to be). The mathematics of this are complicated but the logic is simple. It looks at the relationship between death and being in bed for those with an illness and for those without an illness. Because there is no relationship where there is no illness, being in bed can be discounted as a predictor of death, and the far more important variable of having a serious illness is identified.

Unless noted otherwise, the following variables were entered into the regression model:

- Child characteristics: age, gender, ethnicity;
- Parental and social issues in household: learning difficulties, mental illness, violence, parent in care, parent known to social services as child but not in care, housing difficulties, parent/s first generation immigrant;
- Type of substance misused: alcohol, heroin, crack/cocaine;
- Who misused substance;
- Whether the child was a 'baby at risk of harm';
- For welfare outcome, whether the child remained with the same main carer or moved.

These variables were chosen because they were identified as both likely to be important in understanding either parental substance misuse and/or the workings of social services departments and as it was possible to collect information on them from files.

WHERE WERE CHILDREN LIVING TWO YEARS AFTER THE REFERRAL TO SOCIAL SERVICES?

A key finding of the study was that more than half of the children (54%) no longer lived with their main carer (almost always the mother) at follow-up (see Table 5.1). Even this figure underestimates the extent of child separation

Table 5.1　Where were children living two years after referral?

	n	%
Same main carer (usually mother)	86	46
Father (where mother was main carer at stage 1)	18	10
Kinship placement	30	16
Foster care	30	16
Adoptive placement	15	8
Other	6	3
Total	185	100

over the two years, because several children had been removed temporarily from their primary carer and then returned. Only 40% of children remained with the same main carer throughout the two years.

The extended family played an important part in providing a new home for the children. By the end of the study, 10% of the children had gone to live with their fathers and a similar number were with grandparents (9%), 5% were with aunts and uncles and 2% were with other carers (e.g. great-aunts). But the formal care system played an equally important role. Slightly over a quarter of children were cared for in placements found and funded by the local authority. Most (16%) were in short-term foster care, while 8% were in adoptive placements and 3% were in other placements (e.g. residential or semi-independent).

The living arrangements at the two-year point bring out forcefully just how significant a role parental substance misuse plays in separating children from their carers. In many cases removal is the best, and sometimes the only, way of giving children a chance of a safer and more stable future.

The process of moving away from main carer

The vast majority of the children who changed main carer did so as a direct result of social services' intervention. Indeed, only 6% of the sample moved carer without social services instigating the move. These were usually moves to fathers that were agreed within private proceedings. For one third of all children the move was because of care proceedings, while a further 12% moved because social workers had identified serious concerns about the children, with the possibility of care proceedings being raised for most of these families.

The pattern of moves from main carer over time was also of considerable interest. A high proportion of moves occurred in the first three months: 10% of all children moved within 24 hours of the referral and 26% moved in the first month. This might be expected, as families tend to be referred at a point of crisis. However, what was surprising – and in our view of concern – is that the numbers coming into care did not continue to reduce over time. One would hope that over time social workers would either succeed in helping families or would identify children at risk, and that fewer children would enter care as time went on. In fact, we noted the opposite: 18 months post-referral the number of children moving or being removed began to increase. Furthermore, while we had a cut-off point of two years post-referral for tracking, it was clear from the file studies that the number of children coming into care increased into the third year after referral.

This is of potential concern. It opens up the possibility that following social work interventions children are experiencing inadequate parenting for months or years before they enter care, perhaps with serious problems. We explore this pattern further below. However, first it is worth unpacking the differences between alcohol and drug misuse in the timing of children's moves. Put simply, when both alcohol and drugs were misused, children tended to move carer within six months. If only illegal drugs were involved, most moves occurred within the first six months, though a substantial proportion occurred between six and 18 months. Thereafter the numbers who moved or came into care were much lower. In stark contrast, when only alcohol was misused a comparatively small number moved during the early months. Instead, the numbers coming into care rose over time.

This difference was particularly striking in relation to care proceedings. With the exception of one family, if illegal drugs were an issue care proceedings started *within* nine months of referral for every child: where alcohol alone was identified 62% of the proceedings started *after* this point. This suggests major issues around how social workers and other agencies understand and work with alcohol misuse. However, to interpret this picture better we need more information on the ways in which patterns of moving relate to the welfare of the children. This is discussed below.

WHAT FACTORS WERE ASSOCIATED WITH CHILDREN REMAINING AT HOME OR MOVING TO ALTERNATIVE CARE?

The variables found to be significant predictors of children remaining at home are set out in Table 5.2. Some of these might have been expected. For instance, the carer identified as misusing substances at initial referral proved an important determinant of where the children were living at follow-up. If both carers misused, children were particularly likely to move and also to come into care (whether the father was resident or not). Two-parent families in which only the mother misused also proved an important sub-group. This is because the father frequently left home and the children went to live with him, either at the same time or subsequently. They thus moved but remained within the family.

Moving main carer can also be readily understood for one other group. These were 'babies at risk of harm' who were particularly likely to be placed away from the main carer. Their age and consequent vulnerability, and the

Table 5.2 Factors associated with children remaining at home at follow-up.

	Total	Remaining with same carer			
	n	*n*	%	*p*	OR
(Two-parent family) Only mother misuses	18	1	5.6%	0.003	0.030
(One-parent family) Mother and non-resident partner misuse	10	1	10.0%	0.001	0.019
(Two-parent family) Both parents misuse	33	11	35.5%	0.002	0.154
Baby at potential risk	39	8	20.5%	<0.001	0.101
Heroin misuse	51	25	49.0%	0.003	4.895
Domestic violence	67	39	58.2%	0.001	3.824
First-generation immigrant	25	17	68.0%	0.002	7.449

processes by which these children are identified, mean that they are a group at particularly high likelihood of removal.

The remaining variables associated with children remaining with a main carer at the end of the study are more unexpected and difficult to explain. Parental heroin misuse was linked to children remaining at home, even though around half of these children were not at home at the end of the study. Why? The regression analysis helps to explain this. It showed that heroin misuse interacted with other factors and was particularly strongly associated with a sub-group defined as 'babies at risk'. Just over half of this sub-group (54%) was exposed to parental heroin use. However, once this association was allowed for in the analysis, heroin misuse made it more likely that children would *remain* at home. Babies exposed to parental heroin misuse were more than twice (29%) as likely to remain at home as babies (11%) for whom heroin was not involved. This trend was also true for the other 30 children whose parent misused heroin. Almost two-thirds (63%) of them remained at home, compared to half (51%) if no parent misused heroin.

Another unexpected predictor of children remaining at home was the group of parents who were first-generation immigrants. A higher proportion of these parents significantly reduced their usage (33% compared to 7%). But this does not wholly explain the relationship. Almost half of these children were Asian, though others were found in every ethnic group and the pattern appeared comparatively consistent across the different ethnicities. In many of these families there was also at least one non-misusing parent (52% compared to 18% of other children). In addition, there was often support from the wider family which helped the mother to maintain care of the child, and in some instances assisted or pressurized the misusing parent (usually the father) to address his substance misuse. These seemed to be key factors.

However, most surprising – and most concerning – was the relationship between violence and children remaining at home. The presence of domestic violence made it *more* likely that a child would remain at home. Indeed, where it was present children were almost four times more likely to remain at home. We return to this unexpected finding when looking at the qualitative data, but for now we review the children's welfare outcomes.

WHAT DIFFERENCES IN CHILDREN'S WELFARE WERE THERE IN THE TWO YEARS AFTER THE REFERRAL?

Based on social work files, a judgement was made about welfare in relation to three domains:

- educational performance;
- emotional and behavioural development;
- health and development.

In each of these areas a simple judgement was made at the point of allocation and two years after the referral to establish whether there was an identified problem (to avoid overuse of the term 'problem' the words 'difficulty' or 'issue' are used interchangeably in the following discussion). The files did not reliably record sufficient information for a more nuanced judgement. Nonetheless, this did provide the opportunity to compare the welfare of children at the point of allocation and two years post-referral. To check that there was some reliability 19 cases were independently double-checked by the researchers and high rates of inter-rater agreement were found. For 12% of children there was insufficient information on file to make a judgement on welfare at follow-up, usually because the file was closed quickly or the family moved out of the authority.

The analysis was carried out in two stages. First, an assessment was made of the changes in the two-year window in each domain (education, EBD and health and development). These results were then used to arrive at a composite picture of well-being. Three categories were developed.

The findings relating to the three individual domains make two important points. First, the pattern was dynamic. Just over half the children (52%) experienced a change in the number of dimensions in which they had a

Table 5.3 Definitions of welfare outcome.

Type of outcome	Definition
'Good'	No problems in any domains at follow-up
'Mixed'	Problems in the same number of domains at follow-up
'Poor'	Developed problems in more domains at follow-up than at referral

problem rating. However, the number whose welfare improved was very similar to the number whose welfare deteriorated. This is why there was virtually no change in the average number of domains with a problem for each child (an average reduction of −0.07). Second, the pattern of change varied by domain. Overall there was a slight reduction in the number of children with educational concerns (−3%) and a more noticeable one in relation to health (−11%) (due principally to the fact that babies who were born withdrawing from drugs overcome their initial difficulties). But for children with emotional and behavioural difficulties the proportion of children with problems increased (+7%).

The composite results at follow-up provide a mixed picture:

- Good outcome: Just under half (47%) achieved this, split evenly between:
  - children who had no problems at either stage (23%);
  - children who stopped having a problem (24%).
- Mixed: Just under a third (31%) were in this category.
- Poor outcome: About a fifth (22%) fell into this category.

WHAT FACTORS PREDICTED WELFARE OUTCOME?

The outcomes outlined above provide important feedback but they are a starting point only. If they are to be really useful, it is crucial to understand what lies behind the results. We therefore carried out a further regression analysis to discover what was associated with welfare outcome (good/mixed/ poor). This found that four factors were clearly associated with outcomes. The presence of the following was associated with poor outcomes (their absence was linked to better outcomes):

- children who remain at home;
- alcohol misuse;
- violence in the home;
- being a boy.

Table 5.4 Factors associated with welfare outcome at follow-up.

	Total	No problems		Problems continued		Problems developed or more problems			
	n	n	%	n	%	n	%	**Beta**	p
Alcohol	121	42	40%	39	37%	24	23%	0.148	0.049
Domestic violence	39	22	34%	26	41%	16	25%	0.159	0.039
Girl	87	43	56%	20	26%	14	18%	−0.175	0.022
Child at home	86	29	38%	23	30%	25	33%	0.221	0.004

Even if the variable 'at home' is removed so that we can concentrate on variables that social workers would have been able to include in their assessment at stage 1, then domestic violence, alcohol and gender remain the three variables with significant relationships to welfare outcome. Interestingly, only violence in the home could have been predicted from the qualitative interviews with the social workers exploring their predictions. The other variables, despite their strong statistical link to poor outcomes, did not feature as risk factors in the talk of social workers. This in itself is an important finding.

Individually, the strongest relationship was between children who remained at home and poor welfare outcomes. Thus, only 13% of children who moved main carer had poor outcomes compared to 32% of those who remained at home; 56% of those who moved had good outcomes compared to only 38% of those who remained at home. This result is troubling because it raises questions about the decisions that were being taken by the professionals to safeguard and promote the children's well-being. It is even more concerning when the links between children remaining at home, domestic violence and alcohol misuse are understood. In these circumstances children were most likely to have poor outcomes because although individually each factor had some predictive power, none had an exceptionally strong relationship. However, when considered cumulatively, the significance of the factors emerges. Alcohol misuse correlated with domestic violence and, as noted earlier, children who stayed at home were far more likely to be in an environment where they were exposed to domestic violence. There are important policy and practice implications that need to be examined specifically in relation to responses to domestic violence and alcohol misuse. Indeed, these results are all the more striking when it is recalled that section 31 of the Children Act 1989 definition of significant harm was amended in 1998 to include witnessing domestic violence. The results are also particularly unexpected when the findings from the predictions analysis in Chapter 4 are recalled. Domestic violence was routinely recognized as one of the factors that would lead to serious consideration of alternative care. So what explains these results? To understand the issues we need to turn to our qualitative analysis and the case studies.

But first, we comment on the relationship between gender and outcome. Various studies have suggested that girls tend to be more resilient in the face of adversity in childhood, and in particular parental alcohol misuse (Velleman and Orford, 1999). However, it is equally possible that boys' tendency to externalize problems through challenging behaviour might more readily be recognized and noted on social work files. A longer-term follow-up that gathered information directly from the children might identify greater difficulties for the girls.

However, it is important to emphasize that it is the cumulative picture that is important rather than attention to a single factor. This is shown clearly in Table 5.5 (being a boy is considered a 'risk' factor). The pattern is striking. Taken together the risk factors powerfully differentiate between children who

Table 5.5   Number of risk factors and welfare outcome.

Number of risk factors	Good, mixed or poor outcome					
	No problems		Problems continued		Problems developed or more problems	
	n	%	*n*	%	*n*	%
0	9	100%	0	0%	0	0%
1	24	65%	7	19%	6	16%
2	29	45%	21	33%	14	22%
3	15	33%	19	42%	11	24%
4	0	0%	3	37.5%	5	62.5%
	77		50		36	

had poor outcomes and those who had better outcomes. For instance, none of the nine girls removed from home where alcohol misuse was not an issue and there was no violence had problems at follow-up. In contrast, all boys remaining at home with alcohol and violence concerns at stage 1 had problems and almost two-thirds had developed problems in new areas.

Having identified the overall profile of outcomes for children, including whether they remained at home and their welfare outcome, and explored the factors linked to these outcomes, we now turn to the more qualitative analysis. In this analysis we explore and illustrate these findings in greater depth to develop a more nuanced appreciation of the ways in which outcomes for the children were shaped. We are particularly interested in describing the impact of interventions by Children's Services.

THE CASE STUDY ANALYSIS

The quantitative analysis gives some important clues to the factors linked to particular outcome patterns, but these clues only provide a part of the story. To understand better the complex interactions that influence outcomes for children, we carried out a further analysis of children by exploring the features of children with 'good', 'mixed' and 'poor' outcomes. This was done in two stages. First, a descriptive case study analysis was undertaken of the features of the children, their families and social work involvement with children in the different groups. Second, the case studies were grouped according to the children's welfare outcomes. We then attempted to explain the ways in which the profile of the children related to their outcomes. These often capture important issues that are not readily identified through the quantitative analysis even though it must be recognized that not all pieces of the jigsaw are available – or indeed ever could be. That is because it is easier to look back and find potentially important themes than to identify them prospectively. If this limitation is recognized, then the case studies can prove a helpful way of shedding some light on the quantitative information.

In the presentation and discussion of the data we focus on factors associated with children achieving good welfare outcomes. To a large extent the factors associated with poor welfare outcomes were the absence of the factors linked to good welfare outcomes. To avoid repetition we then discuss more briefly, and with a particular focus on social work intervention, issues related to poor or mixed welfare outcomes.

Throughout we try to illustrate the points we make with summaries of individual families. These have been anonymized and details have been changed in some instances to ensure confidentiality. In the case studies ages refer to age at allocation (i.e. stage 1), and therefore information about previous contact refers to when the children were younger, while the children were two years older at the follow-up point.

GOOD OUTCOMES: COMMONALITIES AND DIFFERENCES

Children with good outcomes fell into distinctive groups, as can be seen in Figure 5.1. A key factor was whether the children moved or remained with their main carer and for this reason we discuss each sub-group separately.

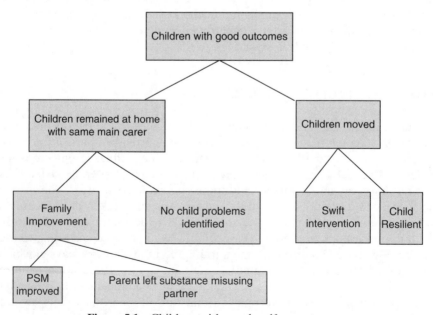

Figure 5.1 Children with good welfare outcomes.

GOOD WELFARE OUTCOME – SAME CARER

A unifying feature of this sub-group was that the children had far fewer identified difficulties at allocation than was the case for children whose outcomes were mixed or poor. Only 7% had educational problems, 14% had health or developmental difficulties and a further 14% had emotional or behavioural problems. The comparatively low rate of problems was related to the children's young age (62% were 4 or under, and a fifth (21%) were 'babies at risk').

At follow-up there were also some commonalities in this sub-group. Far fewer had experienced significant harm than other children who remained at home (21%). In comparative terms this is positive, but the fact that one fifth had experienced significant harm at follow-up gives little cause for complacency. Moreover, for nearly half the children (48%) there were still concerns about the family situation.

While these broad patterns were consistent across the group, the reasons for them varied. We had assumed that within this group there would be a number of children allocated for comparatively low levels of concern, who had made good progress. In fact, this applied to only one family (with two children). Children's Services simply did not allocate families with low levels of concern. Most of those allocated as 'children in need' had serious concerns, and many had had case conferences with a deferred decision to register.

Instead, we found that the children who had good outcomes fitted into two sub-groups:

1. Families with initially high levels of concern, but where significant changes for the better were made.
2. Children who did not have apparent problems despite serious concerns about the family situation.

These were not exclusive categories, as illustrated by the case study on the James family, but there were sufficient differences in their profiles to categorize them separately. For ease of presentation we have decided which factor was most important and categorized children accordingly in Figure 5.1.

Families that changed

Families that manage to change are a group of particular interest because they can provide important lessons for practice and they predominated within the category of children with good outcomes who were still at home. There were two types of change: families in which parents stopped misusing substances and those where the parent separated from a partner who was misusing drugs or alcohol. These two groups accounted for all the families that changed. In the study as a whole, only 10% of parents managed to address their substance misuse satisfactorily. They were concentrated in this good outcome sub-group: 41% (12 of the children) had a parent who had 'significantly reduced or stopped' their drinking or drug-taking – a much higher proportion than any other outcome group. Nine children had parents who left their partner because of misuse. Although the small numbers must be borne in mind in the sub-categories when considering their implications, exploring how parents achieved this improvement is important. In general, we know far more about failure than success.

Understanding why both these types of change were linked to good child outcomes is not difficult. An example of a couple separating is the Patel family. They were an Asian mother and father and their young child. The father's drinking and crack cocaine misuse were causing the mother serious concerns. She left him and returned to her family. This was a big step for her but it led to a transformation in the situation of the baby and rapid social work case closure. The baby was removed from a dangerous father and the mother had the support of her extended family. The main practice point is clear – separation is sometimes the best way ahead. But we are left with an important question for practice: how did this mother reach the point where she was able to separate?

Even more intriguing are the cases where parents overcame their misuse, sometimes in the most unlikely situations. In some cases this was compara-tively clear-cut (we discuss some examples of such changes later). However, often social workers were dealing with ambiguous or relative improvement, and it is much less easy to be certain about the changes that have taken place. This is really important for understanding the complex nature of practice in the real world, but it is of equal relevance for unpacking the difficulties and limitations of research in such situations, for it highlights that many of the categories we are using are provisional and contestable. The use of statistics should not mask this. The variables being studied are open to debate and discussion, and one of our purposes in this chapter is to make this explicit. Take the following case example:

The James Family

The James family consisted of a lone mother and her four children (aged 12, 11, 4 and 2). All family members were Black British. There were a number of refer-rals from the school, culminating in one from the Educational Welfare Officer who said that the children had stopped attending school and the mother was 'drinking heavily'. A superb duty assessment identified that the mother was depressed as a result of social difficulties (she was experiencing severe housing problems and had been racially harassed). To cope with the depression she had started drinking quite heavily (six cans of strong lager a day) and was physically dependent (experiencing shaking and nausea if she did not drink). She felt sui-cidal and the interview was conducted in an almost completely dark room. The duty social worker recommended that the family should be allocated for 'support' through a 'multidisciplinary' approach. The first allocated social worker became very concerned for the children – none of whom was attending school – and sug-gested a child protection case conference. When she did this the mother stopped cooperating with her. The case conference noted concerns around school attendance, however the mother insisted that things were improving – for instance, she said she was not drinking and was going out shopping. It was agreed to defer the decision to register the children's names and a new social worker was allocated. At the deferred conference some three months later the new social worker noted an improvement, including the fact that the family had been on holiday and mother had met a new boyfriend. The children seemed to be doing well and had started to attend school. The case was closed.

We have chosen this case for several reasons. First, the caseworker's prediction indicated that the caseworker thought it unlikely the mother would be able to change within the necessary timescales. Yet she did. We know from other studies that a change of partner can radically alter people's behaviour and the new boyfriend may have been an important influence on the mother's progress. Second, outcomes are dynamic. This point was well made by Roy Parker, who noted that there may be marked variations in outcome profiles depending on the cut-off point taken. It is possible that some of the children who fell into the category of 'good' outcomes may have had hidden problems that did not emerge until later. For instance, in the James family there was a referral 12 months later when the second eldest child shot another child in the face with an air gun. The police described his room as a 'filthy untidy jumble … the bed had collapsed and I would believe it is impossible to sleep in. Kitchen lights were missing and the house was in virtual darkness.' A letter was sent by social services to the mother offering 'support', but when she did not respond no further action was taken. Under our categorization scheme this child was identified as having emotional/behavioural difficulties, but the other three had no identified problems. However, one might justifiably question whether this was likely to be true in the long term. It may not even have been a true reflection of the children's needs at the time of case closure.

Notably, the prediction only dealt with the eldest boy. The other children were invisible and here the relationship between gender and outcome that emerged from the quantitative analysis may be relevant. The eldest child was a girl. We have little information on her. The second eldest was a boy, and he acted in an aggressive manner which brought him to the attention of services. It is possible that the daughter was internalizing difficulties that might manifest later in life. On the other hand, it is possible that this was a one-off incident with the boy. In other words, social work records – and child welfare agencies generally – seem likely to underestimate the extent of difficulties for girls and may also overestimate them for boys. This appears likely to explain the very heavy over-representation of girls in the good outcomes category (62% of children at home with no identified problems were girls).

A third issue that recurs throughout the qualitative analysis is the difficulty social workers have in engaging parents. This was discussed at length in Chapter 4. In the case file there was no evidence of the allocated social worker talking to the children. This seemed to be because all worker's energies were focused on engaging the parent. It is almost always impossible to work with children if you have not worked with the parents. These two issues – the problem of unpredictability and the challenge of engaging parents and their children – are returned to throughout this chapter and the rest of the book.

At a broader level, it is difficult to see what positive impact Children's Services had on the James family. Their primary role was monitoring the situation to see whether there was deterioration. However, in the absence of sufficiently serious concerns they provided little input to actively create positive change. At most they acted as an implicit threat, as their presence held the possibility of the children being removed if the situation worsened. This strategy is often used in the hope that it might contribute to positive change, but it is a fairly limited role for Children's Services. It was usually unclear how social workers were trying to make a positive difference in families with less serious concerns, and it was often unclear how workers were trying to help families, apart from the threat or actuality of care proceedings.

The responsibility of taking a case to court was a better guarantor of active input by the social services and nowhere was this clearer than when care proceedings – or the possibility of care proceedings – were under consideration. This could result in very significant input from social services and sometimes striking change. Yet care proceedings were something of a 'kill or cure' approach, particularly around substance misuse. For most families, initiating care proceedings did not result in positive changes in the family, and therefore for the vast majority permanent alternative placements were sought (only 13% returned home, though for a further 28% proceedings were ongoing at follow-up). However, of the 58 children subject to care proceedings, five were at home with good outcomes. In addition, there were six children for whom Children's Services had raised the prospect of proceedings. Again, a case study illustrates some of the issues for these families:

The McDonald Family

The family consisted of the mother (Kate) and two children (Elizabeth aged 13 and Rhianna aged 2). All were White British. Kate was known to social services as a child, when they had been involved because she had experienced sexual abuse and had then spent time in care. There had been some contact with the hospital social work team after Rhianna's birth as mum appeared depressed and spoke of panic attacks. However, no further action was taken. One year later Elizabeth phoned the NSPCC alleging physical abuse. The police found Kate intoxicated and took the children into protective custody. The emergency duty team provided a foster placement and social services became involved. Two visits in the next two days found mum 'drunk', not certain she wanted the girls home and the house with no electricity. Care proceedings were started and the girls moved to stay with their grandmother. This was the point of allocation.

The care proceedings led to a psychiatric report, which identified Kate as having a 'recurrent depressive disorder and anxiety' which led to her drinking and suggested a good prognosis if the anxiety and depression were treated. Plans for Elizabeth's return were made, with Rhianna to follow later. Over the next six months the police were called to the flat four times for issues relating to drunkenness, often when one or both girls were present, including one occasion five days prior to the girls being returned home when Kate was arrested for being drunk in charge of Rhianna. In the first week after the girls returned Kate rang emergency social workers on five nights saying she could not cope. On the seventh night she was found drunk and Rhianna was returned to the grandmother. As a result a new psychiatrist completed an assessment and concluded that Kate 'has a serious and long-term alcohol problem' which needed to be addressed before she could deal with her depression. This contributed to Kate deciding she would become totally abstinent. The next six months saw Kate remain abstinent and there was major improvement in her care for the children and for herself (her depression also lifted). The case ended with a long letter from Kate reflecting both on how unhelpful social services were initially, but how ultimately the experience of care proceedings – both in the threat of losing her children and the expert assistance she received – led her to make a huge positive change in her life. Both girls were at home with no identified problems.

At the point of allocation the prognosis did not appear promising. Kate's drinking appeared to be out of control and the decision to return the girls seemed unrealistically optimistic. However, ultimately Kate decided to address her drinking. Positive results followed. While it is not possible to be sure that there will not be lapse or relapse, the changes made, and the familial support associated with it, seem to be very positive factors. In this instance, the involvement of Children's Services, and the instigation of care proceedings in particular, seemed vital elements in creating positive change.

GOOD WELFARE OUTCOMES – CHILD MOVED

The second group of children with good outcomes were those who had moved main carer by follow-up. At stage 1 they tended to be young (63% were aged 4 or less), with most of these being 'babies at risk' (40% of this group). A high proportion of the parents misused illegal drugs (31% heroin and 44% crack cocaine), with poly-drug use being particularly common. For many of the children (46%) care proceedings had been started by the point of allocation. Fairly large numbers had identified problems at stage 1 (one third had educational or learning difficulties, one third had health problems and 17% had behavioural or emotional problems). However, by follow-up these had disappeared.

As a group, the pattern of placements at follow-up was different from other children who moved. Children were mainly in kinship placements (35%), living with their father (23%) or adopted (23%). Only 19% were in foster care. Their levels of permanency were also high: 75% were in permanent placements. A majority of these children were in stable homes conducive to promoting their well-being.

What information did the case study analysis provide about how this pattern of outcomes was produced? Again, there seemed to be two main sub-groups:

1. Swift action which prevented children experiencing harm or helped them overcome difficulties;
2. Children who appeared resilient in the face of difficulties.

Swift action that prevented children experiencing harm or helped them overcome it

Most of the children who had moved and had no problems at follow-up had been the subject of comparatively swift action by social services: 83% had been moved by three months after the initial referral. This was generally because the family situation – and in particular the drug and alcohol misuse – was so extreme, and the child so vulnerable because of their age, that the decision to move the child appeared comparatively straightforward. Most of these children were babies at risk but there were also five children aged 5 years old or over for whom swift action was also taken. For two of these children the situation was so serious that it required immediate protection and the child was never returned. One involved a mother who overdosed while in charge of a 5 year old while the second case concerned a serious assault in a public place of a 9 year old. The three other children were moved to their father, which resulted in a speedy reduction in levels of concern.

However, despite the issues in these families being among the most straightforward that one could imagine in that the concerns were so great, the complexity, cost and time involved were often striking. An example is the Frame family, who share many of the characteristics of the children with the most positive outcomes. In particular, the concerns were very serious, Brandy was a newborn baby and ultimately the combination of serious concerns and her age and vulnerability led to her being permanently removed. Once removed, she seemed to make good progress. Yet the case study highlights that this process is rarely straightforward. The hard-headed approach of the local authority was rejected by the court which insisted on further input. This led to a protracted and expensive process lasting several months. More importantly, it contributed to Brandy being very distressed and upset when she was eventually moved. On the other hand, there was obviously something about the mother that indicated she might have what it took to change. In both care proceedings for her previous two children (who had been removed shortly before the birth of Brandy) and for Brandy residential assessments identified positives about her parenting. It was her ability to sustain these positives in the community that did not materialize.

The Frame family highlights many of the challenges that social workers face in carrying out work in these complex situations. They have to give parents opportunities to change while protecting children who are often very vulnerable. There are key issues about timescales, such as the impact on a rapidly developing child of giving a parent time to change. Furthermore, social services operate within resource constraints. Their decision in the Frame family not to offer a residential unit may have been reasonable, but it appeared influenced in large part by resource issues: such placements are extremely expensive. In fact, at a conservative estimate the court's decision to insist on a residential assessment cost several hundred thousand pounds. Was this money well spent in protecting the rights of a vulnerable mother? Or was it money wasted on a hopeless family – money that could have funded interventions for dozens of other families? There are no answers to these questions; they simply form part of the complex background for social work with such families.

Children who appeared resilient in the face of difficulties

Children with good welfare outcomes who had not been protected through comparatively swift action tended either to appear to be resilient despite the difficult circumstances that they had been in, or overcame the problems they were demonstrating at home once they entered care. A brief example of the former was 11-year-old Lydia. Lydia entered care due to very serious alcohol misuse by both parents, which came to the attention of social services when her brother was born. During plans to return her home she disclosed that she had been sexually abused by her father, as well as having witnessed many alcohol-related arguments (which were sometimes violent) and missing a lot of schooling. Despite these obvious difficulties at home, Lydia did not exhibit any overt problems. She blossomed in foster care and was doing well at school where she was both academically able and popular. When the follow-up file study was completed the plan was for both Lydia and her brother to be placed in the wider family.

Lydia had sufficient problems at home to cause her serious difficulties and yet they did not exhibit themselves in any obvious way. It is certainly possible that she was internalizing to some degree the consequences of the difficulties that she had been through. But there is also a danger in pathologizing children (or adults) who have faced serious difficulties and looking at them as victims. Lydia was a resourceful, bright and socially able child who actively managed to overcome some very difficult experiences. This is as much part of the picture of Lydia as the negative impact of the abuse and neglect she suffered. Her case bears out the lessons from research into resilience, showing that social skills and talents can often provide a safety net and escape route for children who might otherwise go under. The important point for practice is how much money social services will spend supporting children to create new opportunities if there is no obvious need. The decisions here are often political and economic rather than driven purely by welfare considerations. Although resilience is very important to understand it can sometimes be used to justify not giving assistance.

An example of a child who overcame difficulties once they entered care is Shane in the Robin family:

The Robin Family

The mother (Sharon) and her newborn baby (Shane) were both White British. The family was well known to social services. They had been heavily involved with mother's previous child who had gone to live with her father following concerns about mother's drinking.

Shane was born with a medical condition affecting his appearance. The hospital was concerned that Sharon misused drugs. For 14 months the family was supported at home, amidst steadily escalating concerns about Sharon's drinking and drug-taking and Shane's welfare. At a case conference the health visitor noted that Sharon had not cooperated in arranging surgery for Shane's condition and he was now failing to thrive and on the 2nd percentile of height and weight. Nonetheless, care proceedings were not started until six months later when Shane was taken to his GP. The doctor noted a number of cigarette burns to his leg which were likely to be non-accidental injuries. He was initially placed with Sharon's daughter (now aged 17 and living on her own), followed by a foster placement. The foster carer noted that Shane's behaviour was extremely demanding and attention-seeking.

By follow-up, a full care order had been granted and the plan was for adoption. Shane was exhibiting no behavioural problems and had already had surgery to rectify his medical condition. There was very little information on his mother.

As happened for a number of children, initial problems on entering care reduced or disappeared in the first few months. This is a common pattern for children and indicates that care is not perhaps causing the difficulties that it is often associated with (Forrester *et al.*, 2009).

Discussion of children with good welfare outcomes

Overall, then, most of the children with good welfare outcomes had moved main carer, and this had generally helped them to overcome or avoid potentially serious situations. For those who remained at home, it was particularly likely that the parental substance misuse had been addressed, either directly by the parent changing their pattern of misuse or indirectly by the parent leaving. A minority of the children appeared to be exhibiting no difficulties despite living in difficult situations. This may have been because the children were genuinely resilient, it may have been because we did not have sufficient information on these children or it may have been because their difficulties were hidden or internalized and likely to emerge when the children were older – or perhaps even when they were adults.

We now turn to the analysis of children with poor or mixed welfare outcomes. However, to a large extent the picture for these children is the opposite of that for children with good welfare outcomes. Thus, most of them remained at home, relatively few lived in families in which the substance misuse was reduced and all were exhibiting difficulties which generally were linked to the abuse or neglect they had suffered. To avoid providing a description and analysis that is in many respects a mirror-image of that for those of children with good outcomes, we instead focus on key issues with a particular interest in evaluating the interventions of social workers and other services.

CHILDREN WITH 'MIXED' OR 'POOR' WELFARE OUTCOMES

Overall children in these groups had a profile that will be familiar to many social workers. Most had difficulties at the point of referral to social services and for most the difficulties worsened over the course of social work involvement. The vast majority (82%) were previously known to social services. The families tended to have complex and interrelated problems, with violence, depression and neglect being particularly common features. Alcohol (74%) and crack cocaine (40%) were comparatively common in this group, though the way that they interacted with other difficulties meant that the substance misuse appeared to be a 'key issue' for a lower proportion of children in this sub-group (56%).

At follow-up there were ongoing concerns for 83% of the children and most who remained at home had suffered significant harm (62%). Substance misuse remained a key issue for almost two-thirds of the families (62%) and it was very rare for it to have been reduced or addressed by the misusing parent leaving the home. More than half the children (54%) had suffered significant harm.

Overall, these figures suggest a group of children who have usually experienced serious abuse or neglect, who come from families well known to social services and who have relatively serious difficulties both at stage 1 and follow-up. They have the complex, interrelated issues characteristic of families receiving long-term social work intervention (e.g. described by Devaney, 2009; Ferguson, 2004).

How did social workers work with these families? One striking feature was that despite – or perhaps because of – the complex issues and well-known nature of the families, social workers seemed reluctant to start care proceedings. They were taken far less often in this group than those with good outcomes. However, even more striking was the fact that when care proceedings were started it tended to be at a much later point. Most of these children entered care after months or even years of social work allocation. All too often, this meant that they entered care following serious deterioration in the family situation and only after the children had been seriously harmed. Unsurprisingly, the children had far higher levels of difficulties and were more likely to be in temporary placements at follow-up. They were, in short, the sort of children who pose real challenges within the care system. What is more, many of the children who remained at home seemed highly likely to enter care at a later date. This was supported by the timing of care entry. For this group, the increased rate of care entry over time noted at the beginning of the chapter was particularly pronounced. More than any other group these are the children who will drift into care after years of social work involvement. This is a bleak conclusion, but one that is hard to avoid.

CHILDREN WHO WERE WITH THE SAME MAIN CARER

Having painted a concerning picture about the children who entered care, what tended to happen with the children who remained at home? It was difficult to identify any clear differences between the children with poor/mixed outcomes who entered care and those who remained home. The picture of complex families, usually known to social services and where alcohol (in particular) interacted with depression, violence and difficult social situations, was fairly consistent across the two groups. So were the high rates of significant harm and serious concerns about the welfare of the children at follow-up.

These figures point to the challenges and complexity of these families and suggest that the children might be suffering significant harm, but this is better brought to life through actual examples. The Blackburn family was not untypical of cases where the children with poor outcomes remained at home:

The Blackburn Family

The family comprises the mother (Dora) and her 5-year-old son (Ryan). Dora also has an older child (Cara, aged 15) who is living with her father. All are Black British.

The family's first contact with social services was when Dora was expecting Ryan. She was referred because she was experiencing harassment from Ryan's father and was depressed. However, after a visit by social workers no further action was taken. In the two years after Ryan was born there were three sets of referrals. The GP said that Ryan was being cared for by a mentally ill person, Dora was drinking heavily and there was continuing violence from Ryan's father. An anonymous source alleged that Dora was drinking heavily and hitting Ryan and Cara, and Cara's school referred the case, saying Dora had force-fed Cara paracetamol to show her how unpleasant it was. Each referral resulted in a home visit and case closure. One year later Cara came to social services and asked to be taken into care and disclosed sexual abuse over the last seven years by a 'family friend'. Her request was refused when mother promised to prevent contact with the 'friend' and, following investigation, no prosecution was considered likely. The criminal case and the social work file were both closed.

The next 18 months saw 12 referrals, generally relating to fights between Dora and Cara. Dora was described as being 'under the influence' or 'drunk' on several of these occasions. The family was allocated and the focus of work was managing the relationship between Dora and Cara. At the end of that year Cara went to live with her father, and the case was closed.

There was no contact for a year, until the referrals that led to the current allocation. In the first Ryan was sick, but when the ambulance attended the paramedics found Dora to be drunk and threatening to Ryan. On the second occasion Ryan was taken to hospital as he was vomiting. Mum was described as 'under the influence' and was seen to slap and threaten him repeatedly. The social worker assessed the family and concluded: 'In general [Dora's] care seems good enough, but when she is drinking she seems odd and often quite inappropriate.' However, it was difficult to get much information because Dora was 'reluctant to engage ... and actively denied the need for social services' involvement'. As a result Ryan's name was put on the child protection register, though at stage 1 there was little information about his welfare.

The next few months are difficult to summarize succinctly. The school reported significant and increasing worries about Ryan. They said he was unhappy, underperforming and missing a lot of school. Dora became anxious and said she was being stereotyped as an alcoholic single mother, however she did agree to attend alcohol counselling. Following a couple of months of comparative improvement, mother suddenly went to school and took Ryan out. The school reported that she smelt of alcohol. The social worker made an emergency visit and found mother 'agitated' and saying she was going to drink over the weekend. The worker arranged for the Emergency Duty Team to visit. They tried but with no success.

Two weeks later the social worker met with the legal team and agreed to start care proceedings with a plan that there would be 'eventual return back home ... if [Dora] beats her addiction to alcohol'. However, for reasons that are not clear care proceedings were not started for a further two months. This appeared in part to be because mother went to a drugs counsellor who said that she was not 'dependent' but was a binge drinker. At this point both Dora and Ryan started to refuse to talk to the social worker.

However, the beginning of care proceedings was a turning point for the family. Dora attended and completed first a community and then a residential treatment facility. For the first time thorough assessments of Ryan were carried out. These revealed that he had complex problems in part likely to be related to Dora drinking during pregnancy but also exacerbated by his experiences since birth. He thus had identified developmental delay, behavioural difficulties and health problems. Nonetheless, the overall picture at closure was of a family situation that had improved considerably since the initial referral.

This family shows a number of features that are important. First, it once again sheds light on the difficulties in discussing welfare outcomes. In part the reason why Ryan's welfare appeared to get worse was that by stage 2 problems were identified that were almost certainly present but not identified at stage 1. However, that is not the whole story. Ryan's behaviour certainly deteriorated over time and it seems likely that the extremely disrupted home situation had contributed to this. This highlights a second issue common in most of the children in this category, namely that during most of the time that social services were involved the children's welfare deteriorated – until serious action was taken. This may not be unreasonable. Social services are allocated to families where there are serious concerns and where parents (in particular) may be reluctant to engage. In such situations, our legal system appears to be geared toward waiting until things are serious enough to warrant legal action. In later chapters – Chapters 7, 8 and 9 in particular – we consider effective ways of working with families in such situations. However, even with the best practice engaging a family may be difficult and in such situations social workers and other professionals may be left to wait until they have evidence to justify legal action. On the other hand, the Blackburn family does suggest that waiting can be a lengthy process. It appears from the outside that legal action could and should have been taken more swiftly. However, while this appears to be true to us in terms of good practice for this family, it is important to consider the policy implication of this. Such an approach would result in more use of care proceedings and would increase the number of children in care. It is possible that this would be a short-term increase (i.e. bringing children into care earlier rather than bringing more children into care), however there can be no guarantee of this. There were many families where social workers were waiting and children would not ultimately have entered care.

Third, the Blackburn family highlights the difficulty in evaluating the interventions of social services. During most of Ryan's life social services appeared to have achieved little, and there is evidence to suggest that they were slow to react to serious concerns (this was often a feature of families in which parents misused alcohol rather than illegal drugs), however once they did take a very active and assertive position this did contribute to considerable positive change for this family and for others. How might one evaluate such a pattern of contact?

Finally, the Blackburn family illustrates well the complex nature of alcohol misuse within the families. On the one hand, in this family – as in many others – it is tempting to believe that if everything else was exactly the same but alcohol was replaced with heroin or crack, then the response of social workers and other services would have been very different. (It is worth re-reading the case study and mentally substituting the word 'alcohol' with 'heroin'; for most of us it has a strong tendency to make the concerns seem more serious.) This suggests that perhaps most of us – and social workers are no exception – underestimate the risks alcohol poses to children compared to illegal drugs. On the other hand, it was actually rare for drugs to be woven into the fabric of concerns in the way that alcohol was in the Blackburn family (and many others). Instead, where parents misused illegal drugs this tended to be a major preoccupation for them and everyone else. The situation that the Blackburn family exemplifies, in which alcohol was one important issue among many, was rather rare in relation to drugs. There are many possible explanations for this. However, the key practice point is that alcohol misuse became part of a pattern of problems, rather than a primary focus, in many of these families.

This point is also relevant in relation to domestic violence. Domestic violence was not a key issue at the time of the referral in the Blackburn family, however it had been a feature of earlier involvement with them. An inexplicable finding in the quantitative analysis was the relationship between violence in the family and a *reduced* likelihood of children moving or being removed. The concerning nature of this finding was reinforced by the link between violence and poor welfare outcomes for the children. There seem to be two main reasons for this. The first is illustrated by the initial stages of the work with the Blackburn family, and that is that violence was often part of a complicated family situation. Social workers often did not focus on the violence as such. This emphasizes the crucial importance of social workers always taking violence in the home extremely seriously and recognizing it as a crucial risk factor. The second reason that violence was often not tackled was not explicit in the case studies, but was touched on in the interviews with social workers, and that was that social workers were often afraid to work with perpetrators of violence. This is understandable. However, effective services need to find ways to help workers to be able to work with violent men. After all, if a worker is afraid to enter the house, what is it likely to be like for the child living in the home?

DISCUSSION

Overall we found the picture that emerged deeply concerning. The families had such profound problems and the consequences for the children were so often deeply and lastingly damaging that it is difficult not to be anxious about the situation in many of these families. However, we were particularly concerned about the ways in which social services responded to the families. In a nutshell, social workers rarely did anything to create positive change. Instead, they waited and monitored. Some families changed for the better on their own. In others there was a watchfulness from social workers and other professionals, often characterized by anxiety and sometimes by interagency disagreements, until something went wrong and children were moved. In some families social workers seemed unrealistically optimistic and supported families or returned children despite a situation that seemed extremely unpromising. On the other hand, when social workers tried to intervene proactively their hands were often tied. Courts were very reluctant to remove children permanently, and social workers would be criticized for having given parents insufficient chance to change.

In general, there appeared to be a strong institutional tendency towards under-responding to alcohol and drug misuse. It was thus perceived by social workers to be difficult to start care proceedings, and there were numerous instances of local authority solicitors insisting that there was insufficient evidence or courts insisting on further assessments or opportunities for families that supported this. In many ways this was reminiscent of Dingwall *et al.* (1995), who identified the pervasive influence of a 'rule of optimism', which led professionals to work systematically towards the most positive interpretation and to give parents many opportunities despite an often apparently poor prognosis.

In part the reason is that assessing risk is difficult. In fact, it is impossible to be fully certain what will happen in the future. As a result assessment strategies often appeared to be more about giving parents opportunities to change rather than actually assessing risks. This is a rather different conception of the nature of assessment from that often put forward and is explored in greater detail in Chapter 6.

However, underlying everything in this chapter and in Chapter 4 was a pervasive sense that social workers did not know how to work with parental alcohol or drug problems. In general, they were working alone with often complicated and serious situations, yet they had received minimal training and often had limited supervision and support in their current role. This is a toxic cocktail that is almost certain to tend to produce poor practice. The fact that many workers managed to work well with families despite these problems is testimony to their individual resilience in the face of systemic adversity.

Having identified a deeply troubling picture of practice and outcomes for children affected by parental substance misuse in these chapters, the following chapters turn to the more difficult question of what good practice – and the systems to support it – might look like. In Chapter 6 we consider some of the key challenges in effective assessments. The subsequent chapters review what is likely to work in engaging with parents and families affected by substance misuse. We conclude with a critical review of the policy structures and make a series of recommendations for ways in which practice could be improved through better policies.

Part 3

6 Assessment

The interviews with the social workers discussed in Chapter 4 found that assessment was central to their work with families, but that they struggled to carry out and be confident about their assessments. The case studies highlighted both the consequences of getting an assessment wrong and the difficulties involved in accurately predicting future behaviour. This chapter is an attempt to consider assessment in ways that might be helpful to practitioners wrestling with the challenges described by the social workers in the research. It starts with a review of key issues in assessment generally which concludes that risk assessment is an inherently difficult activity and does not have a strong theoretical or empirical basis. In the second part of the chapter we outline some key issues in carrying out assessments as well as is possible. Three areas are focused on: how to analyse information; what information to collect; and sources from which information can be obtained. This order is deliberate. We believe that having a clear plan for how information should be analysed should shape the information that is gathered, and that too often in guidance on assessments analysis is added as an afterthought. In each area key issues and suggestions for good practice are outlined.

A POVERTY OF THEORY: ASSESSMENT IN CHILDREN'S SERVICES

Until the late 1980s there was virtually no central government guidance on assessment. From the perspective of the twenty-first century this seems a strange absence. It is redolent of a different approach to Children's Services, or the work of social workers more generally. Specifically, it was considered that the professional training and expertise of social workers furnished them with the skills and knowledge to carry out assessments. From the 1970s government guidance and requirements for child protection specified timescales and urged interagency cooperation, but Government did not set out how social workers should carry out their professional duties in relation to assessment.

Parents Who Misuse Drugs and Alcohol. Effective Interventions in Social Work and Child Protection, 1st edition.   By Donald Forrester and Judith Harwin.
© 2011 John Wiley & Sons, Ltd.

This began to change during the 1980s. The most important catalyst for this change was the inexorable series of inquiries into child deaths, and then the inquiries into over-reactions by social workers (Ferguson, 2004; Parton, 1985; 1991). Some of these reports specifically urged more risk assessment and cited research of dubious methodological rigour that was felt to indicate the possibility of accurate – or at least better – assessment of future risk of harm to children (Brent, 1985). As a result, 'risk assessment' in child protection began to receive attention from Central Government. The most obvious manifestation of this was *The Orange Book* (Department of Health *et al.*, 1988), a guide to comprehensive child protection assessments published by the Government under section 7 of the 1970 Local Government Act (which means there is an expectation that the guidelines will be followed unless there are compelling reasons for not doing so). This may be seen as marking a new stage in government attitudes to assessment within Children's Services: Government was interested in supporting and improving social work assessments where there were child protection concerns, but had little or nothing to say about other forms of assessment. For instance, the 11 volumes of guidance accompanying the 1989 Children Act have essentially nothing to say about how individual social workers should assess need or risk outside child protection situations. The sum total is five paragraphs, most of which relate to procedural or legal issues.

This started to change in the mid-1990s, which saw sustained policy attention directed at improving social work assessment and recording processes. One of the starting points for these changes was the combination of research and policy that became known as the 'looked after children materials' (LAC) (Ward, 1995). These materials involved researchers identifying key areas of child development and working with Government to develop forms and procedures based on these areas. The Government developed the LAC approach further, to include assessments for children still living in their families. It did this through the Assessment Framework and accompanying forms and guidance. The Assessment Framework was developed to provide guidance based on an ecological approach to child development. It is discussed further below. However, the Assessment Framework provided more than guidance. Like *The Orange Book* which it superseded, the Assessment Framework was released under section 7 of the 1970 Local Government Act. It not only introduced new ways of conceptualizing assessment, it also incorporated clear timescales for different parts of the process, and forms and paperwork to guide each stage of the assessment. It was supported by a new edition of the *Working Together* guidance and by several other publications (Department of Health, 2000a, b, 2001). In addition, the Government brought in a number of performance indicators aimed at ensuring that assessments were completed within set timescales. Taken together, these form a sustained attempt to reform assessment processes within Children's Services.

However, the Government's zeal for increasing the regulation of assessment within Children's Services did not stop there. The Assessment Framework was followed by the Common Assessment Framework (CAF). This rolled out the Assessment Framework across a range of different agencies working with children or families, and placed the onus on these other agencies to complete initial assessment forms. This in turn was swiftly followed by the implementation of the Integrated Children's System, a computerized version of the CAF forms which was designed to encourage greater sharing of information across agencies.

What appears certain is that assessment is no longer solely the professional provenance of social workers; Government has taken considerable responsibility for attempting to delineate how assessments should be carried out. Yet if the various government strategies and forms are studied in detail a curious fact emerges. There is now a bewildering and quite an extraordinary array of guidelines and timescales for assessments; and an enormous number of tick-boxes asking about specific pieces of information. Yet despite all of this there is remarkably little guidance on how social workers or other professionals should make decisions using the mass of information they have gathered. Ironically, despite the consistent findings from government inspectors and researchers that social workers are very good at gathering information but are less good at systematically analysing it to make robust decisions (Cleaver *et al.*, 2004; Department of Health, 1991), this is precisely what the government guidance tends to encourage. To understand why the heart of assessment has been left to professional discretion it is necessary to consider the nature and history of assessment within Children's Services.

HISTORY AND THEORY OF ASSESSMENT

Assessment is a comparatively recent phenomenon. Originally it related to making a judgement about an individual's liability to pay tax. It is a relatively easy step from assessing liability for tax to welfare professionals becoming involved in making judgements about individuals' rights to benefits or services. The process essentially mirrors that of a tax assessment: information is collected about the circumstances and resources of an individual or family and a decision made about their eligibility.

Yet this conception of assessment – essentially assessing whether people needed specific resources – changed fundamentally during the 1970s and 1980s. Parton (1985, 1991) provides a detailed account of this change. In brief, social workers were increasingly held responsible for the bad things that happened to children. Assessing the risk of negative outcomes therefore became a central element of social work practice.

This is profoundly problematic, for it repeatedly runs into a serious and irreducible fact: it is impossible to predict the future with complete accuracy.

This is true even in situations in which professionals have perfect information. Ultimately, individuals have – to at least some degree – free will. Even if one holds that individuals' actions are determined by prior events and not acts of will, the factors determining them are so complex that it is impossible, both theoretically and in practice, to predict with high levels of accuracy what individuals will do. As a result, even the most apparently hopeless drug addict sometimes turns their life around. Conversely, an apparently happy and safe child may be killed by a loving parent in what appears an unpredictable moment of madness. As if this did not make risk assessment problematic enough, the truth is that social workers never do have perfect information; often they have very limited and partial information to make judgements on. In such circumstances, it is not possible to make accurate judgements about what is going to happen to a child.

This no doubt contributes to the Government's focus on gathering information and the comparative lack of guidance on what should be done with that information. Ultimately, despite the proliferation of governance around assessment within Children's Services, professionals are left with the responsibility to draw conclusions from the information that they have collected. Yet how should such complex decisions be made? What does research and theory tell us in relation to assessing risk of future harm?

RESEARCH ON RISK ASSESSMENT

One of the features of 'risk assessment' in the area of child welfare and child protection is that incorrect decisions in either direction can be harmful. Assessing a child as being at risk of harm who would not actually experience harm (a 'false positive') runs the risk of disrupting family life, legitimating unwarranted intervention and perhaps a child entering care who does not need it. On the other hand, a failure to identify a child who is at risk (a 'false negative') may result in a child experiencing abuse and neglect, and at the extreme end, dying. Thus at the heart of risk assessment in child protection work is balancing potentially negative consequences in either direction.

This makes accurate risk assessment particularly important. Yet such research as there is in this area is not encouraging. One of the features of 'risk assessment' is that it is used to cover a wide variety of approaches to assessing future harm. At one extreme are research-based 'actuarial' models. These use standardized information and formalized information management processes (such as mathematical formula) to assess risk. For instance, most insurance companies use such approaches to calculate premiums, and in some American studies a similar approach has been tested for assessing risks to children (Baird and Wagner, 2000). However 'risk assessments' are also undertaken by expert clinicians whose judgement is informed by, but not confined to, research evidence and by practitioners who assess risk in ways that are only loosely based on research evidence. Research on both of these approaches consistently highlights their comparatively low level of success.

Since Greenland's research was used to argue that the death of Jasmine Beckford was 'predictable and preventable' (Brent, 1985) there has been a search for risk indicators that will make identifying – and therefore preventing – serious harm to children possible. Yet to date the search has produced little evidence that risk indicators can be used to identify children at risk. For instance, Peters and Barlow (2003) reviewed research on identifying risk of maltreatment for infants. They found only eight prospective studies. These varied widely in their success, and only one of the screening instruments identified 90% of children at risk. However, even with this instrument 75% of those identified as 'at risk' did not experience subsequent abuse. A difficulty in identifying children who are subsequently harmed has been found in other attempts to develop risk indicators. In American studies of risk assessment schemes within child protection work there do not appear to be any studies that have achieved even this level of accuracy. Camasso and Jagannathan (1995) compared two risk assessment systems against re-referral and substantiated re-referral rates for families known to Child Protective Services. Their findings indicated identification higher than chance, but not by much. Baumann et al. (2005) examine the predictive power of clinical and actuarial estimation of risk. They present their results as correlations. These ranged from around 0.3 to about 0.5. These levels would generate very substantial numbers of false positives and false negatives for both methods. Sheets (1991, reported in Baird and Wagner, 2000) found no relationship between identification of 'risk' and likelihood of subsequent maltreatment. Baird and Wagner (2000) compared three of the most rigorous and widely used risk assessment schedules in the USA. The best of these, the Michigan Risk Assessment Model, identified 14.9% of children as at 'low risk' and 58.1% as at moderate risk. The rate of substantiated recurrences of maltreatment for this measure was 9% of low risk cases and 21% of moderate risk. The other models had recurrences of harm for 18% and 22% of low risk cases. These do not appear to be very successful models.

Even retrospective studies to identify risk factors, which should have considerably higher levels of accuracy because the factors are specifically identified from the sample being studied, rarely achieve high levels of accuracy. For instance, in an American community sample Brown et al. (1998) identified a list of risk factors. Where there were four or more, 24% of children experienced abuse. The converse of this is that 76% of those identified as at 'high risk' were false negatives. In one of the few British studies in this area Hamilton and Browne (1999) reported on a study of re-referrals to police child protection units. Retrospective identification of risk factors allowed a model to be created to predict 'high risk'. This research not only specified 'risk factors' but also retrospectively created a method to weight and combine them, thus creating the most accurate model possible based on the data available. In this way the researchers were able to develop a model that achieved an overall level of accuracy of 84.2% for re-referrals, with a specificity of 85.7%. However, these levels would not be found if the model were applied prospectively – and even these retrospective attempts to model risk factors produce considerable levels of false identification. Thus, even the best actuarial-based systems for identifying risk of abuse have high levels of false positives and false negatives, and there is always a trade-off between 'false positives' and 'false negatives' in that to miss fewer children who are abused, more children who are not abused are identified as 'at risk'.

What should be clear from the discussion so far is that in this highly sensitive area very accurate risk assessment is required, and that at present research-based actuarial tools are not able to provide this. Is it therefore possible that clinical assessment by a human expert might be better than purely research-based risk assessment? A clinical approach involves the collection and analysis of information around risk by a human, generally an expert in their field. This allows the expert leeway to ignore certain information and to give more weight to other facts, for instance unique or unusual circumstances. It can also allow them to make use of gut feelings and emotional reactions, which are not available to the mechanical approach. There would appear to be good reasons for relying on clinical judgement within social work. Each child and family is unique, and mechanical approaches do not seem to have the capacity to deal with this. However, this begs the question: are clinical approaches better than mechanical approaches at predicting risk?

The answer suggests potentially serious problems for the clinical approach to risk assessment. The research evidence strongly suggests that clinical decision-making is rarely as good as mechanical assessment. Grove and Meehl (1996) and Grove et al. (2000) discuss this evidence at length. They present a meta-analysis of 137 studies comparing clinical and mechanical decision-making. They come to a strong conclusion in favour of mechanical assessments:

> All policy-makers should know that a practitioner who claims not to need any statistical or experimental studies but relies solely on clinical experience as adequate justification, by that very claim is shown to be a nonscientifically minded person whose professional judgements are not to be trusted.
>
> (Grove et al., 2000, p. 320)

They then defend this conclusion against a range of possible objections. They make a convincing case that human decision-makers are typically prone to a range of decision-making errors. One of the most important is that we have great difficulty holding a range of information in our heads at one time. Humans have a strong tendency to deal with this problem using various cognitive strategies, such as trying to simplify situations and being influenced by whatever is immediately before us or was last seen. These bias our assessments of risk. We also tend to gather information to support our hypothesis and fail to revise our risk assessment accurately in light of new information.

These failings in human reasoning explain the consistent ability of even relatively simple mechanical calculations of risk to be more accurate than human estimations. Munro (2002) has discussed these failings at length and concluded that they present important challenges if we are to improve the accuracy of child protection risk assessments.

However, some caution should be taken in applying these findings to social work assessments. Only one of the studies included in Grove *et al.*'s (2000) meta-analysis related to social work. Many of the studies comparing mechanical and clinical decision-making are based on medical diagnosis or future job or academic performance. It seems likely that these are easier areas in which mechanical decision-making can be used and in which its benefits over human decision-making will be clearer. The research basis for decision-making in these areas is stronger, and less importance is generally placed on issues that may be difficult to assess, such as parents' motivation, acceptance of responsibility or degree of harm. In particular, the 'meaning' of situations, which is considered of central importance in social work risk assessment, is difficult (though not necessarily impossible) to incorporate into any mechanical risk assessment process.

Support for this more sceptical approach to actuarial risk assessment is provided in a series of studies reported by Baumann *et al.* (2005). Baumann and colleagues developed a checklist of indicators for the likelihood of a referral being 'substantiated' as involving maltreatment based on an analysis of social work records. Their studies report on a pilot scheme to measure the accuracy of this risk assessment checklist compared to clinical decision-making in predicting whether an initial referral of alleged child maltreatment would be 'substantiated' (i.e. confirmed by workers) or subsequently re-referred. Two findings from these studies are important. First, to the evident surprise of the researchers, clinical estimates of risk were somewhat more accurate than those obtained through actuarial methods. Second, while Baumann and colleagues do not comment on this, the general correlation between the estimation of risk, whether by worker or computer, and for all types of maltreatment, was not high. It ranged from 0.3 to 0.5. When the fact that this was a dichotomous decision (substantiated or not) over a relatively short period is taken into account, this generally low level of correlation, rather then the relatively small superiority of the clinical judgements, appears the most important finding.

It should not therefore be concluded that clinical risk assessment is better in child protection settings than mechanical risk assessment. The limited literature in relation to social work has tended to find that mechanical decision-making is better than expert decision-making (Baird and Wagner, 2000; Shlonsky and Wagner, 2005). However, as Munro argues, while we do not know that mechanical assessments are better, there is certainly a strong body of evidence suggesting that clinical decision-making is poor. While social work may be different, we do not have much evidence to suggest that in fact it is, and what evidence exists suggests that we should be very cautious about the ability of any sort of risk assessment to predict whether a child will experience harm.

> The question of the viability of actuarial risk assessment systems in child welfare practice remains a matter of dispute. The issue is less a matter of the comparative merits of actuarial and clinical judgments than a question of whether there is any known method of assessing risk in this context.
>
> (Baumann *et al.*, 2005, p. 466)

This goes to the heart of the matter. Social workers are asked to assess risk, but is there any evidence about how this can be done effectively? Or are social workers being asked to do the impossible?

ARGUMENTS IN FAVOUR OF RISK ASSESSMENT

The theoretical problems in assessing risk should give practitioners, policy-makers and researchers pause for thought. They have profound implications for how professionals should carry out assessments. For instance, they suggest that a humble approach to undertaking risk assessments, which places at its heart the impossibility of being certain of the future, is necessary. Below we explore what this might mean in practice. However, before abandoning even the possibility of risk assessment it is necessary to consider the other side of the argument. There are practical and theoretical arguments that suggest that social workers should be prepared to undertake the best possible assessments of risk.

The most important of these is that while it is impossible to be sure what will happen in the future, it is nonetheless possible to indicate general tendencies. We do not live in a completely chaotic world. People are predictable to some degree. If this were not so planning for anything would be impossible: we would not know whether our colleagues would be at work, whether children would attend school or whether our friends would turn up to a party; it would not be possible to develop relationships or make commitments for the future. There is overwhelming evidence that much of human behaviour is, broadly and in general terms, predictable. It is nonetheless impossible to be sure what will happen for any given individual. For instance, in giving a lecture to a class I may be able to predict on the basis of what happens every week that about 30 students will turn up. This may not always be the case. The week after a particularly dull lecture perhaps fewer will be there; if people heard that excellent tips on passing the exam were to be given at the next lecture perhaps attendance would be higher. However, overall the best predictor of the numbers attending will be the pattern of attendance in previous weeks. It is also possible to predict with some accuracy the attendance of individual students. The keen student who has attended every lecture will probably be there again; the one who finds the course dull and has come to no lectures will probably not be there this week. Yet, who knows? Perhaps this week the keen student will be ill, and they will convince the uninterested one to attend and take notes for them.

These examples suggest that people are broadly predictable, but that such predictions can never be wholly accurate. Of course, for the lecturer idly speculating about attendance at their lecture such considerations are of no importance. The problem is that in the field of child protection assessments the accuracy of predictions is vital. Child protection assessments are literally life-and-death issues. Error is potentially disastrous.

It is this fact that provides the second compelling argument in favour of risk assessments. They may be fraught with theoretical and practical challenges, yet ultimately accurate assessments by social workers have the ability to save children from serious abuse or even death. The challenge is therefore to carry them out as well as possible, and to minimize the number of false negatives and false positives. This is no trivial challenge. The conclusions of risk assessments often have massive implications for parents and children. Getting them right – or at least as 'right' as is possible – is therefore crucial for the welfare of the individuals concerned. It is also a moral imperative. Removing children from families, or deciding that they can remain in concerning family situations, or even making a decision about whether a concern requires a family to be allocated, are hugely important decisions. As such, professionals have a duty to ensure that they are made as accurately as possible, that individuals are provided with opportunities to change, but that this does not result in unhelpful delays for children.

In many ways therefore social workers are attempting to carry out an activity that most theorists consider impossible to do perfectly, and very difficult even to do well. The rest of this chapter is devoted to considering how social workers might do this. In particular it considers how social workers and other professionals use, or might use, pragmatic approaches to cope with the uncertainty inherent in any risk assessment. In essence we argue that practitioners have developed methods for coping with the uncertainty involved in risk assessment. These methods do not eliminate uncertainty, but they provide the opportunity to manage and cope with it. We argue that making them more explicit provides an opportunity to carry out better risk assessments, to integrate risk assessment with understanding needs and services, and to deal with the theoretical, practical and moral limitations inherent in risk assessment as currently formulated.

APPROACHES TO ASSESSING RISK AND NEED WHEN PARENTS MISUSE DRUGS OR ALCOHOL

We shall considers three issues:

1. How should information be analysed?
2. What information should be collected?
3. Where should information be collected from?

It has been noted that much guidance has concentrated on what information needs to be gathered and spends little time considering how it should be analysed. Social workers have also been criticized for this (Department of Health, 1991). We attempt to address this problem by starting with a consideration of how information should be analysed. Key information in relation to parental substance misuse is then considered. However, we also think it important to look at how information is obtained. It is rare for a parent to be completely candid about their substance use and its impact on their child. Understanding the nature of these issues and how to work around them in an assessment is as important as knowing what information to gather.

ANALYSIS IN ASSESSMENT

Thus far we have – in common with many social work commentators – been critical of Government's attempts to reform assessments within Children's Services. We have also highlighted the shortcomings in both actuarial and clinical approaches to risk assessment. Yet, while it is easy to critique approaches to assessment, it is more challenging to outline helpful ways that social workers or other professionals should undertake assessments. So, how should practitioners approach undertaking an assessment?

In this section we propose an approach that developed from our reflections on the interviews with social workers for the current study. It is not a description of what they were doing, but it does incorporate elements from their responses into a more systematic attempt to address some of the many challenges in assessments outlined above. Essentially, it arose from our attempt to address the issues that they were raising in their interviews. The model we propose is an attempt to articulate an approach to assessment that takes into account the theoretical discussion above and the practice challenges identified by social workers. In doing this it has three main components. These are:

1. Specifying a range of outcomes;
2. Testing capacity for change;
3. Giving meaning to information.

Crucial to this approach is that assessments should specify a range of possible outcomes – from a 'worst-case' scenario to a 'best possible' scenario. This is an important approach to assessment for both theoretical and practical reasons.

Specifying a range of outcomes

The idea that assessment should aim to consider a range of outcomes rather than identifying a single 'outcome' emerged from social workers' answers to the final questions in the interview schedule, as outlined and discussed in Chapter 4. They were asked what we would find when we came back to look at the family in a year's time. Respondents generally began their answer with some version of 'Well, I hope that …' and would then outline a comparatively positive scenario. This might include parents continuing to cooperate or obtaining treatment, or the case being closed because there was no need for further social work involvement. After noting this answer, the researcher would ask whether this was what they thought would happen. Sometimes it was, but this was in fact rare. Far more common was a less positive scenario. This would often include relapse, failure to engage with services or an inability of services to make a difference.

This pattern of answers led us to characterize the social workers as 'optimistic cynics'. They appeared simultaneously to hold optimistic views about what they hoped to achieve and what they thought might happen for the family, and cynical views about what was likely actually to happen. On reflection, such an approach appeared likely to be helpful in certain respects. It is difficult to achieve much in working with people if one does not hold out at least the possibility of change. Optimism may well be necessary to be an effective worker. The powerful impact of expectation effects in both teaching and counselling situations have been demonstrated in research studies (Asay and Lambert, 1999; Rosenthal, 1994). Yet to rely wholly on optimism is profoundly dangerous if vulnerable young children are involved. It may lead to them being exposed to unacceptable levels of abuse or neglect (Dingwall *et al.*, 1995). Balancing optimism and cynicism therefore seems a central part of the social work role.

There was no evidence that social workers systematically made explicit these potentially conflicting approaches to the family. Indeed, there was evidence that they did not as none of the files outlined a range of possible outcomes. However, holding in mind a range of outcomes seems a very promising way to approach assessing families, for several reasons.

First, it addresses the unpredictability of human behaviour. As discussed above, predicting what will happen for any particular person or family is very difficult to do accurately; predicting a range of outcomes, on the other hand, does seem possible to do accurately. As such, it forms an important starting point for responding to the criticisms of risk assessment discussed earlier.

Second, making explicit the possible range of outcomes deals with some of the key shortcomings identified by Munro and others within human reasoning (Munro, 2002). In broad terms, these all result from attempts to simplify complicated situations and so all tend to lead to professionals forming an inaccurate judgement and sticking to it. As an antidote to this Munro suggests that social workers should take a more scientific approach, in that they should explicitly test and try to falsify their picture of what is happening and what is likely to happen. Incorporating doubt – for instance, through considering a range of outcomes – into assessments is therefore helpful. It has the potential to help practitioners avoid the failures in reasoning associated with both child death inquiries and instances when social workers have overreacted. Explicitly outlining both a best and worst-case scenario is likely to help in developing such habits of thinking, for it attempts to avoid social workers becoming blinkered about what is likely to happen within a family. It incorporates testing out what is happening rather than narrowing down to a single picture of the family.

Third, identifying a range of outcomes explains and to some extent addresses one of the core challenges social workers talked about when we interviewed them about assessing and working with parental substance misuse (see Chapter 4). This is the fact that when parents with substance misuse issues are not using or are using in a stable manner many of them are very good parents, but that when their use is problematic – when they lapse or relapse – their care can be very dangerous and harmful. To paraphrase the nursery rhyme:

> When they were good, they were very, very good,
> But when they were bad they were horrid.

This is a particular challenge in working with parental substance misuse. For many issues that a social worker assesses – for instance, a parent with a learning difficulty, children with special needs or complex social problems – the presenting issues are relatively consistent. The difficulty with substance misuse is that often patterns of misuse change over time, but how can decisions be made about whether positive change will last? This is a key challenge in assessment. Attempting to make explicit the possible range of outcomes does not prevent this from being a difficult judgement to make. However, by making explicit the issues concerned, it allows all those involved to work towards the best possible outcome without ignoring the very real risks of a relapse.

Fourth, making explicit this range of outcomes has practical benefits in working with families and with other services. It creates a link between needs and risks, rather than allowing them to exist as parallel discourses. This is worth considering further. An explicit positive goal for work allows family members, the lead professional and other services to be clear about what the aims for work are. It identifies the needs that must be met if a family is to achieve a particular goal. It also provides the essential element of hope that is central to good work of all types. However, an explicit articulation of what the concerns are is equally important. It identifies – for the family, the lead professional and other agencies – what the concerns relate to. This allows the changes that need to be made to be identified. However, it also allows appropriate monitoring and identification if things are not going well to be put in place. If there was a relapse leading to poor care for the children, how would we find out?

Such an approach also incorporates both risk and need. The needs of the child, the parent and the family are the things that must happen to achieve the positive goals of work. This might include resources for the family (for instance, being rehoused), for the parent (for instance, accessing a regular methadone prescription) or for the child (for instance, the parent ensuring that they get to school regularly and on time). It can also include tasks for the parent (for instance, not using heroin as well as a methadone prescription). These are what are needed to achieve the positive goals. The risk is that the positive goal is not achieved and that in fact progress falls so far short of the positive goal that the child is placed at risk of harm or significant harm. In this model, needs must be met to achieve specified positive goals; risk is the likelihood of positive goals not being achieved. This may be because needs are not met (for instance, the family is not rehoused) or for other reasons (perhaps unexpectedly a supportive grandparent dies leading to serious problems in the family). The core of this approach to assessment is that specifying a range of outcomes is the key to analysing the information within an assessment and to putting together interventions aimed at making a difference. This approach is outlined in Figure 6.1.

Testing capacity for change

A crucial aspect of this model – which also appeared to be implicit in the comments of the social workers whom we interviewed – was that it does not see assessment as static, but as fluid and occurring over time. A key element of this is that the ability of parents to change is not simply assessed, it

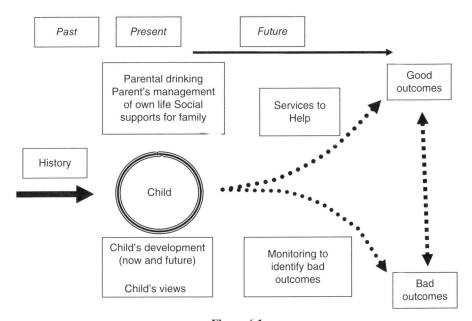

Figure 6.1

is tested. Ideally, this should be done by providing the services and supports that parents need and assessing whether they are able to make use of them and whether the necessary changes occur. This is a complex process in practice, but at this point it is more important to consider its importance from a theoretical point of view. As we discussed above, social workers are faced with making incredibly important decisions in a situation in which they cannot be certain whether they are right. One key strategy for dealing with this is to assess and work with the range of possible outcomes for any particular family. A second, is to use this as a process that tests out the parents' ability to change.

The most obvious example of such testing out occurs in more serious cases, such as those subject to care proceedings. In such circumstances, the commitment of parents to use treatment and address their drug or alcohol use is often a key element of the assessment process; their ability to make and sustain changes is central to the proceedings. Yet even when care proceedings are not started and when children are not at such great risk, the process of testing out over time may still be a central part of the process of assessment. For instance, a family may be offered services and if they do not use them, the case may be closed provided the children do not seem to be at too great a risk; or the parent's ability to work with services around a child protection plan may be tested out over time.

This conceptualization of assessment as a process that is carried out over time is crucially different from the rather static models inherent in the discussions and research relating to 'actuarial' or 'clinical' assessments. Indeed, while change over time is explicitly discussed within the Assessment Framework guidance, the forms that accompany the Framework militate against such an approach. Thus the box ticked for substance misuse should perhaps be cleared after a period of treatment, but this would not be straightforward. Central to this testing out over time is that for most assessments the decision is not a binary one, it is not a matter of a child being at risk or not at risk. Instead, assessment processes involve a substantial area of uncertainty. In practice they often involve not knowing – for instance, not knowing what will happen in a residential or community treatment. As a result, assessments can – and should – wrestle with this lack of certainty by providing opportunities for change and testing out what happens. We suggest that making explicit the range of possible outcomes as outlined above is one way of actively managing uncertainty.

Giving meaning to information

Social work assessment is not simply a matter of collecting information and making a judgement. The meaning of the information needs to be understood – and understood from different perspectives. What meaning does it have for the parent? For the child? For the social worker? For other professionals?

Perhaps the best example of the importance of meaning is provided in the work of Reder and colleagues (Reder *et al.*, 1993; Reder and Duncan, 1999). They analyse child death or serious injury inquiries. What Reder and colleagues emphasize is understanding the meaning of the child for the parents. At the broader level this is about understanding what caring for a child may mean for a parent and the issues around care and control that it may have for them. More specifically, it may be about what this particular child means for a parent or a step-parent. However, this is just one example of meaning. In fact, social work assessments are saturated with meaning.

Parental substance misuse is a good example. Let us consider a family in which the mother drinks heavily and her 5-year-old daughter appears to be neglected. What is the meaning of this woman's drinking? For the woman herself it may be a way of dealing with difficult feelings – perhaps a way of 'coping' with abuse she experienced, or feelings of worthlessness or depression; perhaps she cannot imagine a life in which her feelings are not dulled without drinking, and she does not feel that she could change. On the other hand, what is the meaning of the mother's drinking for her daughter? Is it something she fears and hates? Is it something she takes for granted, part of everyday life? Is she already learning that drinking is a way of coping when she is unhappy? Or is it something she welcomes? Perhaps her mother becomes more relaxed and affectionate when she is drinking.

The importance of meaning is not confined to clients. What does the mother's drinking in this family mean for the social worker? In other words, what are our own feelings, values and experiences, and how might they shape the way we understand the world of the client? For instance, a social worker who had a mother who drank very heavily causing the social worker unhappiness as a child might feel very differently about the above family from one who was drinking heavily at home to cope with the stresses of the job. These value differences are at least as pronounced with illegal drugs. Some workers have extensive personal experience of using a range of substances, others have none. Neither experience places one in a better position to work with drug misuse. What is crucial is a self-critical approach to one's own values and feelings and how they might shape the act of understanding (i.e. giving meaning to) information within an assessment.

Finally, the meaning of drinking (or anything else) will vary among professionals involved with a family. This will be in part about individuals and their experiences, but it will also be shaped by professional understandings of particular issues. Thus, the substance misuse professional may understand the mother in this family to be depressed and may see the drinking as an outcome of that. The health visitor may see the mother as neglecting the needs of their child. Furthermore, it is not just professional frameworks that can influence understanding. A feminist would point to the absence of the father and the focus on the mother and her drinking. Someone who was active in Alcoholics Anonymous might think the mother has to 'hit rock bottom' in order to realize that they have to abstain. The list is literally endless, because the interactions of values, emotions and frameworks for interpreting information are infinite.

In facing this complexity two things are crucial. The first is space to reflect critically on the meanings and their interplay. There is a variety of ways in which this can be done. However, we would emphasize the central importance of reflective professional supervision. By this we mean supervision that discusses the dynamics of working with families, including the emotional significance and meaning – for the social worker and others – of information. Such supervision allows space for the exploration of ambiguity and for emotional support for the worker. There is a widespread perception that in recent years such supervision has been in decline, with an increase in managerial supervision that focuses on task completion. This is unfortunate, as reflective supervision has been shown to be associated with social workers remaining in frontline work and significant reductions in turnover of staff (Zlotnik *et al.*, 2005). Little wonder. Given the complexities of the work and the impossibility of certainty a focus on task completion appears to miss the very nature of the complex business of child protection social work.

The second key element of responding to the complexity involved in understanding the meaning of information is to try to remain open to multiple interpretations. Munro (2002) has done social work a great service in highlighting the dangers of premature closure in making decisions. Similarly, with understanding the different meanings of behaviours and events it is important to remain open to the complexity of that which is being assessed. For this reason, perhaps more than any other, tick-box forms are not simply an annoying additional task social workers have to complete when doing an assessment, they are a fundamental failure to understand the nature of social work assessments.

Having considered issues in analysing information within an assessment in some depth, in the next section we turn to consider what information social workers should collect when assessing children's safety and welfare.

WHAT INFORMATION TO COLLECT?

There are many places offering advice – or even expectations – about what information social workers and other professionals should gather to make an assessment. The Assessment Framework sets out three domains in which workers should gather information. These are:

- Child development;
- Parenting capacity;
- Social and environmental context.

These broad areas are supplemented by copious paperwork. The standard forms accompanying the Assessment Framework identify many pieces of information that should be gathered for a Core Assessment. We do not consider this a particularly helpful way of structuring an assessment, for a number of reasons. First, the highly structured nature of the government guidance leads to a centralized and bureaucratic style of information-gathering. The most important problem with such an approach is that it is not led by the individuals involved in the assessment, namely the professional, the parent/s and the child. The information to be gathered has been determined by 'experts'; it is not up to the client or the social worker to decide what information should be gathered. Second, the increasingly structured nature of these assessments can easily encourage shallow and unhelpful information-gathering. For instance, asking individuals whether or not they have a drink or drug problem is unlikely to be helpful. Asking them open-ended questions about how they are finding caring for their child, how they cope with the pressures of life or what a normal day is like generates far better quality information. No doubt skilled practitioners gather information in this way and then fill in the necessary forms; however, all too often the forms structure the interactions between professional and service users, and they do so in ways that risk dehumanizing the assessment process. Finally, the structure of the Assessment Framework, the CAF and the ICS does not allow the exploration of meaning. This requires a story to be built up about what is happening in the family and why (Reder *et al.*, 1991; Reder and Duncan, 1999). Collecting discrete pieces of information does not facilitate this approach.

Quite apart from such considerations, there have been criticisms of the Assessment Framework as a basis for assessing parental drink or drug-taking as issues. Murphy and Harbin (2000) highlighted that very little information is specified in relation to substance misuse issues and has suggested that the Assessment Framework could be supplemented by material relating to substance misuse. In the families in the current sample drug or alcohol misuse by a parent was usually a key issue, yet the Assessment Framework provides very limited information on how to gather or analyse information on this area.

A useful checklist for gathering such information was developed in the late 1980s by the Standing Conference on Drug Abuse (SCODA). These questions have been adapted and reproduced in later publications and can often be found in the child protection procedures of local safeguarding boards or Children's Services Departments. They are outlined in Box 6.1. The SCODA guidelines provide a very useful aide-mémoire or prompt for the types of issues that may be of relevance for assessing drug-using families. While the guidance was not developed with alcohol misuse in mind, many of the issues can also be applied to alcohol. However, it has a number of shortcomings. Kroll and Taylor (2002) note that the views and opinions of the child do not feature in the guidelines. There is also little consideration of broader structural issues, such as the ways in which gender, race or class may be of relevance in understanding patterns of substance use. However, perhaps most important of all is the difficulty involved in actually gathering the information

Box 6.1　The standing conference on drug use guidelines for professionals assessing risk when working with drug using parents.

Parental drug use

1. Is there a drug-free parent, supportive partner or relative?
2. Is the drug use by the parent: experimental? recreational? chaotic? dependent?
3. Does the user move between categories at different times? Does the drug use also involve alcohol?
4. Are levels of child care different when a parent is using drugs and when not using?
5. Is there evidence of coexistence of mental health problems alongside the drug use? If there is, do the drugs cause these problems, or have these problems led to the drug use?

Accommodation and the home environment

6. Is the accommodation adequate for children?
7. Are the parents ensuring that the rent and bills are paid?
8. Does the family remain in one area or move frequently? If the latter, why?
9. Are other drug users sharing the accommodation? If they are, are relationships with them harmonious, or is there conflict?
10. Is the family living in a drug-using community?
11. If parents are using drugs, do children witness them taking the drugs, or other substances?
12. Could other aspects of the drug use constitute a risk to children (e.g. conflict with or between dealers, exposure to criminal activities related to drug use)?

Provision of basic needs

13. Is there adequate food, clothing and warmth for the children?
14. Are the children attending school regularly?
15. Are children engaged in age-appropriate activities?
16. Are the children's emotional needs being adequately met?
17. Are there any indications that any of the children are taking on a parenting role within the family (caring for other children, excessive household responsibilities, etc.)?

Procurement of drugs

18. Are the children left alone while their parents are procuring drugs?
19. Because of their parents' drug use are the children being taken to places where they could be 'at risk'?

20. How much do the drugs cost?
21. How is the money obtained?
22. Is this causing financial problems?
23. Are the premises being used to sell drugs?
24. Are the parents allowing their premises to be used by other drug users?

Health risks

25. If drugs and/or injecting equipment are kept on the premises, are they kept securely?
26. Are the children aware of where the drugs are kept?
27. If parents are intravenous drug users:
    Do they share injecting equipment?
    Do they use a needle exchange scheme?
    How do they dispose of the syringes?
    Are parents aware of the health risks of injecting or using drugs?
28. If parents are on a substitute prescribing programme, such as methadone:
    Are parents aware of the dangers of children accessing this medication?
    Do they take adequate precautions to ensure this does not happen?
29. Are parents aware of, and in touch with, local specialist agencies who can advise on such issues as needle exchanges, substitute prescribing programmes, detox *and* rehab facilities? If they are in touch with agencies, how regular is the contact?

Family social network and support systems

30. Do parents and children associate primarily with:
    Other drug users?
    Non-users?
    Both?
31. Are relatives aware of the drug use? Are they supportive?
32. Will parents accept help from the relatives and other professional or non-statutory agencies?
33. The degree of social isolation should be considered, particularly for those parents living in remote areas where resources may not be available and they may experience social stigmatization.

Parents' perception of the situation

34. Do the parents see their drug use as harmful to themselves or to their children?
35. Do the parents place their own needs before the needs of the children?
36. Are the parents aware of the legislative and procedural context applying to their circumstances (e.g. child protection procedures, statutory powers)?

set out in the guidance. If one had full information on each of these areas, one would certainly have enough information to complete a very thorough assessment. But that is very unlikely to be the case. This key issue is returned to in the next section.

More recently, Alcohol Concern (2006) has developed excellent guidance that can be used when completing CAF materials, and the same organization has devoted a whole website to helping professionals work better with alcohol issues in the family. This is particularly useful for a review of risks and strengths in family situations. Hart and Powell (2006) have also produced excellent materials for the National Children's Bureau for practitioners undertaking assessments where parental drug misuse is an issue.

All of these contributions provide helpful pointers for the types of information that might be considered when undertaking an assessment of parental drinking or drug-taking. Rather than replicating such excellent sources of information about drink or drug problems and their impact on family life, in this section we aim to identify four key issues to focus on in deciding what information is needed to make an assessment. (These are an adapted version of guidance previously published in Forrester, 2004.) It is hoped that these may undergird and inform the more specific indicators of which information can and should be gathered. These are:

1. Focus on the child not the drug or alcohol problem.
2. Information – particularly information around concerns – should be specific and concrete.
3. It is important to understand the everyday life of the family.
4. The best predictor of future behaviour is past behaviour.

Focus on the child not the drug or alcohol problem

All too often anxious practitioners focus on trying to understand how much or when the parent is drinking or taking drugs. This is understandable. As noted above, one of the anxiety-provoking issues where there is substance misuse is trying to understand what may be happening behind closed doors. However, there are four important reasons why focusing on drug or alcohol misuse is inappropriate. The first is that it is very difficult to obtain such information accurately. It has long been recognized that individuals seeking treatment for drug or alcohol use issues tend to understate the extent of their misuse. How much more likely is it that they will do this when the individual's care for the child is likely to come under scrutiny? Put crudely, information from parents about their drug or alcohol use is extremely unlikely to be reliable – at least in the early stages of the relationship. Second, on its own, information about patterns of substance misuse tells us little. It is the person's response to the substance, the context in which it is taken, the sacrifices that are made to obtain it and similar considerations that are crucial.

Third, an excessive focus on substance use patterns may well antagonize the parent, who may feel – with some justification – that they are being judged. Finally, and most importantly, it is not the role of child welfare professionals to assess or make judgements about drug or alcohol use. The child is the focus of the assessment, and it is the impact of the substance misuse on the child and their welfare that should be the focus of concern.

This is not of course to suggest that child welfare professionals should not talk to parents about their drinking or drug-taking. This is a legitimate and necessary area for discussion when talking about child welfare and family functioning with a parent who has a drug or alcohol problem. Understanding patterns of use, how they have changed over time and how they impact on children is crucial to assessment where there is parental substance misuse. However, this is a different conversation from one focused on drug or alcohol misuse *per se*. The key issue here is to understand why information about drug or alcohol use is needed. The key questions fall into two areas:

1. How does the drinking or drug-taking impact on the family's functioning or the child's welfare? For instance, are there particular times when the drinking or drug-taking is particularly likely to harm the child? When are they? What can be done about them?
2. What does the pattern of substance misuse tell us about the best ways of helping the family? For instance, what is the parent's perception of their drinking or drug-taking and its role in their life? Is the drinking or drug-taking dependent or occasional? Steady or prone to binges? What is the history of substance use and of help around substance use? What help, if any, would the parent like for their substance use?

Throughout, the key issue is to be clear about why information needs to be collected and how it relates to the welfare of the child and/or the parent.

Information – particularly information around concerns – should be specific and concrete

This crucial fact shapes the entire nature of the assessment. Thus, it is not sufficient to conclude:

> Jenny's (the mother's) drinking leads her to neglect Dylan's needs.

More acceptable would be:

> When she drinks too much Jenny does not make sure Dylan goes to bed at a reasonable time; he often does not get enough sleep and school say he cannot concentrate. Jenny also finds it difficult to get up and make sure Dylan has breakfast and gets to school on time if she has a hangover; Dylan has been reported by the school often to be hungry at school (which makes it difficult for him to concentrate). Dylan also sometimes comes to school in dirty clothes and the other children tease him.

Obtaining such specific and concrete information is more difficult than making general statements, yet it is vitally important. First, it provides parents with a clear account of what the concerns are. This may be difficult for them to hear, but it is far more understandable than 'neglect' or 'emotional abuse'. Second, it provides the basis for creating plans for change. In the above example, it is easy to see the sort of agreement that Jenny and the social worker might make to produce clear and tangible change for Dylan. However, collecting such specific information is not easy. It requires detailed information-gathering from a variety of sources to produce a composite picture of family functioning.

It is important to understand the everyday life of the family

Assessments do not just require – or even primarily require – an understanding of all the 'facts' required to complete a Core Assessment form. Rather they should be based on understanding what normal days and weekends are like for families. In this respect, simply asking for information about such things is crucial. Helpful prompts might include:

- What did you do on Saturday?
- It would help me if you could tell me what a typical day in your family is like. How does it start? [*listen*] Then what happens ...?
- What are your plans for this weekend?
- Tell me about a good time you had as a family recently.

The best predictor of future behaviour is past behaviour

It is an old and oft-repeated adage within social science that the best predictor of future behaviour is past behaviour. If social science teaches us anything, it teaches us this. This has profound implications for assessment. It underscores the vital importance of chronologies and social histories. Each of these is worth considering. A chronology is a collection of key information about a family's history. It should include key dates, changes and events for the family and relating to the involvement of professionals. Ideally, the chronology should be checked with the family and developed collaboratively. Chronologies allow social workers and the families that they work with to recognize patterns and their likely consequences.

Social histories are essentially the story behind the chronology. Whereas a chronology outlines what happened, a social history focuses on why it happened. It is particularly important that it links and makes sense of major changes in the life of the individual or the family, such as changes of partner, moves or the birth of children. Social histories are crucially important because the statement that 'the best predictor of future behaviour is past behaviour' does not do justice to the complexity of human experience and the capacity of humans to change. A woman may have lived with three men all of whom were violent to her, but this does not mean she will necessarily do so again. Crucially, to evaluate whether people may change it is necessary to understand their interpretation of events and the actions they intend to take in relation to them. For instance, imagine that the woman concerned now says she is going to make a change in her life. Previously, she had always felt that she needed a man – any man – and had ended up with men who were violent and controlling, but now she understands the underlying reasons for her doing this and has decided that she is going to learn how to live happily on her own. Such an account might offer the hope – though by no means the guarantee – that the woman might avoid another violent relationship. A social history provides the opportunity to understand the story of the family.

However, there are pitfalls in the stories people tell us. It is certainly true that people should not be condemned purely on the basis of past behaviour; on the other hand, their stories are not necessarily good predictors of what will happen. Holland (2004) makes the point that social workers' tendency to emphasize the stories told by clients means that they are more likely to give eloquent and intellectually able clients extra chances. This can certainly be the case where someone is struggling with an addiction. A story of change can be all the more convincing because the person telling it truly believes it. The task of the social worker is to hold in mind both the objective facts and the client's account (Forrester and Pitcairn, forthcoming). Again, the space of reflective supervision is crucial here.

WHERE SHOULD INFORMATION BE COLLECTED FROM?

As a rule of thumb the more different sources of information an assessment is based on the better. Talking to parents and accepting their account is not sufficient. Some key sources include:

- The views and experiences of the child;
- The parent's views and experiences;
- Other members of the family, particularly those involved with the children on a regular basis;
- Members of the wider community, for instance friends and neighbours;
- Information from other professionals;
- Information from files;
- Workers or others previously involved with the family.

In addition, much can be obtained through direct observation. For instance:

- How do the children present? Do they seem well cared for? Healthy? Are their responses appropriate to the circumstances that they find themselves in?
- How does the parent appear? Do she appear coherent and able to participate appropriately in conversation with the worker? Is she reasonably

dressed, relatively clean and giving an appearance of being able to look after herself?

- What is the home like? Are the levels of cleanliness and safety acceptable? Are there toys and/or books? Where do the children sleep and what is it like?

Finally, an important source of information is how one feels about the family. Hunches and gut feelings are too open to bias to record in a formal assessment, but if critically examined they are appropriate for informing an assessment. In particular, you may want to consider the following questions:

- Am I afraid of this parent? If so, are there indications that the child appears afraid?
- Do I feel uncomfortable about the safety of the child in this family? If so, what leads me to feel that way?

DISCUSSION AND CONCLUSION

This chapter has explored the complex process of assessment where there are concerns about a child. It has emphasized two issues that make this a particularly challenging area. The first is that incorrect decisions in either direction are potentially extremely serious. The second is that it is impossible to predict the future with very high levels of accuracy. Taken together, these two conditions create a highly stressful and challenging environment within which social workers operate.

There have been a range of responses to these difficulties. These have included academics who have criticized the very concept of a risk assessment, and government responses which have – perhaps inadvertently – created a bureaucratic and managerial approach to assessment. We have tried to propose a different approach. Central to this is acknowledgement of the importance of the space for professional decision-making and judgement. We also proposed a model of decision-making in assessments that found space for both optimism and cynicism by incorporating a range of potential outcomes into both the assessment and case planning. We hope that practitioners find this a useful way of conceptualizing the assessment process, and one that is compatible with guidance such as that in the Assessment Framework.

However, a key element in any assessment is obtaining the information. It is therefore particularly important to engage the parent in the assessment, so that their views and understanding can inform decision-making. Yet as we saw in Chapters 5 and 6, this is all too often highly challenging. In Chapter 7 we explore the issue of engaging parents in some depth.

7 What Works in Engaging Parents Who Misuse Drugs or Alcohol?

A key issue identified in interviews with social workers in Chapter 4 was the challenge of working with parents who so often deny or minimize their misuse of drugs or alcohol. Our research is not unusual in finding this to be a common difficulty with a major impact on work in this area. Kroll and Taylor (2003) reported on 40 interviews with workers from a range of agencies that dealt with parents who misused drugs or alcohol. They found that 'denial' was a central issue for workers. They expressed the difficulties thus:

> Secrecy and denial seemed central and pervasive characteristics of both the relationship between parents and children, and between parents and professionals. In some ways an atmosphere of secrecy and distrust in the home could often be mirrored in relationships between clients and workers. What appeared to emerge here was a problematic dynamic. Professionals were attempting to help, conscious that the first step in the process needed to be proper engagement. However, they were being viewed by parents as intrusive and potentially threatening, in terms of their child protection role. Although parents often seemed to want to sort things out, their natural fears frequently got in the way of real disclosure.
>
> (Kroll and Taylor, 2003, p. 221)

Denial is clearly an issue of central importance in working with parents with drug or alcohol problems. In the current study the presence of denial often led social workers to feel 'stuck'; unsure how to make progress with parents, they sometimes found themselves waiting for something to go wrong for the child. Denial also makes carrying out the sorts of assessment discussed in Chapter 6 very difficult. If the parent cannot be engaged in the assessment, or if their account of their substance use is so at odds with other evidence that it is clearly untrue, then gathering the information required for a good quality assessment becomes difficult.

Denial may be considered to be one manifestation of a broader problem in engaging and working with non-cooperative parents. For the purposes of this discussion we shall describe the full gamut of client non-cooperation as

Parents Who Misuse Drugs and Alcohol. Effective Interventions in Social Work and Child Protection, 1st edition. By Donald Forrester and Judith Harwin.
© 2011 John Wiley & Sons, Ltd.

'resistance'. This includes denial and minimization, but also covers aggression, non-communicativeness and any other aspect of non-cooperation. These behaviours are not confined to clients who misuse substances, though they may be particularly important for working with them. Indeed, 'resistance' is a common, perhaps even a ubiquitous, feature of social work practice in a wide range of settings. It is therefore likely that effective ways of understanding and working with resistance will be of more general applicability than just with work with substance misuse.

This chapter starts by considering how resistance is understood in basic social work textbooks. It is argued that most have remarkably little to say about the concept, with the relationship between client and social worker often portrayed as comparatively unproblematic. Similarly, there is very little research that looks directly at how social workers talk to parents about child welfare or child protection issues. This leaves a significant gap between social work theories and methods and the realities of practice. We then consider three different understandings of the nature of resistance from clients, namely:

1. Resistance as a client trait;
2. Resistance as an (understandable) response to social work intervention; and
3. Resistance as a product of interaction between social worker and client.

We conclude that all three explanations may contribute to the resistance that clients exhibit, and understanding and reflecting on this is crucial in assessing risk for children. However, we think it important to focus on resistance as something that can be increased or reduced by the social worker. Focusing on this area provides insight into the nature of effective communication in social work settings. Crucially, while professionals cannot reduce resistance arising from client 'trait' and have minimal control over resistance as a response to social work intervention, they can control the degree to which their own intervention is likely to increase or reduce resistance from parents. Given the central place of client denial and minimization in work in this area this is an important focus.

In order to explore how the skills of social workers influence interviews we report in detail on research that looked at interviews between social workers and actors playing a mother with an alcohol problem. This analysis identified some key elements in effective communication in order to reduce resistance created by social workers. We conclude the chapter by drawing out the lessons for good practice in working not only with substance misuse but also a range of child welfare concerns.

CURRENT SOCIAL WORK THEORIES AND METHODS AND WORKING WITH RESISTANCE

In order to consider this issue we reviewed some of the most widely used and highly respected basic introductions to social work theories, methods and skills to see what they had to say about working with resistance. The texts we chose were Trevithick (2000), Davies (1994), Payne (1997) and Coulshed and Orme (1998) because they not only represent excellent introductions to social work, but are also some of the most widely used in recent years. The criticisms below are aimed at the current state of social work theory, rather than at limitations in these texts.

The most startling finding was how little these key texts had to say about the resistance or non-cooperation. For example, Trevithick, Davies and Coulshed and Orme barely touch on working with resistant or uncooperative clients. This is on the face of it remarkable. It does not take an in-depth engagement with social work to realize how much of the work is with reluctant or resistant clients. The absence of discussion or guidance on this in the key texts for social work students appears little short of extraordinary.

A possible reason for this gap becomes clearer if the theories and methods that most commonly provide a basis for social work intervention are considered. Payne (1997), which is perhaps the most widely used British introduction to social work theory, lists nine theories or methods that are used particularly often in social work. Seven of these theories were developed in therapeutic settings, primarily or entirely with clients who wished to have help. They have little or nothing to say about working with people who are resistant. Two approaches discussed by Payne were developed specifically for social work settings: these are task-centred and radical approaches. However, both of these methods explicitly exclude working with reluctant or resistant clients. For instance, Payne says of task-centred work that is concerned with problems that 'clients acknowledge or accept' (1997, p. 104) and that it 'should not be used where authoritarian protection or social control are the main priorities' (1997, p. 108). Radical approaches such as Marxist, feminist and anti-racist views provide invaluable correctives to individualistic models of social work problems and interventions. However, by their nature they say little or nothing about how to work with reluctant or resistant clients. In general, they frame the system as the problem and an oppressed client's resistance as an understandable and often laudable response. This is an important insight and one that we return to below. However, on its own it is often likely to be of limited usefulness for workers trying to work with someone whose resistance cannot be wholly attributed to systemic oppression. As a result, in Payne's text there is no discussion of ways of working with reluctant or resistant clients.

In *Counselling Skills in Social Work Practice*, Seden (1997) acknowledges that social work clients are frequently not voluntary and that this may add 'barriers of reluctance, hostility and resistance to many encounters' (1997, p. 22). She continues:

> The ability to communicate and establish relationships, to establish purpose and to engage people in effective working in these circumstances needs acutely developed and refined skills, especially as anxiety and anger are likely to be very much in evidence.
>
> (1997, p. 22)

Seden advocates a person-centred approach, involving empathy, a non-judgemental attitude, understanding why people are defensive and avoiding 'simplistic labelling' (p. 122). Seden's acknowledgement of the reality of many social work clients is refreshing and the values that she suggests appear likely to be a good place to start in working with resistance. However, what these 'acutely developed and refined skills' *are* is not outlined.

The relative absence of theory and guidance for social workers on how to work with resistance is surprising. It creates a paradox at the heart of social work practice. Workers are expected to work with often, perhaps generally, resistant clients, but how to work with resistance is given little attention in social work theory. There are some texts that provide more focus on working with resistance. For instance, Trotter (1999) outlines how task-centred approaches might be used with 'involuntary' clients, and Turnell and Edwards (1999) have adapted a solution-focused approach for child protection. These are interesting and helpful contributions, however in some respects the presence of specialist texts in this area underlines the lack of attention to working with resistance in the main body of social work theory.

It is obvious that this gap between theory and practice is undesirable. It is also possible that it contributes to wider systemic problems within social work. For instance, it is common for practitioners to find that college teaching is remote from the realities of practice; equally, academics often find the failure of even qualified Practice Assessors to use established theories or methods difficult to understand. It seems likely that the failure of the theoretical resources to conceptualize how to work with resistance contributes to this gap.

Social work theories and methods are strikingly silent on the issue of client resistance. Yet it has been repeatedly identified as an issue within empirical research. In the next section three approaches to understanding the phenomenon of client resistance are considered.

DIFFERENT APPROACHES TO UNDERSTANDING CLIENT RESISTANCE

Despite the fact that resistance does not have a central place in most social work textbooks it is such a common phenomenon, one it has often been identified as an issue in research. However, writers have tended to describe and understand it in very different ways. We think it useful to think of three broad types of understanding of client resistance. As noted above, these are:

1. Resistance as a client or family trait;
2. Resistance as an (understandable) response to social work intervention; and
3. Resistance as a product of interaction between social worker and client.

Each of these is worth considering in greater depth.

Resistance within the client or family

In some ways the 'common-sense' way of understanding resistance is as something within the client. All social workers, or other helping professionals, must on occasion have concluded an interview with a client believing there was nothing they could have done or said that would have got through to the client. The parent – or sometimes the young person – was simply being difficult. There can be many explanations for such behaviour: they were having a very difficult day; something bad had happened before the interview; or possibly, they were hung over or 'coming down' after taking drugs.

Sometimes the problem is not a single event, but a persistent issue in work with an individual or family. Whatever the social worker does, the client does not seem to engage. Here too there may be explanations within the client or the family situation. The first attempt to understand the phenomenon of resistance was aimed at understanding such behaviour.

Freud saw resistance as a central aspect of psychoanalytic work. For him it was one part of making unconscious motivations conscious:

> The discovery of the unconscious and the introduction of it into consciousness is performed in the face of a continuous resistance on the part of the patient. The process of bringing this unconscious material to light is associated with pain, and because of this pain the patient again and again rejects it. It is for you then to interpose in this conflict in the patient's mental life. If you succeed in persuading him to accept, by virtue of a better understanding, something that up to now, in consequence of this automatic regulation by pain, he has rejected (repressed), you will then have accomplished something towards his education. For it is an education even to induce a person who dislikes leaving his bed early in the morning to do so all the same. Psychoanalytic treatment may in general be conceived of as such a re-education in overcoming internal resistances.
>
> (Freud, 1959, pp. 261–2)

In other words, we have deliberately chosen to make some of our motivations unconscious, perhaps because they were too painful or challenging to be considered by our conscious mind. As a result, while making these conscious may ultimately be helpful it is likely that it will be a painful process for an individual. This is why clients may be resistant.

Many others have identified reasons why individuals or families may prove resistant to help at a more prosaic level. Taylor and colleagues (2008) discuss a number of reasons in families in which parents have serious drug or alcohol problems. In such families the complex and overwhelming nature of the problems may make the families resistant to help. They may feel helpless and may be using drugs or alcohol as a way of coping with these difficulties. Taylor and colleagues echo Freud's view of resistance and then give it a social context by stating that an attachment to a substance as a way of coping:

> may also result in closing down contact with others by constructing defensive barriers. What may then start out as a barely conscious psychological tactic used

by parents experiencing stress can be reinforced by other factors such as stigmatization and social exclusion. These barriers keep at bay professionals who may be trying to offer safety, respite or protection.

(p. 860)

They go on to discuss 'family types' associated with misuse which may be linked to difficulties in engaging families. They identify two in particular that may be problematic:

The first is the 'enmeshed' family pattern characterized by denial, in which the coping strategy limits contact with others outside of the family. The second pattern is 'unorganized', in which the family structure may be more open, but potentially disorganized due to a multiplicity of problems, and in which children may be more vulnerable to issues of neglect and taking on the parental role.

(p. 861)

At the most extreme end there are examples of families in which serious abuse or neglect is deliberately hidden by parents or carers. In recent years this happened in the well-known cases of Victoria Climbié and 'Baby P'. However, concealing abuse or neglect is likely to be a common reason for resistance for clients.

Thus there is a variety of explanations for resistance which see it as something within the client. These range from Freudian theories of intra-psychic resistance, through resistance as a product of a dysfunctional individual or family, to resistance as a deliberate attempt to hide abuse of a child. These widely differing views have two things in common. First, client resistance is a significant sign of underlying problems. Second, they say relatively little about how to work to reduce resistance. We return to these issues below, but first it is important to consider other explanations for resistance.

Resistance as an (understandable) response to social work intervention

In some of the explanations discussed above, the idea of resistance being an understandable response to social work intervention was acknowledged. However, it is worth considering this further. When considered in any depth it becomes understandable that clients may resist social work involvement. This is particularly likely because they fear the social workers' involvement as social workers have powers to remove children. In reality these powers are defined and circumscribed in law, but in both the public imagination and in practice social workers have a key role to play in placing children in 'care'. A parent with a drug or alcohol problem may therefore find engaging with such a professional particularly difficult. Many parents have on occasion done things they are not proud of. A parent with a drug or alcohol problem has probably done many things they feel ashamed of. In such a context, the involvement of social workers is likely to create fear and anxiety, and this may well manifest as aggression or active attempts to lie or prevent engagement with the social worker. It is certainly a challenging point from which to build a trusting relationship.

In addition, research suggests that substance misusing parents may fear that child protection services will respond to them inappropriately. Elliot and Watson (1998) identified among drug-using parents not only a fear that children would be taken away, but also a fear of negative stereotyping, anxiety that confidentiality might not be maintained and that inappropriate treatments would be offered. Bates and colleagues (1999) interviewed parents and professionals and found that assumptions about drug misuse being associated with poor parenting were considered particularly unhelpful.

However, both studies identified key ways in which social workers could work with parents in order to reduce the impact of such fears and anxieties. In particular, professionals who were non-judgemental and did not dictate to people what to do, while being open and transparent about their power and authority, were what parents felt that they needed. Features of successful services that engage parents with drug or alcohol problems seem to include just such an approach to communication (see Forrester *et al.*, 2008c; Taylor *et al.*, 2008). A fascinating study by Platt (reported in Platt 2006a and b, 2007, 2008) confirmed these findings. Platt found that while there was a relationship between the level of concern that the professional had about children's welfare there were many instances in which successful relationships were built despite high levels of professional concern, and equally there were instances of low levels of concerns for children nonetheless being linked to poor professional relationships. Platt (2007) goes on to consider the significance of the congruence between the social worker's perception of issues and that of the family and the level of cooperation.

These findings indicate that social worker response can influence levels of resistance from clients. This fact points to a third explanation for client resistance: resistance as a response to professional communication.

Resistance as a product of interaction between social worker and client

A third explanation for resistance is that it is not something that resides 'within' the client, but is produced through the interaction between client and worker. For instance, the research noted above suggests that coming into contact with social workers may be a situation with a high potential for resistance, but that where workers are non-judgemental and open and combine this with skilled listening, this is likely to reduce resistance.

This is supported by research from the substance misuse field. A dominant belief in the literature until the 1980s was that denial was a symptom of the disease of addiction. A confrontational approach to overcoming this denial was often used. Yet careful research suggested that this was not an appropriate understanding of resistance, and indeed that active confrontation was rarely helpful. First, research found that the level of resistance in therapy sessions could be increased or reduced through the actions of the therapist. In particular, a confrontational approach led to greater resistance while empathic listening reduced confrontation. Second, the level of resistance predicted client outcome. Where there were high levels of resistance, clients were less likely to reduce their drinking; where it is lower, they were more likely to change (see Miller and Rollnick, 2002). These are important findings. They suggest that – to some degree at least – client resistance is something that may be influenced by the way we talk to clients.

DISCUSSION

For any individual or family it is likely that resistance will come from all three sources. The individual may have done things that they do not wish social workers to know about, they may be anxious of and fear social work involvement and their level of resistance may be increased or reduced by the social worker's response. These reasons for client resistance may also interact. For instance, a client's anxiety about a child protection investigation may be exacerbated by a judgemental or thoughtless response. In practice, unpicking the reason for resistance in any single instance may be difficult.

In the rest of this chapter we focus on social work communication in difficult child protection situations. In doing so we aim to identify the ways in which social workers might minimize the resistance they encounter. The most important reason for this focus on the third type of resistance is because reducing client resistance is the most important first step in effective work, including assessment. It is impossible to understand the situation people are in or to help them change if the encounter is characterized by high levels of resistance. Effective communication appears to be the primary skill that social workers bring to engaging around resistance. A thorough exploration of the skills involved therefore appears to be an appropriate way of addressing the denial and minimization identified in Chapters 3 and 4 as so important in social work with parents who misuse drugs or alcohol.

It is worth noting as an aside that whatever the reason for resistance, it seems likely that effective communication by the social worker is most likely to be the best way of reducing resistance. However, this does not mean that skilled communication will always result in engaging parents. In some instances, parents may remain resistant. This may happen when the parent has such profound issues that they will respond in a non-cooperative way whatever form of intervention they encounter. Parents experiencing paranoia as a result of mental illness or excessive use of certain drugs may be in this category, as may parents deliberately hiding serious abuse. In circumstances like these the skills of the social worker will not reduce or eliminate parental resistance. However, knowing that high levels of skill had been used to engage parents is still useful, for it identifies the parental issues rather than the social work intervention as likely to be the primary cause of the resistance. Thus, to identify systematic deception or profound personal difficulties social workers with excellent communication skills are necessary.

Skilful communication appears to be at the heart of working with client resistance. Yet what does 'skilful communication' involve? In particular, what are the skills needed to carry out effective child protection and child welfare work, with its combination of social control and social care? In the next section we consider the research on social work communication and then present in some detail research by the first author and others on how social workers manage such challenges.

RESEARCH ON SOCIAL WORK COMMUNICATION

Since the publication of Mayer and Timms' classic study *The Client Speaks* (1970) there have been many studies that have talked to clients about what they value in a social worker, and the findings are relatively clear and consistent. Thoburn and colleagues offer a useful summary:

> The particular characteristics associated in many studies with higher levels of satisfaction with social workers and other professional helpers … are accuracy, empathy, warmth and genuineness. These are demonstrated when the worker is reliable, a good listener, honest, gives accurate and full information about services available and agency processes, and puts him or herself out to be available at times of stress.
>
> (2004, p. 176)

These findings are based on interviews with service users. They are not therefore able to explore the complexity involved in being 'honest' or 'warm', and they cannot analyse the ways in which such characteristics are manifested in interviews and the impact they have on the process of the interview. For that research that directly observes social work communication skills is needed. However, there is little research that appears to do this. In searching for literature that looked directly at social work communication we found only three studies published in the last 20 years. One of these was carried out more than a quarter of a century ago, one was in the Netherlands and one was based on a single interview. There is therefore a remarkable gap in research looking at key skills that are at the heart of social work. Nevertheless, while the literature is limited, the existing studies have a number of interesting findings.

In the first study, Lishman (1988) videotaped 47 'early', 'middle' and 'final' interviews between nine social workers and parents in 22 families. Lishman explored the relationship between social worker behaviours and outcomes (as judged by researcher, social worker and client after the intervention). She found that positive remarks, nodding, smiling and laughing were associated with positive outcomes, while unchecked interpretations, confrontation, criticism and hostility were associated with negative outcomes. This is a really important study, as it is the only published research that explores the relationship between social work skills and the process and outcome of interviews. However, the numbers are very small and the research was carried out over 20 years ago.

A more recent study was carried out by Nijnatten and colleagues (2001) in the Netherlands. Nijnatten *et al.* videoed 51 interviews between social workers and clients and analysed them using Conversation Analysis (an in-depth qualitative method for describing dialogue and other communicative interaction). The researchers concluded that in general the social workers in their sample tended to understate the power they had and that this could confuse the parents. This study offers important insights, but it is important to bear in mind that the research was carried out in a very different context. Hetherington *et al.* (1997) and others have noted the profound differences between the UK and continental Europe in relation to child protection. In general, practitioners in England and Wales (there are important differences in the approach in Scotland) appear to be part of a far more confrontational system than that found in continental Europe. Thus, while Nijnatten *et al.* identify some important issues, it cannot be concluded that social workers in England and Wales would behave in the same way.

The only recent study looking directly at social work communication in a British context was carried out by Hall and colleagues (2006). They provide an interesting interpretation of a single interview that focuses on the ways in which the social worker and the mother attempt to frame and define their roles and actions. As with the Nijnatten *et al.* (2001) study, their findings highlight the subtlety of the interaction between social workers and clients, and the complex ways in which power is negotiated. However, their approach is not to evaluate what 'works'. They do not therefore draw clear conclusions in relation to social work communication skills.

These three studies provide some indication of the potential contribution that research in the area of social work communication might make. However, they provide remarkably little up-to-date information on how social workers do communicate and very little evidence on what works in difficult interviews such as those where parents misuse drugs or alcohol and there are concerns for a child's welfare. How do workers manage such challenging interviews? And what approaches seem to produce better – or worse – outcomes?

RESEARCH ON EFFECTIVE COMMUNICATION AND CHILD PROTECTION

To address this gap in the literature Forrester and colleagues carried out a small-scale research study that involved taping 24 interviews between social workers and an actor playing a mother with an alcohol problem. In this chapter we explore qualitatively the nature of the interaction between the social worker and the 'client' in these interviews. It is hoped that this will allow us to explore how social workers dealt with issues of resistance from clients, and what social workers did that worked or did not work.

The interviews carried out in the study related to the same scenario, but with two levels of concern (see Forrester, 2010, for a full description). The actors playing the client were prepared for their role in a half-day workshop. The main focus was to encourage them to respond to what the social worker did rather than following a script, as it has been suggested that following a script is a weakness in the use of simulated clients (Miller *et al.*, 2004). Overall, the interviews were rated by social workers and researchers as highly realistic. Nonetheless, a limitation of this study is that it used actors rather than real clients. On the other hand, this means that if the interview goes well – or badly – this can be attributed to the approach taken by the social worker. It is not just a 'difficult' or 'easy' client that is making the difference.

A quantitative analysis of the interviews is reported in Forrester *et al.* (2008a). Overall, the social workers asked a lot of closed questions, few open questions and rarely used reflections. They tended to raise concerns often, particularly as the interview progressed, but were considerably less likely to identify positives. The level of empathy was generally low, though there was very high variation between social workers (see Box 7.1 for the levels of empathy used in the ratings).

Box 7.1 Carkhuff's levels of empathy.
(based on Carkhuff, 1969, pp. 315–17)

Level 1: The helper does everything *but* express that he is listening, understanding or being sensitive to even the most obvious feelings of the helpee in such a way as to detract significantly from the communications of the helpee (referred to as 'obstructing').

Level 2: The helper tends to respond to other than what the helpee is expressing or indicating (referred to as 'not listening').

Level 3: The helper … does not respond accurately to how that person really feels beneath the surface feelings; but he indicates a willingness and openness to do so. Level 3 constitutes the minimal level of facilitative interpersonal functioning (referred to as 'minimal listening').

Level 4: (In addition to Level 3) The helper's response adds deeper feeling and meaning to the expressions of the helpee (referred to as 'empathic listening').

Level 5: The helper is responding with a full awareness of who the other person is and with a comprehensive and accurate empathic understanding of that individual's deepest feelings (referred to as 'highly skilled listening').

Every social worker successfully raised issues of concern and most achieved clarity about what was expected of the 'parent'. However, the way in which this was done varied enormously. The most important factor that influenced this was the level of empathy. Some social workers expressed very little empathy. The 'parent' tended to respond to them with high levels of resistance, and in particular denial or minimization around substance misuse. In contrast, those social workers who raised concerns in an empathic manner generated far less resistance and the 'parents' disclosed significantly more information to them. These findings are important because they suggest that the skill of the social worker may influence the amount of resistance that they encounter, and that some social workers may be inadvertently contributing to the amount of resistance that they experience. However, in addition to the quantitative attempt to map relationships between what social workers did and how parents responded, we also carried out a qualitative analysis using Grounded Theory (Strauss and Corbin, 1989). In summary, it involved researchers repeatedly listening to and reading the interviews in order to develop an agreed theory that answered two key questions:

1. What were the social workers trying to do?
2. What worked well in achieving the social worker's aims? What tended not to work well?

In the next two sections we present evidence from the interviews in relation to each of these questions.

WHAT WERE THE SOCIAL WORKERS TRYING TO DO?

The qualitative analysis suggested that in broad terms social workers were trying to do two things in the interviews. These aims were to:

1. Gather information; and
2. Create client cooperation, particularly to go to the local 'alcohol service'.

They tried to achieve these aims using a variety of approaches.

HOW DID SOCIAL WORKERS TRY TO GATHER INFORMATION?

Information was gathered using three main approaches:

1. Basic information-gathering;
2. Raising concerns;
3. Asking for the parent's perspective.

Each of these is worth considering in turn.

Basic information-gathering

Typically, basic information-gathering occurred towards the beginning of an interview, though it could occur later. This type of information-gathering was characterized by short, closed questions and usually generated short, closed answers. For instance:

Social Worker: All right. First, can I ask how you are generally, your health?

Parent: All right.

Social Worker: OK. Employment?

Parent: All right.

Social Worker: OK. How is Charlie's health?

Parent: He is all right.

Raising concerns

A second form of information-gathering involved raising specific concerns. All the social workers in our sample addressed the child protection concerns raised by the research scenario. Most of the interviews raised concerns at an early stage, all but two within the first five minutes. This also often marked a change in the tone of the interview, the introductory stage (of introductions and basic information-gathering) being concluded and a new focus on the social work agenda. A fairly typical example was:

Parent: Charlie is doing very well, with Charlie, he's doing well in school, and things are fine. I think things that is going around is just purely exaggeration. Charlie is doing well in school, he's happy and I'm still so proud of him.

Social Worker: Right. OK, OK. I mean obviously you're aware with the previous social worker and because of Charlie being on the child protection register we have to liaise with other agencies.

Parent : Right.

Social Worker: Which obviously includes school, and I mean you're saying he's doing well at school. I mean, the most recent information I've had from school is saying that Charlie's attendance is actually pretty low, he's around about 50% attendance and he's often late as well, so for us that's a real, that's a real concern. I mean, will your – what's been happening?

Parent: I think it's not true, I just …

This exchange is typical of many, in that the initial raising of concerns leads to denial by the parent. There has been little time to engage the parent and the positives that the parent does raise (she is proud of her son) are ignored.

These types of interaction were typical of most interviews and they highlight the complex nature of the interaction. The social worker must raise issues of concern and yet doing so tended in this research to be met with resistance. We discuss further below how some social workers managed to raise concerns without creating as much resistance.

Asking for the parent's perspective

A third way in which social workers tried to obtain information from parents was by trying to elicit their perspective. This might relate to the presenting concerns, their reasons for drinking or life more generally. There were some excellent examples of the use of such an approach. In the following extract the social worker probes the parent to identify their reasons for not attending the specialist alcohol service:

> *Social Worker*: When you say that, would you be able to tell me a bit more? When you say it does not work out, what do you mean?
>
> *Parent*: Well, I don't think it's really the right thing for me to go down there.
>
> *Social Worker*: When you say right thing, what do you mean?

The social worker continued to try to ascertain the parent's reasons for not attending the alcohol service. The parent gradually disclosed these, allowing the social worker to explore her concerns rather than focus on the agency's concerns about the non-attendance. By the end of the interview, the parent had agreed to attend the service.

However, rather to our surprise, this was not the way in which the parent's perspective was usually used. Instead, it was common for the social worker to ask a question relating to the parent's point of view, particularly at the beginning of the interview, but they rarely followed this up with further questions. Instead, the parent's views were used as an opportunity to raise concerns; they acted as a contrast to the professional concerns rather than appearing to be of interest in their own right:

> *Social Worker*: Well, what do you think is happening in your home? What is your point of view? How do you see it from your side?
>
> *Parent*: I think everything's great. I think we have a great relationship, I think he's a very happy young boy. I think he's a very bright young boy, he does well at school, you know. All right, it's not the easiest of home life, it's just me, we've got no money, but, you know, all right we're struggling in some ways, but as far as love and whatever else and care for my child, that's all there.
>
> *Social Worker*: Well it's because we are concerned about – what about these – obviously these phone calls, you realize what they are about, do you?

Opportunities to acknowledge the positives in the families' circumstances presented by the parent are not pursued by the social worker. Instead, the social worker, having asked the parent's point of view, ignores the response and immediately raises concerns. The response from the parent is to deny the concerns:

Parent: Well, it's bullshit saying that I've been drinking or whatever.

This was the primary pattern for eliciting parental views. In general, a question that appeared to be aimed at eliciting the client's viewpoint was followed by raising concerns. The parent's viewpoint was sought so that it could be contrasted with the concerns from agencies rather than as something of value in its own right.

WHAT WORKED IN OBTAINING INFORMATION FROM CLIENTS?

Raising concerns repeatedly was associated with high levels of resistance and low levels of disclosure of information. The comparatively few interviews in which social workers obtained high levels of information about parental drinking or child welfare were characterized by *sustained* attempts to understand the parent's point of view. In other words, social workers did not simply ask one question about how the parent perceived the situation, they spent some time exploring the parent's views. An example of this can be seen in the following interview:

Social Worker: ... But what about you, what have you felt like? What do you feel like now? What do you feel has happened for you over the last three months?

Parent: Well, obviously it was shit when it all started kicking off again, you know.

Social Worker: Yeah, what do you mean, what started kicking off again?

Parent: Well, when all you lot got involved and everything and it was probably the worst time of my life I would say. But like what you say, things have been a bit more positive recently. I feel like I am a bit more on top of things and things are going a lot better.

Social Worker: OK, what sort of things are you finding easier now? Because before you were both well aware of the things that were happening – you were drinking a lot, Charlie was getting neglected a bit. What sort of specific things are you finding it easier to do, because as far as we can see, you are not drinking so much. I don't know what your level is, but you are not drinking. What's improving for you now specifically with regard to getting Charlie moving and looking after him?

Parent: Well, you know, it just has to have been a bit of a – I don't know, a bit of a change, maybe I have had a bit of a wake-up call, you know what I mean?

Social Worker: Yeah.

Parent: So you know I haven't necessarily been doing things very differently, but maybe I have been just seeing where I was lacking a bit before and like getting him to school and all that. Maybe before if he told me that he was ill I would just let him have the day off, but now I am being a bit more firm with him really, taking on my role.

Social Worker: OK, and are you finding it easier yourself to get up in the mornings and get him moving?

Parent: Yeah, yeah, you know. As I said, I have cut down a lot on my drinking and I guess in some ways maybe that does make it a bit easier in the mornings getting up, I can get up that bit earlier and I am a bit more awake, you know.

Such an approach did not seem to be associated with 'collusion' or a failure to raise concerns. Rather, obtaining the views of the parents in some detail was part of the process of the interview. As we discuss below, it formed a crucial basis for successfully engaging the parent in plans to improve the child's welfare. For instance, the following interview was rated as having some of the highest levels of empathy from the social worker and low levels of resistance from the client. Yet within a short period the social worker manages to raise a number of key concerns very clearly:

Social Worker: I appreciate that you – I mean in no way are we questioning your love for your son at all, but what we are getting is concerns about him and multiple concerns about him. I just wanted to run through that with you. His attendance, his attendance is too low, it should be at 93% but it's at 50%. ... And for a child of his age, I mean, kids get sick, absolutely, kids get sick and they need time off school, but you need to communicate that to the school ... So, if he is taking that much time off to sickness then that is concerning in itself. I understand that you haven't made any appointments or made any of the appointments made for you at the Alcohol Service. ...

Then, a few moments later:

Social Worker: ... because you know that within the last two years we have had seven concerns relayed to us by the police about your drinking. They are focused in on your drinking and also on Charlie being seen wandering around on the estate. You know, concerns around Charlie being home alone but in actual fact you were there ...

Parent: Yeah, see he wasn't alone ...

Social Worker: ... but when the police went to the home they deemed that you were intoxicated ...

Parent: Yeah ...

Social Worker: ... and not able to care for your son. Now, we want this to work; we want you to be able to care for your son; we want your son to grow up in an alcohol-free environment; we want him to get to know his mum ...

Parent: He does, he knows me ...

Social Worker: … we want you to be able to spend time together. What we need from you is a commitment, we need a commitment from you to go to Alcohol Service and do the alcohol and drug treatment.

Parent: Yeah.

Social Worker: And if you are saying to us there is no problem we need that evidenced, do you know what I mean? We need that evidenced from the alcohol and drug advisory service and we need them to show us if there is a problem – then you are going to get support. If there is not a problem, then we can go on a different path, but right now there is too much information to say that there is a problem.

This social worker appears fairly clear and uncompromising in setting out both the concerns and what she thought the parent needed to do. However, it differed from less successful raising of concerns in two important ways. First, even when concerns were being raised the social worker exhibited an understanding of how the client might be feeling. Evidence for this can be seen in the above excerpts from comments such as 'in no way are we questioning your love for your son at all'; 'And if you are saying to us there is no problem'. Both these comments related to comments that the mother had made. Second, and probably more importantly, having raised the concerns the social worker spent much of the rest of the interview – and particularly the portion that followed the raising of concerns – exploring how the mother understood the situation and what they intended to do. In other words, they made an attempt to understand the mother's point of view.

Another way of looking at this is that in less successful interviews social workers asked for the parent's point of view and then contrasted the evidence of concern from other sources with the parent's account. This tended to put parents on the defensive and led them to minimize or deny problems. A more successful strategy appeared to be to raise concerns and then listen in depth to the parent's response.

WHAT WORKED WELL IN ACHIEVING THE SOCIAL WORKER'S AIMS? WHAT TENDED NOT TO WORK WELL?

Social workers were very interested in engaging the client in cooperating with them and with the child protection plan as set out at the previous case conference. In particular, a focus in almost all interviews was on getting the mother to attend the specialist alcohol service. Again, there were three main ways in which they tried to do this.

1. Advice/persuasion;
2. Raising consequences/threats;
3. Support for client-identified goals.

Each of these is described before an analysis of what worked is presented.

Advice and persuasion

In most interviews, following the information-gathering and the initial raising of concerns stages, the social workers' aim appeared to be to try to create change via the use of advice, persuasion or even coercion. This type of activity was most evident in the main body and towards the end of interviews. It was also more likely to be used repeatedly, with social workers spending sustained periods trying to persuade clients to undertake particular actions.

For instance, in this fairly typical example the social worker is trying to persuade the parent to attend Alcoholics Anonymous meetings:

> *Social Worker*: Yeah, there are meetings all over the city, so let's make an agreement that you are going to go to at least four meetings a week.
>
> *Parent*: Right, what about my housework? I have got a lot of things to do.
>
> *Social Worke*r: I think the thing is, is that when you are battling with a disease and you are really battling a disease.
>
> *Parent*: Why do you call it disease? Nobody has ever called it disease, you are making me feel like I am suffering from some kind of illness …

This type of dialogue continues with the social worker trying to persuade the parent to adopt a particular course of action, but with little exploration of the parent's specific circumstances, point of view or explanation of how this would relate to the needs of her child. Indeed, a feature of this attempt is to impose a disease model of addiction that is contentious (as discussed in Chapter 1). It is in fact a rather ineffective attempt at persuasion.

Persuasion was sometimes used for other purposes. In the following example, it was used in an attempt to get the parent to see things differently. However, as often tended to happen, when the parent resisted an attempt at persuasion this easily escalated into argument.

> *Parent*: Nobody has worked together with me. Everybody has told me what to do.
>
> *Social Worker*: I think from the seven referrals, what has happened before, social workers have come out, they have visited you, they have talked to you, you have denied that you have had a drink problem, that you don't need help.
>
> *Parent*: Yeah.
>
> *Social Worker*: Those are the opportunities where people have tried to help you and even at the case conference –
>
> *Parent*: I don't call that help you know, I don't call that help, when somebody comes telling you what everybody is seeing, nobody is asking me my side. I don't call that help, I call that everybody is telling me what to do and I am beginning to feel you are doing the same thing, you are going by everybody, everybody. I am sitting here and you are telling me what everybody – and this is what's getting to me.

Social Worker: But even when the social workers came out on the other seven incidents they would have asked you your point of view and what happened.

Parent: Were you here? Were you here? You weren't here.

Social Worker: I have reports upstairs.

It is difficult to see what the social worker has achieved – or was trying to achieve – in this interchange. Ultimately, the parent is saying that she does not feel anyone is listening to her; but rather than showing that they understand this, the social worker also does not listen and instead tries to prove that previous social workers did listen. This attempt to persuade the person ends with 'I have reports upstairs' – a comment that effectively reinforces the very point being made by the parent, namely that nobody is listening to her. For what the social worker is arguing is that the parent is wrong and to do so is privileging the other social workers' reports over the views of the parent.

Raising consequences/threats

A second way in which social workers would try to create change was by explaining the consequences of non-cooperation to parents. Being clear about the nature of concerns and what might happen if there is a failure to address them is obviously an important part of safeguarding children's welfare. It is also necessary if parents are to be clear about where they stand and the possible consequences of different actions. However, in this area, more perhaps than in any other, there were widely different approaches from different workers.

Some workers appeared capable of being clear about the seriousness of concerns without becoming threatening:

Parent: Would it help you to stop taking him away from me? Charlie is the only thing I have. He's the only one and I'm holding on to him.

Social Worker: Yeah, I think that's the worst thing that could happen isn't it, that we would have to think about taking him into our care and I am not saying that that's going to happen, but I think if things don't start to change, then – we are very worried about Charlie. We are worried about you as well, and we need to think about what's the best way to help you out here.

However, it was more common for social workers to turn to raising consequences when persuasion had not worked or had started to veer towards argumentation. For instance, in the next excerpt the social worker starts by trying to persuade the mother to attend the alcohol service:

Parent: … you think it's just walking into the door. It's not that easy to walk into a place …

Social Worker: That's one appointment, make a call, make an appointment, go there and that's it, OK?

Parent: If it was that easy I would have done it long time ago.

Social Worker: So I mean, how, how can we do it then? How can we do it?

Parent: I don't know, what …

Social Worker: Do you want to, do you want to go up because you can use a phone now upstairs and just ring them, book an appointment today, you could get an appointment this week, OK? Is that all right with you? Yeah? Just before you leave we can make a call here, you actually make the call, I'll give you the number, just book an appointment, all right? Have you got, you know, any relatives, anyone that could just come and, if you don't want to go on your own you can ask somebody to assist you there …

Parent: I don't have anybody, I don't have any family near.

Social Worker: You don't want nobody? OK, so you could book an appointment, and go up there and I'll give you a call afterwards to find out how it went, OK? You could tell me more about it, how it went, because we need to g … really get these things off, OK? Because these concerns are very serious, very serious concerns. OK? We don't, we don't want to wait until tomorrow for something to happen to Charlie and I'm sure you don't either, OK? So we really need to get through this because when I say care proceedings, you know, we might initiate care proceedings. You know what care proceedings is?

Parent: No, nobody told me before.

Social Worker: They told you that?

Parent: Nobody …

Social Worker: Well I mean due to the nature of this, you know, initiating care proceedings is basically we will have to go to court for the court to decide who to look after Charlie, OK? That's what we might – that's, that's …

Parent: You see I find all of this so – this is what gets me, so base, it's so ugly. What has Charlie done to be taken somewhere else? It's …

Most of the rest of the interview continued with the social worker using a mixture of attempts at persuasion and threats of consequences, while the mother expressed her unhappiness and anger at what is happening. The social worker evaluated themselves as having worked hard to ensure the parent had a variety of support options; the actor said that if she had been a real parent she would have felt like killing herself or the worker, or both.

Support for client-identified goals

The third way in which social workers attempted to engage parents in change was by supporting the mother to identify and work towards her own goals. This was comparatively rare, but it was a crucial marker of the most effective interviews. In this example the social worker tries to move the conversation away from the 'child protection plan' to a discussion of what the parent wants to achieve:

Social Worker: Obviously, the local authority has said 'these are the things you need to do', but my question is, did they ask you what would work for you? ... Because I think what happens a lot of the times in child protection conferences – I don't like child protection conferences, I would not want to be a parent in a million years on one of those, I don't like being a professional in them. So I think what happens is professionals sit there and say 'you should do this' and never say to you 'is that going to work for you?'

Parent: Yeah, that's what they did to me.

Social Worker: And you don't feel very – my guess is, and you can tell me if I am wrong, but you sit in those things and there is probably whatever, 10 other professionals, and you feel very disempowered, you are not feeling like you can say anything?

Parent: Feel so small, I am nobody, I am just here to be told what to do and walk out.

Social Worker: Exactly, and that's what I don't like about them, I am from [a different country] and we deal with child protection in a very, very different way and it is not so punitive, and I have very hard time with the punitive [approach].

Parent: Yeah, yeah.

Social Worker: So to me I would much rather hear from you what you think is going to work. I am hearing you say you don't think you have a drinking problem, however, at the same time, whether you know you are a full-blown alcoholic or not, is neither here nor there, the point is if Charlie, for whatever reason, they are saying isn't doing well in school.

This led in to a long discussion of the parent's views on their drinking and why they were finding it difficult to stop or to access services. It concluded with the parent saying:

Parent: No, I am just so surprised, I was just sitting there thinking – as I said, originally I didn't think I got problems so that's why I don't go to those people, the Alcohol Service and the AA. Then from the way you talk maybe I will give them a call and see, just to see about it.

WHAT WORKED IN CREATING COOPERATION IN 'PARENTS'?

From the above discussion some key elements of effective engagement of parents should be clear. Workers who attempted to obtain the view of parents through at least some sustained attention to their views were more likely to gain information useful for their assessment. This also formed a stronger basis for developing a plan with the parents. Those who expressed empathy and tried to identify the parents' goals were also more likely to engage parents successfully. However, these factors did not explain all the interviews in which parents appeared to be successfully engaged. In particular, there were a small number in which workers talked a lot and did not spend much time listening to the parents, and yet they appeared to have had some success in engaging the parents. These interviews were generally carried out by more experienced workers or managers.

Following repeated reading and listening to the interviews in which parents were considered to have been most successfully engaged, we concluded that the key issue was whether the social worker was able to *demonstrate an understanding of the parent's point of view*. This was usually done through the empathic listening and consequent sharing of the agenda for change as illustrated in the examples above. However, it could also be done primarily by social workers intuitively demonstrating an understanding of the client's point of view. The following is an example of this:

Social Worker: ... Maybe there is something that pushes you maybe to drink a little bit more often than you should do. Maybe you are a bit unhappy or lonely and this is normal. People do end up doing what you do ... whatever people say that you're supposed to be doing.

Parent: Yeah, yeah.

Social Worker: So maybe there is something that upsets you. Is there?

Parent: Well, no. I do find it hard being on my own and, you know, it's like everybody's turned against me and that's why all these phone calls are coming into you lot and I do feel – I don't even know the word for how I'm feeling. Yes, maybe you're right, maybe I do reach out for the bottle a bit more than maybe at other times in my life when I've been a bit happier or things have been a bit more settled, you know, then I would be drinking less. It's like smoking, I'm the same with smoking. I'm smoking a lot more at the moment because, you know – I don't know why.

Social Worker: Well you see, for example, if this is the case then maybe because you feel a little bit unsettled or unhappy or lonely or things are not going quite right – and this is normal for a lot of people – by drinking it makes you feel a little bit better because you can forget and so your mind relaxes, but then that doesn't solve your problems.

Parent: No.

Social Worker: So when you come round afterwards, what do you find?

Parent: It's just the next day and I've got a headache. I'm not saying I drink every day, you know, I'm really not saying this but yes, sometimes I do regret having a drink because I'm not as focused as I should be, I'm not as motivated.

Social Worker: Well you see what I was trying to say was that what you're trying to do, which is perfectly fine because if you've got something that upsets you or you're not quite happy, you want to find a way of stopping those kinds of feelings and make you feel better. That strategy, you know, what you try to do, you go to the alcohol or whatever. I'm suggesting that it's maybe not the right strategy because it doesn't resolve the problem. As you say, you've got a hangover afterwards, you don't feel that well and then you're back again to the same sort of problem. So, you know, that is not necessarily the best strategy, the best way to cope or to find ways of coping with what you feel. I think that it would be a good idea for you to think that, you know, you've got to find another way to cope with those kinds of feelings because you've got a child.

Parent: Yeah, yeah.

This excerpt was taken from one of the interviews in which the client spoke the least (the social worker spoke for 80% of the time). Yet the social worker's ability to demonstrate accurately an understanding for the feelings of the parent, and to reflect that in a non-judgemental way, allowed them to build an effective working relationship with them.

It is hard to argue that this is how social workers should behave; after all, it relies heavily on accurate intuition and listening to the client's point of view seems a more certain way to ensure that one understands them. Nonetheless, these interviews demonstrate that the key issue is not just to understand the client's point of view; it is to *demonstrate* an understanding of their point of view. This is not the same as agreeing with their point of view. As evidenced in the following excerpt, often demonstrating an understanding of the parent's point of view was a starting point which allowed the social worker to explain their own point of view in a way that was acceptable to the parent (whether or not they eventually agreed with it):

Social Worker: Do you still feel that Charlie didn't need that, that there was no real concern?

Parent: No, because a child who needs protection is, as far as I am concerned, some child who is being hurt or being vulnerable in some way and that's not my kid, he would never come to any harm.

Social Worker: OK, well there were times when you were not properly in charge of Charlie.

Parent: Yeah, but I wouldn't have let anyone hurt him.

Social Worker: OK, well there's different kinds of ways that you can harm a child and it might be anything that you are actually doing but it can be something that you are not doing. And if you are drinking too much and some other thing is distracting you from that and people notice and report it to us, that's where we have the concern, so that's why – and we did have concern that Charlie was being left and that you were being seen fairly under the influence of drink and that's why the child protection proceedings was taken, not because we thought you were going to hurt Charlie, but that's why it happened. Does that seem more sensible to you?

Parent: Yeah, yeah, when you put it like that, that it is like not what I am doing but what I am not doing. That makes a lot of sense to me but, you know, I think that I am doing a lot of stuff. I love him and think that that's really the main thing.

Social Worker: Well, I think you are showing that now because whatever you thought of the action that we took, however much you felt hurt by that and that it is a criticism of you, you have started to change things, so there was something obviously that could be changed. I am a little bit concerned that you don't feel that you had kind of a problem with your drinking because that seemed to be a major factor in what was going on.

This was followed by a sensitive discussion of the place of alcohol in the mother's life, the positive steps that she had already taken and an agreement about what she planned to do to reduce her drinking.

Overall, therefore, *demonstrating* understanding appeared to be a vital foundation for developing effective collaboration between worker and parent. It provided the basis for an ability to agree a specific plan of action.

DISCUSSION OF FINDINGS

The research suggests that the key issues in successfully engaging a parent in child protection situations are:

- A sustained attempt to obtain the parent's point of view; and
- Demonstrating an understanding of the parent's point of view.

However, the research suggested that in the sample studied both of these were surprisingly rare. Instead, social workers tended to spend a lot of time raising concerns and trying to persuade parents to cooperate, and this sometimes escalated into using the threat of legal proceedings or other sanctions.

Underlying both obtaining the parent's point of view and demonstrating such an understanding were key skills (such as using reflections and open questions) and a more general empathic approach. Where social workers were able to use these skills in order to engage parents it appeared to hold the promise of a more successful working relationship. As noted by Forrester *et al.* (2008), highly skilled workers did not become parent-focused and thus collude with parents, nor did they focus solely on the concerns about the child and thus create resistance and a failure to work in partnership with parents. Instead, they seemed able to hold in mind that they were working with both a vulnerable child and a vulnerable adult. They were operating at the level that Forrester *et al.* call 'child-focused plus', in which:

concerns [about the child] are raised but communication skills are used to ensure that the parent is related to empathically even during difficult interviews. Parents can feel confident that the worker will be open about any concerns they have, but strengths and positives are also recognized and highlighted. Workers at this level are often able to build positive working relationships with parents despite the difficulties involved in working with concerns around child welfare.

The key to effective work with resistance, therefore, appeared to involve trying to understand the parent's point of view, to demonstrate to the parent that you understand their view but simultaneously not colluding or agreeing with what they feel. This involved a high level of skill, but some workers seemed able to achieve this.

The next chapter looks at these findings in the light of research on working with individuals with drug or alcohol problems. It considers the social work literature on communication and then at greater length what the substance misuse literature can tell us about issues such as denial or minimization, and key lessons for effective work with parents who misuse drugs or alcohol. Particular attention is paid to Motivational Interviewing (MI) as a communication style (Miller and Rollnick, 2002), as the key elements of MI appear broadly similar to the foundations of effective practice discussed in the current chapter.

8 What Works? Substance Misuse Treatment and Evidence-Based Social Work

The research discussed so far has painted a concerning picture of social work practice. In particular, the findings have suggested that while social workers succeed in protecting some children from harm by removing them, there is little indication that they have a positive impact on children who remain at home. The accounts of social workers suggested that they often struggled to know how to work with parental substance misuse and the tapes of interviews with simulated clients suggested very variable practice, with many social workers demonstrating limited skill in engaging parents or listening to their concerns. These problems were not an indication of poor practice by a few social workers. Rather, we feel that they suggest a systemic problem in working with parental substance misuse, and perhaps more broadly in social work within the UK.

In this and the next chapters we review the evidence base in relation to substance misuse treatment and serious parental substance misuse to identify some key lessons for improving policy and practice with parental substance misuse. In doing so, we make some radical suggestions for new ways of delivering better practice. For if the problem is systemic, then the solution also needs to be. More information or training for social workers, while no doubt a good thing, will not create the sort of radical change necessary to produce more effective ways of working. In order to explore these complex issues we divide the discussion of the evidence into three chapters. In the present chapter we review the nature of 'evidence-based practice' and 'evidence' before critically considering evidence on what works in working with alcohol misuse. We conclude by suggesting that delivering 'evidence-based' interventions is a complex process, but that it offers a profoundly different approach to the delivery of services. Crucially, it focuses on what happens when professional meets worker. This chapter is therefore crucial for understanding the subsequent chapters. Chapter 9 takes the review of the evidence from the

Parents Who Misuse Drugs and Alcohol. Effective Interventions in Social Work and Child Protection, 1st edition.   By Donald Forrester and Judith Harwin.
© 2011 John Wiley & Sons, Ltd.

substance misuse field further by considering in some detail the key elements of effective approaches from the substance misuse field and the challenges and opportunities that they provide for child welfare work. In particular, Motivational Interviewing is discussed at length and it is suggested that it provides a useful basis for child welfare work with parental substance misuse (and possibly with other issues). Chapter 10 considers the evidence on family interventions.

EVIDENCE-BASED PRACTICE (EBP)

Learning from the evidence is not a straightforward matter. First, there is considerable debate about the relationship between research evidence and practice. For instance, should research findings determine the methods used by professionals or should they simply be one consideration in deciding how to work with a family? These debates are considered in the next section, in which we argue in favour of a specific version of EBP that involves professionals primarily delivering interventions that have been shown to work through research. Second, the nature of evidence – particularly around what 'works' – is contentious. The second section considers different types of evidence and argues that some are more robust than others. In particular, we argue that experimental and quasi-experimental methods are uniquely stringent tests of whether an approach works and that they are therefore particularly useful.

Yet while we believe in robust research and in the importance of practice being based on such evidence, and indeed such beliefs seem like common sense, there are very great practical and theoretical problems with such an approach. A practical issue is that there have been few experimental studies of what works undertaken within British social work. The few studies that do exist focus on specific interventions, such as a particular project, rather than normal practice. This makes it almost impossible to suggest with confidence that particular approaches 'work' – and indeed means we have little evidence that social work makes a positive difference.

However, even in areas where much good research has been undertaken the findings prove more complex and difficult to interpret than might be expected. We illustrate and explore this through detailed consideration of the alcohol misuse literature. This is relevant in its own right: the severe limitations in social work research mean that we need to learn about what works from other fields. Our focus on parental substance misuse means that the alcohol misuse literature is a particularly rich source of research evidence on what works. However, it also leads to important discussions about the nature of the interventions that are evaluated. We argue that a true understanding of effective interventions and robust research leads to a profoundly different vision for practice and policy within Children's Services and, indeed, social services more generally. We conclude the chapter by developing this argument further and suggesting that a commitment to EBP requires profoundly different structures and practices from those currently dominant within social services.

WHAT IS EBP?

There is much debate about the nature of EBP. The concept initially emerged in medicine and was based on the idea that treatments chosen should be based on research evidence about what does and what does not work (MacDonald and Sheldon, 1998). More recently, there have been attempts to make social work and social care evidence-based. However, this has proved far more complex – and controversial – than evidence-based medicine. There are a number of reasons for this, and it is necessary to consider these before deciding what the place of evidence is within services for children. First it may be useful to consider what is meant by EBP.

The concept of EBP has been the subject of heated debate within the social work literature. Most of the criticisms relate to the fact that social work and related disciplines require a more complex and critical model than that required in medicine. The medical model requires diagnosis of an illness and selection of an appropriate treatment (such as a particular medicine). This is not necessarily appropriate for social issues, such as parental substance misuse. For these a social model is more appropriate. Crucially a social model requires:

1. A critical view of the nature of the issue being dealt with;
2. An understanding of the social as well as other causes of the issue;
3. A consequent focus on social elements of interventions.

How do such considerations make evidence-based practice more complicated? Each is worth exploring in turn.

First, a critical view of the very nature of the issues that social workers deal with is essential. Deciding about the presence of 'child abuse' involves society defining an issue and sanctioning the way that it should be dealt with. This makes interpreting evidence far more difficult. For instance, child abuse appears to be more common in poor families. This may be in part causal (because the stress and difficulty of living in poverty may make parents more likely to abuse their child) but it could also be *definitional* (we tend to label the parenting practices of the poor or marginalized as child abuse while those of the more affluent tend not to be considered this way). Social workers therefore need to take a critical approach to the social 'problems' that they deal with, which makes the nature of evidence far more complex.

Second, the medical model tends to individualize problems and therefore does not pay sufficient attention to their social context. For instance, Olds' Nursing Partnership is targeted at pregnant women living in poverty. The intervention appears to help many of these women, and experiments have shown this to work, in the sense that there are positive outcomes for both mother and child in the long term (Olds, 2006). However, there remains a mismatch between the presenting issue and the response. Poverty is not a personal problem, it is a social issue. Yet it is difficult to deal with poverty using experimental approaches; one cannot in practice distribute income more equally in some areas but not in others and then examine the outcome. As a result experimental methods – which are the primary basis for evidence-based practice in medicine (and we would argue should be in social care) – often shift the focus on to individuals and ignore the social causes of problems. This is anathema to social work, where we strive not just for individual welfare but also for social justice.

Third, EBP in medicine suggests delivering interventions that work. However, the nature of interventions and what works are very different in the situations social workers engage with. Importantly, experiments in medicine may generate universal truths, but experiments in social situations do not owing to the importance of the context within which interventions are delivered. There are many examples of interventions or services that worked well in one situation but did not have a positive effect in others. Medicines are also mediated by a range of factors, but their mechanisms of action are easier to explore than are social interventions. Pawson and Tilley (1997) argue that because context shapes the effectiveness of social interventions, research does not provide evidence that allows it to be generalized to other situations; thus evidence that a service produced good outcomes in Boston, USA does not mean it will do so in Boston, UK.

Furthermore, social work interventions are very different from medicine or surgery. We do not do social work *to* people (for instance, selecting an intervention and then treating people), we do social work *with* people. Clients' views and opinions are therefore a crucial element in deciding the appropriate course of action. EBP – at least as crudely formulated – tends to emphasize the professional's responsibility for identifying and using evidence. There is little exploration of the role of the service user in this process. Finally, most of the interventions that have been shown to 'work' are focused on individuals or families. Few attempt to change social situations.

As a result of criticisms such as these there has been a movement towards a broader conceptualization of evidence-based practice in social work. Thus people now tend to talk about evidence-*informed* practice (EIP) rather than EBP, to indicate that evidence is only one of the considerations to inform practice rather than being the basis, and that it should be used critically and with understanding. Indeed, Forrester and Pitcairn (2008) go further and argue that social workers are necessary precisely because of the complex multiple issues that need to be taken into account, and that they perform a crucial role in mediating between general research findings and the specifics of an individual situation. Such an approach seems to be a reasonable recognition of the importance of professional judgement in decision-making. It was fundamental to the discussion of assessment in Chapter 6.

However, there are problems with such an approach to the *delivery* of services. Here we are making a distinction between assessment and decision-making on the one hand, and how social workers work with families – the interventions or methods they use – on the other. Of course, both assessment and intervention require professionals to make decisions using evidence, tempered by professional judgement. The above criticisms of EBP as an approach to assessment are well made, and in Chapter 6 we discussed at length the importance of professional judgement in assessments. However, the type of EBP in social care that we wish to discuss is particularly interested in defining and evaluating specific interventions. Thus, for instance, cognitive behavioural therapy (CBT) and systemic therapy are specific types of intervention. In medicine, the interventions may be particular medicines or surgical treatments. The adaptation of EBP for social work does not simply require social workers to be aware of evidence; it requires them to use interventions that have been tested out – generally in ways similar to those used in medicine (e.g. in large-scale trials). This might be seen as the apotheosis of the medical model, with social work interventions being treated as if they were medicines. Given the strong arguments against the medical model, what are our reasons for proposing such an approach?

IN DEFENCE OF EVIDENCE-BASED PRACTICE

There are strong arguments in favour of a more rigorous approach to EBP. Specifically, we argue that:

- Social workers and other welfare professionals should be required to use interventions that have been shown to work.
- Robust evidence of what works can only be obtained using experimental methods (i.e. trials that compare outcomes for those who received an intervention and those who did not).

This is a relatively rare and comparatively radical approach to EBP within social work. There are six sets of arguments to support it.

First, the arguments against a medical model of EBP have many strengths; however, they also have a conspicuous weakness. They successfully pick holes in EBP, but they do not provide a convincing alternative against which EBP can be contrasted. In the absence of this, the most appropriate comparison is current practice. Even if all the criticisms of EBP were correct (and as discussed below we take issue with most of them), if EBP is compared to current practice it appears to be a better way of delivering effective social work. In the first place, almost all of the criticisms of EBP could be applied to much of current practice. Thus, in our interviews with social workers there was little indication that a critical view of the processes that construct the nature of child abuse was being used. There was also limited focus on broader social causes of problems, because social workers tend to work with the family in front of them rather than addressing the social causes of difficulties, and little attention in practice to changing social situations. There is, in short, little indication that social workers currently use a social model. Indeed, the implications of our research are far broader than this. They suggest not just that social workers are not operating a social model, but that social workers are barely using any theory at all and do not systematically use any intervention method in their work. It is this that is contributing to profound problems in how well they are able to carry out the complex tasks involved in working with parental substance misuse.

Of course, critics of EBP may argue that neither current practice nor practice based on EBP is what good social work should be. If they are able to articulate such a vision and convince social workers, academics and policymakers to put it into practice, then this becomes a valid comparison. In the absence of such an alternative we believe a nuanced and critical understanding of EBP provides the best starting place for developing a new vision for effective, critical and humane social work. We are interested in making social work as good as it can be in the real world.

Second, pragmatically, it seems almost certain that many issues that social workers deal with could be handled more effectively if social workers used interventions that have been demonstrated to work. For instance, as we discuss below, there is strong evidence about what does and does not work when helping people with alcohol problems. Currently, the practice and education of social workers tends to focus on approaches that research has demonstrated do *not* work, such as non-directive listening or confrontational approaches. It is therefore hard to argue against the positive impact that training social workers in more effective methods would be likely to have.

Third, the fact that social work has not developed and evaluated interventions with a broader social focus is not solely a failing of EBP, it is at least as much a failing in social work. There are examples of such interventions – for instance, Families and Schools Together (FAST) which combines individual, family and community-level interventions to deliver an effective social work intervention (see FAST, 2008; Kratochwill, 2004). It also involves service users at every level and takes issues of anti-discriminatory practice seriously. It has been shown to work in a variety of experimental trials. There is no theoretical reason why other social work interventions could not be developed and evaluated. For instance, Task-Centred working is a distinctively social work approach. However, there is limited British evidence on the approach, and most of it is over 20 years old (Marsh and Doel, 2005). The lack of evidence for social work interventions is not solely because EBP focuses on individuals; it is also because social work has not taken EBP seriously. Indeed, we can go further than this. Engaging with EBP would allow social work to shape interventions and research in a way that allowed many of the criticisms often made of EBP to be addressed. For instance, social work could develop interventions that paid more attention to the social context in understanding causes, construction and intervention.

Fourth, the criticisms of the medical model caricature medicine rather naïvely. In fact, medicine has a long tradition of addressing the social causes of problems. Public health is one of the most radical areas of current academic endeavour, with a critical view not only of the social causes of health problems but also their roots in inequality and oppressive social structures. However, evidence-based medicine attempts to understand what can make a difference at every level. It can therefore make a contribution to social policy and also provide individual practitioners with guidance to helping an individual problem drinker. Evidence-based social work should also be able to operate at all levels.

The final arguments in favour of EBP will be explored in depth in the rest of the chapter, however they can be summarized here. The fifth is that learning and delivering an evidence-based approach requires the practitioner to develop skills, knowledge and values that make them a better worker. An evidence-based approach is a discipline, and the discipline of delivering such an approach makes social workers better. This argument is perhaps best understood through an analogy. If social work is like a broad area such as music, then a particular intervention can be thought of as a specific musical instrument. It is true that no one instrument can capture the full range of music. Some instruments are particularly appropriate for certain types of music, and often a combination of instruments is necessary. In the same way there are dangers in specifying particular interventions, as social work is a broad activity and needs a range of skills. On the other hand, it is still more foolish to believe that social work can be learnt in the abstract; this would be as silly as trying to teach music without the individual learning how to play an instrument. Thus mastering one or more evidence-based interventions is an important step on the road to being a competent social worker.

Finally, and perhaps most importantly, we believe that EBP offers an opportunity for social work to develop a new vision for the delivery of services that can be operationalized at a policy level. In particular, the focus of EBP on the quality of the interaction between worker and client makes it a potential alternative to visions of policy delivery based on managerial or market-based solutions. We expand on this point towards the end of this chapter.

Much of the rest of the chapter focuses on the substance misuse treatment literature. It critically reviews the evidence for 'what works' and suggests that a more complex understanding of the nature of EBP is required. It argues that this more complex understanding has profound implications for policy development. However, before such arguments can be considered it is necessary to review briefly the nature of evidence.

WHAT COUNTS AS EVIDENCE IN EBP?

Different research methodologies are required for different purposes. To understand meanings and feelings, qualitative approaches are necessary. However, on their own these are of limited use in evaluating effectiveness. This is because people tend to report positively about services, and it is difficult to compare views across services. What then are the key elements of rigorous research on whether interventions work? There are two key elements of good evaluative research.

MEASUREMENT OF KEY OUTCOMES BEFORE AND AFTER THE INTERVENTION

Measuring whether there have been positive changes on key measures is a minimal requirement for evaluation. This does not allow the research to conclude that the intervention is *producing* changes. Often people approach a service at a time of crisis, and even if no service is provided, their problems will have reduced. Furthermore, the extensive evidence on placebos illustrates the power of self-healing for those who believe they are receiving help as just believing you are being helped makes a difference, whatever the actual nature of that help. Thus pills with no active ingredients consistently result in improvements in a range of medical conditions. However, measuring change at least provides an indication that a service is doing no harm and may identify that it is likely to be doing some good.

It is crucial to emphasize, however, that not all measures are the same. The most robust measures use *standardized instruments* – questionnaires that have been tested (i.e. standardized) against large numbers of people. As a result, the scores provide fairly good indications of how the extent, nature or severity of a particular issue compares with that in the general population. Thus, the Alcohol Use Disorders Identification Test (AUDIT) is a 10-item questionnaire on drinking (see Babor *et al.*, 2001). Scores can be compared with the general population and provide an indication of whether drinking is at harmful or dependent levels. Thus a service aimed at reducing alcohol-related problems could give AUDIT before and after an intervention to see whether there was any reduction.

USING A COMPARISON GROUP

As noted above, change often happens anyway. A key challenge is to identify whether the service is producing change or whether it was going to happen anyway. The only convincing way of establishing this is to have a comparison group. Such research is called experimental or quasi-experimental.

The ideal method for such research is a randomized controlled trial (RCT). Essentially, individuals are given either a specific intervention or a control condition. The decision about which they get is random. The control may be normal services, no service or an alternative intervention, depending on the goals of the research. Crucially, because individuals are randomly assigned to receive the intervention or the control condition, the only difference between the groups should be whether they received the intervention (indeed, the equivalence of the groups is generally checked in order to ensure that the only difference is service received). As a result any differences between the groups at follow-up can be attributed to the intervention.

The usefulness of this type of design is illustrated by its ability to identify interventions that do not work, despite appearing to do so. There are numerous examples of interventions in which clients reported positively about the service and before and after measures suggested positive change, but that when experimentally tested found the positive changes were also found in the control group (see Forrester *et al.*, forthcoming). Conversely, it is sometimes found that an apparently negative result (where a problem gets worse or no better) needs to be reinterpreted when the problem gets much worse in a control group. Experimental designs are therefore particularly useful where interventions are designed for chronic and long-term issues that are not easily 'cured'. They therefore seem particularly appropriate for social work services. We often feel that we are making no difference, but in fact social work may be preventing a bad situation from getting even worse. This can only be identified using experimental methods.

There are many variations on the RCT. Most need not concern us, but one major variation is worth mentioning: quasi-experimental designs. For practical reasons it is not always possible to randomize participation in an intervention. For instance, there may be insufficient clients, not enough research funding or the change may be at a level that does not allow randomization. An example of the last would be a systemic change introduced in a small number of local authorities. In such cases it is often possible to identify a comparison group, even if the group is not a randomized control group. For instance, if a change is being evaluated in one local authority, a similar local authority could be included in the research to explore differences.

There is a major limitation in quasi-experimental approaches, namely that any differences found between the groups may be for reasons other than the intervention. For instance, even if similar local authorities are compared, they will differ in particular ways. The same applies to any comparison group that is not randomly identified. For instance, comparing outcomes for those receiving a service with those on a waiting list may be better than not having any comparison, but being on a waiting list is in itself an intervention. It may be telling people to wait to change, whereas people refused a service may decide to find their own ways of changing. Such issues are not trivial; they are an important limitation in quasi-experimental approaches. It is therefore extremely important that such studies explore potential differences between intervention and comparison groups, and insofar as they can allow for them.

Having argued for the importance of specific types of evidence we now turn to review the evidence on alcohol misuse. The findings in this area turn out to be more complex – and more important – than one might have thought. They do not simply point to 'what works' with people who have alcohol problems; rather, they identify key issues in the design and delivery of effective interventions of any kind. We therefore discuss them at length before exploring in greater depth a particularly promising approach from the substance misuse field in Chapter 9.

WHAT WORKS IN HELPING PEOPLE WITH ALCOHOL PROBLEMS?

It is important to consider this question for a number of reasons. One is that knowing which interventions work in different settings is an essential starting point for outlining a vision of how social workers and other child welfare professionals should approach drug or alcohol problems. The review of what works therefore provides a foundation for suggestions below and in Chapter 9 about the nature of effective work with individuals and families affected by substance problems.

There are, however, a number of other reasons why a review of the research evidence is important. An important consideration is that an understanding of what does and does not work in relation to helping people affected by substance misuse sheds light on the nature of alcohol and drug problems. It therefore provides important information in undertaking assessments in such families. It is also likely to be helpful in developing better informed liaison with substance misuse specialists.

Yet the significance of the findings goes beyond such pragmatic considerations. The literature on what works in relation to substance misuse is a comparatively well-developed field (at least in comparison to child welfare and child abuse), and the findings from key research studies throw up some unexpected and challenging results. In discussing these findings we argue that the results have profound implications for policy and practice generally; in essence, they shed light on the key elements involved in producing positive outcomes in almost any setting. As such, they have profound consequences not just for research and practice but also for the development of effective policies in the field of child welfare. In essence, we reflect on the findings from the substance misuse treatment literature and then argue for a fundamentally different approach to service development and delivery, and a more nuanced understanding of the nature of evidence-based practice. An understanding of the alcohol misuse intervention literature is therefore fundamental to our conception of effective child welfare services.

A REVIEW OF THE RESEARCH FINDINGS

There is a vast literature on what works and what does not in relation to alcohol problems. In this discussion we selectively identify the key findings from this literature and then discuss their explanations and implications at greater length.

A helpful starting place is the Mesa Grande project undertaken by Bill Miller and colleagues. (Mesa Grande is Spanish for 'big table'.) The project is an attempt to reduce the vast complexity of the alcohol treatment literature to a manageable size and draw conclusions about what approaches the research suggests do and do not seem to work. As such Mesa Grande uses a comparatively simple approach to grade different studies on particular approaches and then provides average ratings for each approach.

In the latest version of Mesa Grande Miller and Wilbourne (2002) reviewed 361 studies into the effectiveness of alcohol interventions. To be included in the review the studies needed to evaluate at least one alcohol intervention, use a comparison group of some kind, seek to establish equivalent comparative samples prior to the treatment starting and report at least one outcome measure of drinking, or related consequences. They began by grouping together studies with similar interventions. This process resulted in 46 different treatment modalities. Two independent reviewers then assessed and awarded each study scores on the basis of methodological quality and outcome logic. Miller and Wilbourne (2002) also differentiated between the samples used within the studies on the basis of whether or not the samples were treatment-seeking and the severity of their alcohol problems.

It is important to be cautious about the findings of Mesa Grande. First, the approach provides an indication of the strength of research evidence for different approaches and not an indication of the actual effectiveness. In particular, there may be approaches in the middle range that simply do not have good standard studies undertaken. It should not be concluded that they do not work, simply that there is no evidence that they do work. Second, the studies are not necessarily comparing like with like. For instance, some may be dealing with individuals identified by their GP as drinking heavily, others may be delivered to individuals seeking treatment. It is noticeable that some of the best supported interventions seem to be dealing with populations that are drinking at less serious levels compared to some treatment approaches. This is an important consideration when looking at the Mesa Grande. Finally, some of the approaches have had very few studies undertaken on them. To address this issue we are only going to comment on those approaches which had 10 or more studies reporting on them. This ensures that we only comment on interventions with a comparatively robust research base.

Despite these considerations, Mesa Grande usefully differentiates between the types of intervention that work and those that tend not to. Interventions that typically create negative outcomes include:

- Alcohol education;
- General counselling;
- Psychotherapy;

- Confrontational counselling;
- Relaxation training.

It is noteworthy that many of these involve the provider of the service being an expert and delivering an intervention to an individual. This expert approach does not seem to produce positive change, whether it is undertaken in classrooms or with individuals. However, non-directive and psychodynamic approaches are also conspicuous by their lack of success.

In contrast there are a number of interventions that seem to be associated with positive changes. Most strikingly, these include:

- Brief interventions, usually delivered in a Motivational Interviewing (MI) style with feedback on the impact of drinking;
- Motivational Enhancement Therapy (MET) – a brief and structured version of MI;
- Self-help manuals.

Two characteristics of these approaches seem noteworthy. First, they tend to be structured. The sessions have a purpose and are not completely client-directed. Second, despite this they tend to be client-centred and view the client as the person who will make decisions or changes within their own life. It this combination of structure and client-centredness that seems to characterize successful interventions.

Having identified a range of interventions that seem to 'work', the research literature in recent years has moved on to addressing the question of which works best, and for whom. Most conspicuously, two major studies – Project MATCH in the USA and UKATT in the UK – have attempted to compare treatments thought to be effective. In doing so they have been particularly interested in whether different interventions are particularly well suited for individuals with specific patterns of alcohol use or personality types. Thus, for instance, one might expect brief interventions to be more appropriate for less serious or entrenched alcohol problems, or that abstinence-based interventions work better for people with more serious alcohol issues.

The largest attempt to consider such issues was Project MATCH. To explore the impact of different types of intervention on different individuals, 1,726 people with alcohol problems were randomly assigned to three types of treatment. These were:

- Twelve Step Facilitation (TSP), i.e. individual counselling to support the individual in attending AA;
- CBT;
- MET.

For all individuals treatment was provided over 12 weeks; however, individuals received different levels of input. Those in the first two treatment types received weekly sessions (a total of 12 sessions), while those in the third received four sessions (one every three weeks). In addition, TSP worked to encourage individuals to participate in AA and therefore people received significant additional support. A key hypothesis was that MET would have a positive impact, but that for individuals with more serious alcohol problems the more intensive and abstinence-based approaches would work best. In addition, an array of other characteristics and personality issues were hypothesized to be likely to be related to individuals doing particularly well in different modalities of treatment.

The findings of Project MATCH were encouraging about the effectiveness of treatment in general. Overall, there was very significant reduction in levels of drinking across all three interventions. However, virtually no support was provided for the concept of matching. The three types of treatment produced very similar outcomes and there were very few matching effects. This is not simply an unexpected result; it goes against almost everything that alcohol treatment experts would have expected. Yet Project MATCH is not alone in producing such a finding.

The UKATT was the largest British trial of alcohol treatment. It compared MET and Social and Behavioural Network Therapy (SBNT). SBNT is a form of intervention that works to harness people in the family and other networks of the individual seeking treatment to support them in helping the individual change. As in Project MATCH, SBNT was provided as a more intensive treatment than MET and the hypothesis was that it would be more effective for individuals with more pronounced substance misuse problems.

However, the findings of UKATT were broadly similar to Project MATCH. Both modalities produced noteworthy reductions in levels of problem drinking: some 60% of participants reduced their drinking and a fifth were abstinent following the intervention. However, once again there was virtually no difference between SBNT and MET in the outcomes they produced.

If one reflects on these findings they are very surprising. Interventions with very different theoretical approaches and very varied levels of intensity do not differ in their impact. This raises serious challenges for a medical model for understanding experimental research. It is akin to finding out that it doesn't matter what drug you prescribe, as they all work! Indeed, the findings are leading to a major reconsideration of the methods used to identify what works in the substance misuse literature (see Orford, 2008). Given the unexpected and counterintuitive nature of these findings we think it important to explore the results from Project MATCH and UKATT in depth. In doing so we develop an argument that suggests that they provide important indications for the nature of effective practice in human services. At the heart of both projects is the unexpected finding that the nature or intensity of the intervention provided made remarkably little difference to the outcomes. How can this finding be explained?

This is not a new or unusual phenomenon. It has been found in relation to therapies for a variety of problems, where many studies have found that a range of therapies work and there is little difference between them. This characteristic of the findings has led to it being titled the 'Dodo effect' after the Dodo in *Alice's Adventures Wonderland* which stated: 'Everyone has won, so all shall have prizes'.

Yet this is a puzzling phenomenon; apart from anything else, it seems strange that the characteristics of the client, their readiness to change and the extent of their alcohol problem do not have an appreciable impact on which treatment is right for them. How can this finding be understood? And what are its implications for policy and practice?

UNDERSTANDING THE DODO

Mesa Grande demonstrates that some approaches do not work, so why do credible approaches tested in rigorous, large-scale controlled trials tend to produce similar results? Many factors may contribute to understanding the Dodo effect, but they all have in common one thing. In essence they argue that the similarities across the groups were greater than the differences, and that these similarities swamped the differences between the interventions being studied. There are (at least) five types of similarity that may be relevant (and in all likelihood they interact to some degree). These are:

1. The therapist and their skills may be more important than the methods they use.
2. Factors within the client and their situation may be more important than the intervention method.
3. Effective interventions have many shared characteristics and these are more important than the apparent differences.
4. Being in the study may have had an effect on participants in its own right.
5. The study may have created similarities in the therapist across both conditions.

Each of these is worth considering. In broad terms we do not think the first two are likely to explain the Dodo effect, but the other three are likely to be contributory factors.

THE THERAPIST AND THEIR SKILLS MAY BE MORE IMPORTANT THAN THE METHODS THEY USE

It is certainly true that so-called therapist effects are very important. Research consistently finds that different workers using the same method produce strikingly different results. Yet this is an unlikely explanation for the Dodo effect. It would only explain the findings if all of the change was explained by a mysterious therapist 'X' factor and virtually none could be attributed to differences between the interventions. More importantly, if the therapist effect is so influential, this does not explain why in so many of the trials reviewed in Mesa Grande one method proves better than another. To explain the Dodo effect we need to find reasons why many trials find differences between methods, but some do not.

FACTORS WITHIN THE CLIENT AND THEIR SITUATION

One way of approaching this might be to change the focus from what the helper does to what the clients do, and the situation that the clients find themselves in. As such, perhaps a skilled and thoughtful approach that helps them structure the way that they deal with their alcohol problem is all that is needed. The rest is down to whether the individual is ready to change and the effort that they wish to put into changing.

This is one of the explanations that Orford (2008) explores in a thoughtful discussion of these issues. In particular, he highlights a failure to consider the processes of change from the client's perspective. Orford also emphasizes the broader networks and contexts within which treatment and change (or lack of change) occur. The research focus has been on specific treatments and attempts have been made to reduce the impact of other factors through randomly assigning people to particular conditions. It is therefore assumed that as the interventions are the only differences between the groups, exploring differences in outcomes will provide information about the different impact of the interventions. Orford is very critical of the dominant paradigm of experimental studies in the alcohol treatment literature, as he argues that it has failed to explore the complexity of processes of change.

This is certainly true, but it does not appear to provide a convincing explanation of the Dodo effect. For if factors within clients and their situations are so important, then most trials would struggle to produce any effect. Yet this is far from the case. As noted above, any attempt to explain the Dodo effect needs to explain why many trials do produce differences, but why when effective interventions are compared they produce so little difference. There are three factors that might explain this.

EFFECTIVE INTERVENTIONS HAVE MANY
SHARED CHARACTERISTICS

One explanation for the Dodo effect is that effective interventions have common characteristics. This might be a powerful explanation, because Dodo effects tend to be found when interventions that appear likely to work are compared. They are not a feature of trials comparing interventions to normal treatment.

There certainly seems to be some truth to this as an explanation, because the interventions that work with alcohol problems have many characteristics in common. At the broadest level, they tend to be respectful and client-centred, but combine this with some sort of structure to the intervention. They also tend to focus on what the client could or should do now, rather than searching for root causes for the drinking. Thus, Mesa Grande found that interventions that did not work tended to lack the former (for instance, confrontational or didactic approaches) or the latter (for instance, non-directive therapy and relaxation therapy). This might be a factor that contributes to the Dodo effect, but it appears unlikely to explain the whole effect. Should the amount of help provided not make *some* sort of difference – quite apart from the different types of intervention, and their suitability for different individuals? It seems likely that the common characteristics across interventions are important, but it seems unlikely that this is a sufficient explanation for the entire Dodo effect.

BEING IN THE STUDY MAY HAVE HAD AN EFFECT ON PARTICIPANTS

The thorough research design led to a great deal of information-gathering in both studies. Thus individuals were interviewed prior to treatment and at three and 12 months after treatment in Project MATCH and UKATT. In total, they received eight hours of research interview in Project MATCH or twice as much time as the *total* MET intervention. Furthermore, as noted above, this process of an interested individual enquiring in an empathic and non-judgemental way about their drinking might be conceived of as a type of follow-up intervention that was constant across the conditions of both trials. It is possible that it contributed to the similar outcomes across conditions. The qualitative data from UKATT certainly found that being part of the research, and in particular having a research interview prior to treatment, seemed important to many participants (Orford *et al.*, 2006). It seems likely that a 'research only' condition in which only the research interviews were carried out would on its own have demonstrated significant reduction in drinking levels. It is thus possible that in their efforts to be particularly thorough and rigorous, the researchers in these well-funded studies contributed to the Dodo effect.

This certainly seems an important possible factor causing the Dodo effect. It is worth noting a couple of implications. The first is the importance of including consideration of the impact of being in the study itself when carrying out research. This is a powerful argument for including a 'treatment as usual' condition whenever possible. The second is that we are currently concerned about the ethics of research and the potential harm it can produce for participants. The qualitative evidence from UKATT highlights an opposite issue that is not frequently discussed, namely that taking part in sensitive research can actually be beneficial for individuals.

However, there are limitations in this as an explanation. The Dodo trials were particularly well-funded and attempted to be rigorous, and in doing so they tended to collect more information than most RCTs. This seems likely to contribute to the Dodo effect. Yet the impact of being studied does not stop many of the trials in Mesa Grande from producing measurable differences. In part this may have been because the data collection was briefer, but nonetheless the ability of other trials to find an impact suggests that being part of a study is not enough on its own. However, there is a further commonality across the conditions, and that is the selection and support of the therapists.

SIMILARITIES IN THE THERAPIST ACROSS BOTH CONDITIONS

There are two important ways in which both Project MATCH and UKATT may have created similarities in the therapists across the two conditions. The first is that, in their anxiety to ensure that therapists would be able to deliver the intervention, they selected therapists who were skilled. For instance, in UKATT therapists needed to have two years' experience and to submit a tape of their practice that demonstrated skill in Motivational Interviewing. This in itself creates a similarity across the conditions, as MI-competent practitioners were being used in both conditions.

The second commonality is that great time and attention was devoted to ensuring that the therapists were able to deliver the intervention. Tober (2007) has written about this in relation to UKATT. The enormous time and attention paid to supporting therapists in developing skills in the intervention that they were to deliver and in ensuring that they were delivering it is striking. Following an initial three-day course, therapists submitted weekly videos of their practice and received supervision. Only once the videos were independently rated as being competent were therapists allowed to start delivering the intervention. Furthermore, their interviews during the research were taped and if they were found not to be delivering the intervention, then they were given additional supervision and training to enhance their skills.

This attention to the skilful and consistent delivery of the intervention in face-to-face interaction with the client points to a way in which the study may have been creating a Dodo effect, for it is possible that the considerable attention paid to ensuring skilled practice in itself created similar effects across different interventions. In other words, skilled therapists with considerable training and clinical supervision, and knowing that their work will be scrutinized, tend to deliver highly effective interventions. In so far as it is the level of skill that is important rather than the specific type of intervention, then the attention to such issues within these trials may have produced significant elements of the Dodo effect.

WHAT ARE THE IMPLICATIONS FOR POLICY AND PRACTICE?

The failure of key studies to find differences in the outcomes for different methods has been perceived to be problematic from a theoretical point of view. It raises questions about the nature of interventions and how experimental methods can evaluate them. However, what is striking for policy and practice from the findings of Mesa Grande, UKATT and Project MATCH is that credible interventions in well-designed trials all produced very substantial reductions in problem drinking. Furthermore, both trials found that the reductions led to substantial cost savings in health and other areas. What is important therefore is to understand how these studies produced the substantial positive impacts that they did. From the above discussion we would suggest that there are three implications for designing and delivering services.

1. Choose evidence-based interventions.
2. Invest considerable effort in ensuring they are delivered effectively.
3. Evaluate the work being undertaken.

Choose evidence-based interventions

Evidence-based interventions are those that have been found to have worked in experimental trials. The most credible interventions will have been evaluated through a number of such trials and systematic reviews of the evidence will support their effectiveness.

As noted above, they tend to be empathic and client-centred, structured and focused on change now, rather than understanding root causes. However, credibility ultimately comes from an intervention having shown it can make a difference to the lives of individuals and their families. There are interventions that appear to have many of these characteristics (such as Solution Focused Counselling or Neuro-Linguistic Programming) but that do not have a strong evidence base of effectiveness or that have been found not to work. If such an approach were to be used, it should only be done within a carefully evaluated trial of its effectiveness.

In the field of alcohol misuse the strongest evidence is for interventions based on Motivational Interviewing. There are many MI trials, and most have found it is effective and, when compared to other approaches, MI consistently performs as well or better than them. Crucially, MI is often provided in briefer interventions and there is therefore a strong cost-effectiveness argument for choosing it. Furthermore, there is a flexibility about MI that makes it a strong candidate for an underlying communication style. It is interesting to note that in the UKATT trial all therapists needed to demonstrate skill in MI regardless of whether they were to be trained in MI or SBNT. MI can therefore usefully be seen as an evidence-based approach on which others can be built. It is a foundation for good practice. These issues – and the potential challenges of using MI in child welfare settings – are discussed further in Chapter 9. However, other approaches may be useful. In particular, there is a limited but interesting literature on what works with families affected by serious drug or alcohol issues. This literature is considered further in Chapter 10.

A strong focus on the quality of the intervention

There is a danger in believing that evidence-based approaches are easy to deliver. For instance, most social work courses train theories and methods through comparatively brief inputs on a range of different approaches. There is little indication that these are systematically chosen for being evidence-based. More importantly, providing brief input is unlikely to change practice, let alone help individuals become skilled in delivering an evidence-based approach.

A key element in the success of Project MATCH and UKATT – and probably most successful trials – is a focus on ensuring the fidelity of the service delivered. Fidelity is often thought of as a methodological issue whereas in fact it is a practice delivery issue. Fidelity is the degree to which the intervention is being delivered as it should be. There are two key elements in ensuring fidelity of delivery of the service. The first is that there should be considerable investment of time and money in developing skilled practitioners o consistently deliver the intervention chosen. The second is that there should be checks that this has happened. Each of these is worth considering further.

The success of Project MATCH and UKATT involved ensuring that practitioners were able to consistently deliver the interventions that they were meant to be delivering. As noted above, this required considerable investment of time and effort. However, it is not just the focus on developing skills that is worthy of note, it is the *way* in which skills were developed that was striking. In UKATT individuals were recruited with experience and indications of expertise in MI. They were then provided with further minimal training. However, at this stage they were not competent to deliver MI or SBNT. It was only after they had been supervised on videotaped sessions that they developed the skill in practice required to deliver the intervention. This often took some considerable amount of time: generally months of supervised practice before individuals were able to demonstrate skill.

It is also interesting to note that the therapists themselves reported positively on being involved in this process. It was time-consuming and challenging, but they enjoyed the close attention to developing their skills and the sense that they were becoming highly skilled themselves (Tober, 2007). In many ways there are parallels here to Sennett's description of the development of 'Master Craftsmenship' (Sennett, 2003). A focus on doing social work well is likely to be welcomed by practitioners and this is central to evidence-based practice.

Crucial to the intervention was taping some of the sessions the therapists delivered. This is important from a research point of view because it ensures that the intervention that is meant to be delivered is in fact being delivered. However, it seems likely that its significance goes beyond this. As noted above, checking fidelity – and providing feedback on performance – were vital elements in improving the skills of practitioners. Furthermore, it seems likely that knowing they were going to have tapes checked contributed to ensuring that practitioners delivered sessions to the best of their capabilities.

Evaluate the work being undertaken

Finally, evaluation itself seems likely to have made a positive contribution to the success of the interventions in Project MATCH and UKATT. This is worth considering further. Following people up to check how they are doing is likely to influence their behaviour; it may well therefore be appropriate to consider it an intervention in its own right, which contributes to the effectiveness of clinical trials. However, as important as the impact on clients is likely to be the impact on practitioners. Knowing that their work is being evaluated, that their skills are being reviewed and that their impact on clients is being studied is likely to contribute to workers delivering services to the very highest standards. It thus seems likely that investing in evaluation would have a significant positive impact on the quality of the services being delivered.

At the simplest level this suggests that more money should be spent by Central and Local Government on evaluating services. Doing so would not only enable us to have a better idea of what does and does not work, but rigorous evaluation would on its own be likely to improve the quality of services.

Of course, having independent evaluation of services feeding back into management and service development as a standard practice would not be a cheap or an easy option. However, it is worth considering it within a broader context. At present for each person who works in the health service in the UK the Government and major charities invest £1,600 per year in research and evaluation. In contrast, for each person working in social care the figure is approximately £24 (Marsh and Fisher, 2005). If Local and Central Government took evaluation seriously and invested substantially in finding out whether their services worked, it would cost a considerable sum of money. However, it would still be far short of the money invested in health, and the benefits for the quality of services would be immeasurable.

Another way of looking at this is comparing rigorous research with the ways in which the Government currently spends money finding out whether services work. At present the primary ways in which Government ensures standards within social services are by requiring social workers to complete many forms and masses of paperwork – White (2008) estimates that workers spend 80% of their time completing such paperwork – they also use Performance Indicators and an inspection regime that is far more expensive than that of comparable countries. It is difficult to cost these approaches precisely, however if the time spent by professionals on these activities was to be costed, there is little doubt that they would be extremely expensive activities. Yet the outcomes are of dubious merit: there is little or no evidence that they improve performance. A good example is that shortly before the death of 'Baby P'

Haringey had been praised by the inspectors. Indeed, it would be surprising if they did have much impact on practice. In the first place, they do not focus on practice. None of these methods of managing services focuses on what is delivered in practice or on outcomes for clients. Instead, the focus is on process measures, such as Performance Indicators indicating particular types of assessment have been carried out to a certain timescale or inspections of files and procedures. It is telling that none of these ways of evaluating whether services work would be publishable in an academic journal. The lack of rigour would make them unacceptable as a way of studying services; yet we consider them an appropriate way of managing services. Perhaps the extensive resources spent on such approaches would be better spent on undertaking rigorous research.

CONCLUSIONS

The discussion of the research evidence around alcohol misuse has taken us in unexpected directions. We have argued for a vision of social work based on workers undertaking evidence-based interventions. This is not a cheap or an easy option. The discussion of the research suggests that there needs to be a very significant investment in ensuring the delivery of the interventions that are chosen. Deciding a service should deliver an evidence-based intervention is not like buying a ready-made meal. It is more like learning to cook by following a recipe. It requires systemic and systematic focus on developing skills needed to ensure that the intervention is delivered as intended. This requires not only training, but also ongoing supervision focused on skills development and including supervision of direct or recorded practice. It would also benefit from substantial investment in research and evaluation.

These are not easy changes to make. They are likely to require a substantial reconsideration of the nature of Children's Services. However, if Government at local or national level is serious about putting into place evidence-based approaches, then that is the type of change that is required. It is only through such a thoroughgoing approach to evidence-based practice that we are likely to be able to create the types of impressive improvements in client outcomes (and consequent cost savings) demonstrated in large-scale research studies.

We return to explore some of the complexities in developing effective policy responses in the final chapter. However, in Chapter 9 we turn to focus on a specific approach to working with individuals with substance misuse problems that seems particularly likely to be helpful, namely Motivational Interviewing.

9 Motivational Interviewing and Effective Work with Families in which Parents Misuse Drugs and/or Alcohol

The research findings outlined in Chapter 3 identified that resistance from parents – in particular, denial and minimization of the extent of misuse – were key challenges in working with parental substance misuse. Chapter 7 highlighted the paucity of social work research on the communication skills of social workers and the comparative lack of theoretical attention to how resistance from clients should be understood and worked with. The chapter focused on the practical difficulties that these gaps in our knowledge created, as they leave social workers with little guidance on how to manage the complexities of conversations in which they need to combine both the 'care' and 'control' functions of their mandates (Platt, 2007, 2008); in other words, conversations such as those where a parent misuses drugs or alcohol and there are concerns about their child's welfare. In practice, this contributed to social workers all too often failing to listen to parents, working in a non-empathic way and becoming engaged in persuasion and threats in ways that tended to be unhelpful.

These issues are not unique to social work. Indeed, the challenge of working with denial and minimization has been central to approaches to substance misuse for decades. The evidence on what works in this area was therefore reviewed in Chapter 8. Motivational Interviewing (MI) was identified as a particularly effective way of working with alcohol misuse issues. This chapter considers MI in some depth as it appears to be a particularly promising approach for social work with families in which parents misuse substances for a number of reasons. As expanded on below, these include its strong evidence base, its congruence with social work values and the centrality of understanding and working with client resistance. MI is as good as any approach, better than many and – most importantly – we believe provides an effective

Parents Who Misuse Drugs and Alcohol. Effective Interventions in Social Work and Child Protection, 1st edition. By Donald Forrester and Judith Harwin.
© 2011 John Wiley & Sons, Ltd.

communication style which is broadly compatible with all other ways of working with substance misuse. We therefore argue for it as a foundational set of skills for work in this area, rather than as a specific intervention. In other words, we are not suggesting that social workers provide MI as a treatment for parental or alcohol problems. Instead, we are suggesting that MI should be understood more broadly as a set of conceptual resources and skills that provide the basis for skilled communication around problem behaviours such as drug or alcohol problems. As such it is worth spending some time exploring the nature of MI and the challenges inherent in using it in social work. This chapter begins this process. In the next we consider a number of projects that appear to be effective in working with parental substance misuse. One of the recurring features of these projects is that most include MI as a communication style, and for those where it is not explicit many of the fundamental principles of MI appear to be present.

REASONS WHY MI MAY BE AN APPROPRIATE APPROACH

There are four reasons for considering MI to be a useful way of working in child welfare and child protection settings. These are:

1. A strong evidence base that MI is effective, not only with alcohol and drug problems but also with a range of other problem behaviours across different settings and in both brief and longer interventions.
2. Understanding and working with client resistance is central to MI.
3. MI represents the key elements of anti-oppressive theory in practice.
4. MI can be conceived of as a specific intervention or a more general communication style. This flexibility makes it appropriate across the whole range of child welfare work.

Each of these arguments in favour of MI is worth exploring before going on to consider the nature of MI and the opportunities and challenges that using MI within child welfare settings presents.

1. MI is effective, with a range of problem behaviours, across different settings and in both brief and longer interventions.

It was originally developed for working with problem drinkers. As noted in Chapter 8, in this area the evidence for the effectiveness of MI is unparalleled. Not only has MI, or adaptations based on MI principles such as MET or the 'drinker's check-up', consistently been found to be among the most effective way of working with problem drinkers, but large-scale studies comparing different ways of working with problem drinking have found MI to be at least as effective as any other way of working with problem drinking, and better than most.

However, the evidence base provides further indications that MI may be an appropriate method for social workers to use. In recent years the success of MI with alcohol problems has led to it being used in a wide range of other problem behaviours. Thus, there is evidence that MI is as effective as other approaches to working with drug problems (Gossop, 2006). There has also been exploration of the use of MI with other types of behaviour change. MI has been found to be an effective way of working with changes in diet or exercise (Fransen *et al.*, 2008; Garrett *et al.*, 2008; Groeneveld *et al.*, 2008) and with medication adherence, including diabetes and anti-psychotic medication (Greaves *et al.*, 2008). The apparent success of the approach has led to it being tried with issues that might not have been conceived of as problem behaviours, such as depression, attempted suicide and anorexia (see Arkowitz *et al.*, 2007). There are indications that in a number of these areas MI appears to be producing promising results.

The strength of the evidence base for MI can be seen in the fact that at time of writing there are hundreds of RCTs of the effectiveness of MI in a wide range of settings. This evidence base suggests that MI tends to be a helpful approach to working with problem behaviours. This is an important reason for prioritizing MI as an approach within social work. Not all methods have strong evidence bases. Furthermore, the evidence base extends beyond trials to prove that MI does or does not work with particular issues. The strength of the rich tradition means that there are many studies looking at the processes involved in successful MI, including some that have challenged and helped to develop the nature of MI (such as Armhein *et al.*, 2003). However, a strong body of evidence is not just important because it indicates that MI 'works'. It is also important because it indicates when MI does not appear to work. (Indeed, it would be wise to be suspicious of approaches that purport to work with all people in all circumstances.) Thus, in relation to MI there is no evidence that it works better than some other approaches, such as SBNT or CBT, to the treatment of people with alcohol problems. Furthermore, there are some groups for whom MI did not appear to work: one recent study found no impact of MI on pregnant women who were heavy smokers and had tried and failed to give up smoking (though no other approach has been found to work with this particular group) (Tappin *et al.*, 2005). However, it is striking that there do not seem to be any studies indicating that MI was associated with worse outcomes and thus at least seems to be an approach that in general 'does no harm'. Furthermore, even in the study of pregnant smokers the respondents reported positively about the quality of the intervention they received, even if its impact was dwarfed by the many reasons for them continuing to smoke.

The widespread use of MI and its extensive evaluation suggest that it has proved effective in a wide range of settings, used by different professional groups, in different countries for different problems. Furthermore, many of the issues that MI is being used to help with are the types of problems that social workers routinely work with, such as substance misuse, depression, suicide and behaviour change. MI has also been used, with indications of effectiveness, by professionals in roles that, like social work, combine both care and control issues. For instance, it has been used by probation officers, drug counsellors in prisons and prison warders to deal with behaviour problems in situations where the helper has a social mandate to use coercion. This is important because it seems particularly likely to be applicable to child protection situations.

It is also noteworthy that MI has been successfully used by a wide range of different professionals. Some of these have been trained counsellors, but other research has included nurses, doctors, social workers or others in delivering MI-style interventions.

Many of the interventions studied were brief – sometimes as short as one 15-minute session (see Miller and Wilbourne, 2002) – and in general MI appears able to produce measurable change in comparatively brief interventions. This makes MI a particularly useful skills base for initial assessments and interventions in social work. It also highlights the fact that MI is not an in-depth counselling intervention but an approach that can be used in a variety of interactions, from brief meetings to longer-term counselling.

2. Understanding and working with client resistance is central to MI.

It was noted in Chapter 7 that social work textbooks have remarkably little to say about working with non-cooperative clients. This is a major problem. Most social work clients exhibit at least some degree of non-cooperation, and as the research outlined in both Chapters 4 and 7 demonstrated, social workers can often feel stuck when working with such issues. The fact that understanding what causes client resistance and using effective ways of working with it are at the heart of MI contributes to MI having a particularly good theoretical fit for social work.

3. MI represents the key elements of anti-oppressive theory in practice.

One of the advantages of there having been many studies undertaken into MI is that the studies can be statistically combined to identify overall patterns of outcome. This is called a meta-analysis. It allows a great deal of detail and further analysis about the impact of the intervention to be explored. An interesting finding from a recent meta-analysis is that MI is particularly effective with Black and ethnic minority clients. Hettema *et al.* (2005) found effect sizes (i.e. a measure of the impact of MI) that were 2–3 times greater for Black clients compared to White clients. The reason for this needs to be explored further, but the finding has profound implications for anti-discriminatory (ADP) approaches in social work practice. Often ADP is talked about in a rather abstract way. It seems likely that the respectful approach of MI and the focus on trying to understand the client's viewpoint are a way of making ADP a reality in practice. Thus, while MI does not directly address the broader structural causes of oppression, it does provide a way of communicating effectively across differences of power or position.

4. MI can be a specific intervention or a more general communication style.

Finally, MI is an unusually flexible intervention. Some claim it is a philosophy or 'way of being'. Others have used tightly defined versions of MI in controlled trials. It is often used in combination with other interventions. For instance, MI can be combined with CBT or with task-centred approaches. This is particularly appropriate because MI can be particularly helpful in engaging clients and the other intervention can be useful in helping people who have decided to undertake work to change a behaviour.

There are problems with such a degree of flexibility. It can lead to debates about what MI is and how standards of practice can be ensured. Yet it is likely that it is the flexibility of the approach and its ability to produce results when used in very different ways across a range of settings that have led to it spreading so rapidly as a way of helping people. Certainly, it makes it particularly attractive for social work.

These arguments taken together provide a compelling case for the use of MI in child welfare settings. Yet to date there has been limited interest in the use of MI in such settings, and very little research on the challenges or potential that MI has. For it is important to emphasize that using MI in child protection work is not without its challenges. Furthermore, at this stage we have not outlined what is actually involved in MI. In the next section we attempt to do this. This is followed by an exploration of the theoretical and practical challenges that arise in using MI in child welfare and child protection work.

MOTIVATIONAL INTERVIEWING IN THEORY AND PRACTICE

A detailed account of the nature of MI and the skills involved in carrying it out are beyond the scope of this book (see Miller and Rollnick, 2002, for an accessible guide to MI). Instead, we highlight the most important elements of MI in the hope that readers who are interested will be encouraged to follow up by reading the primary text.

MI pays particular attention to skilful ways in which helpers can guide discussions to help clients to explore and potentially resolve *ambivalence*. Ambivalence is seen to permeate difficulties in a wide range of behaviours that people find hard to change. For instance, even if drinking is causing someone enormous problems, it may also have very significant rewards (a social life, a way of escaping bad feelings or just being enjoyable in some respects) or the prospect of changing may have potential drawbacks (the possibility of failing or not being able to imagine life after having changed). This concept of ambivalence was discussed at some length in Chapter 1, where it was proposed to be at the heart of problem drinking and drug-taking. Skilful exploration of ambivalence is at the core of MI.

One way of conceptualizing ambivalence is by thinking of an individual's readiness to change on a spectrum from not wanting to change at all through to being completely committed to changing. In the middle of this spectrum is ambivalence, an area where the individual has reasons for changing and simultaneously reasons for continuing with their current behaviour. The two sets of reasons are unresolved and in conflict. This middle area is of particular significance for helping professionals, as it is generally these people whom we need to work with because people who do not want to change will not in general change. We cannot force people to change, but only help them if they wish to do so. (It is however important to be cautious about deciding that someone is or is not ready to change. As we discuss below, it is possible to make someone sound as if they do not wish to change by talking to them in certain ways. One should therefore avoid labelling an individual as not ready to change. The introduction of the concept here is just to understand the theoretical model underpinning MI.) On the other hand, individuals who are absolutely committed to changing will generally do so anyway. Most people with serious alcohol problems give up without professional help, and this is true of many other types of problem behaviour. For some, professional help can be useful, but if the individual is already determined to change, then the type of help they need tends to be different. It is far more likely to be about structuring the change they wish to achieve through methods such as CBT or task-centred work.

The people whom we are most likely to work with – and who can be the most difficult to work with – therefore are those who are ambivalent about change.

The next important concept within MI is client *resistance*. Resistance means any form of non-cooperation, however resistance recognizes it as an active response, while non-cooperation sounds passive. People with substance misuse problems are often characterized as being 'in denial' if they disagree with professionals about the extent, nature or presence of substance misuse. Indeed, challenging this denial and forcing people to admit to their addiction have been central to some approaches to substance misuse counselling, particularly in the past (Miller and Rollnick, 2002) and is an image of drug or alcohol problems that is still very common in television dramas, perhaps because it lends itself to highly charged and dramatic confrontations.

Motivational Interviewing was developed in response to problems of denial or minimization in alcohol treatment (Miller and Rollnick, 2002). Crucially, however, in MI resistance is conceived of not as a psychological attribute within the person, but as a *product of the client–counsellor relationship*. To support this view Miller and Rollnick reviewed a range of evidence that suggests that counsellors can increase or reduce the amount of resistance

expressed by clients by using different counselling approaches. A confrontational style produces more resistance, such as instances of client's denying or
minimizing their problem. 'Confrontational' styles include challenging clients
at one extreme, but also include attempts to persuade the client that they have
a problem or direct them to take certain actions. In contrast, empathic, non-
judgemental and client-centred listening reduces the amount of resistance in
counselling sessions. One way of looking at this is that the person who is
ambivalent about a behaviour is an expert in the arguments for and against
changing. This is an internal debate that they have often had. If one therefore
makes the arguments for changing, then it tends to elicit arguments for not
changing. This can take the form of an argument between professional and
client, or it can be an internalized response in which the client makes the
counterarguments to themselves.

   This may, on reflection, appear to be common sense. For instance, if one
considers a bad habit that one has, one would be more likely to be resentful
and defensive if confronted than if sympathetically listened to. How much
more true is this when one considers the situation of someone whose use of
alcohol or drugs is leading to them having problems in caring for their child?
It is nonetheless a crucial finding. In the substance misuse field, confrontational approaches were extremely widespread in the 1970s and 1980s. The
evidence discussed in Chapters 4 and 7, along with other research (see Cleaver
and Freeman, 1995; Platt, 2007, 2008), suggests that such approaches may be
common win child welfare social work, particularly when child protection
issues are present.

   Crucially, the way that counsellors (and presumably also social workers)
speak to clients influences the amount of resistance from clients. This is true
when counsellors using different styles are compared, but it has also been
found when the same counsellor deliberately changes the way they talk about
substance use issues (see Miller and Rollnick, 2002). In general, empathic and
non-confrontational approaches produce less resistance. This was also found
in the discussions between social workers and simulated clients reviewed in
Chapter 7. Crucially, however, there is also evidence of a relationship between
the amount of resistance produced and outcomes for clients. The more resistance produced in counselling sessions, the worse the outcomes for clients (see
Armhein et al., 2005; Miller and Rollnick, 2002). Taken together these findings
provide a compelling case for developing approaches to working with substance use that minimize client resistance. This provides a starting point for
understanding MI.

   The foundational skills of MI are essentially those of good counselling with
a specific purpose: to help resolve ambivalence in the interests of behaviour
change. They include asking open questions, affirming positives, reflecting the
helper's understanding of what is being said and summarizing statements.
However, MI goes beyond empathic and client-centred approaches. Miller and
Rollnick, the founders of MI, define MI as 'a client-centred, directive method

for enhancing intrinsic motivation to change by exploring and resolving ambivalence' (2002, p. 35). It is crucial to emphasize that while it is client-centred, MI is a *directive method*. While emphasizing the importance of skilled listening as a foundation for effective engagement with clients, MI remains aware that to help people change their behaviour good listening alone may not be enough. For instance, when talking to someone with a serious alcohol problem, confronting them about it is likely to create resistance, but simply listening to their denial of the problem may be almost as counterproductive. It can often (though not always) lead to them rehearsing the arguments for and against change without resolving them; it allows them to share their ambivalence without helping them to resolve it.

One of the insights of MI is that it is very difficult to be non-directive, and indeed it is often not appropriate. (Even Carl Rogers, who developed the humanistic approach to psychology, differentially reinforced some things said by clients as opposed to others.) Within MI a range of ways of responding to clients are developed in depth. These are intended to be used to minimize the amount of resistance expressed by clients and to maximize the amount that clients talk about the reasons for or commitment to changing. However, undergirding these skills is a set of values, referred to as the 'spirit of motivational interviewing'. Miller and Rollnick stress that MI is more than a set of techniques: it is a 'way of being with people' (2002, p. 34). There is a fundamental spirit underlying MI, a key component of which is the non-judgemental, collaborative nature of the interview: 'the counselor avoids an authoritarian one-up stance ... communicating a partner-like relationship' (2002, p. 34).

The skilled helper needs to be able to direct the discussion in a way that not only reduces resistance, but also encourages people to talk about reasons to change their behaviour. To this end they actively elicit arguments for change. Such arguments for change are called 'change talk'. In a number of important respects they can be thought of as the opposite of resistance statements. MI has evolved a wide variety of ways of eliciting change talk, and methods from other approaches can also be included. Thus eliciting change talk might involve asking someone for their three best reasons to change or it could use the 'miracle question' from solution-focused approaches (a version of 'If you woke up tomorrow and this problem was no longer there, what would life be like?'). Miller and Rollnick (2002) discuss ways of eliciting change talk in some depth. For our purposes it is most important to understand that as a directive method a practitioner using MI would strategically elicit change talk.

Ambivalence, resistance and change talk are the key concepts within MI, and the skills involved in reducing resistance and eliciting change talk are central to it. It is, however, worth noting a couple more features of MI. First, change is the choice and responsibility of the individual. This is recognized throughout MI, but perhaps particularly powerfully in the 'key question'. The key question generally follows a summary of the client's position which identifies all the reasons for change that they have noted and then simply asks the client what they are going to do now. Second, MI has two stages. The first is about establishing rapport and exploring ambivalence. The second is an agreement around what will be done. This division makes MI potentially compatible with other approaches (such as CBT or task-centred therapy) (see Arkowitz *et al.*, 2008), as MI focuses on effective ways of helping the individual resolve ambivalence and other approaches may be particularly good ways of working with someone who has resolved to change.

We hope that this brief introduction has provided sufficient information about MI to allow those not familiar with it to consider its use in child welfare settings. In the next section we consider the challenges involved in using MI in child welfare and child protection work.

CHALLENGES FOR MI IN CHILD AND FAMILY SOCIAL WORK

There are a number of challenges for MI approaches within social work settings. These can be grouped into theoretical and practical challenges. The main theoretical challenges are first, that using MI with a parent in a situation where there may be concerns about a child may lead the social worker to collude with the parent; MI is client-centred and it might erroneously be thought that the parent is the client. Second, MI is essentially individualistic. This is not only inimical to the social model at the heart of social work, it also fails to address the broader context which causes and sustains substance misuse.

The risk of an inappropriate focus on the parent is a genuine challenge for the use of MI in child welfare. However, it is a challenge for many approaches that are taught to or used by social workers, as most of these focus on helping individuals, and even those that are focused on families tend not to concentrate on how statutory protective duties and therapeutic interventions can be effectively combined. Furthermore, provided there is an awareness of these as challenges it seems possible that they could be addressed through imaginative and skilled practice. For instance, MI is widely used by professionals in the criminal justice system in Sweden, and workers appear able to sustain their responsibilities to the system while being client-centred.

In a similar way, most social work approaches are individualistic and in reality there is little indication of a genuinely psycho-social approach in common practice. However, this is not to argue that MI should be used in an individualistic manner. A weakness in MI is that it focuses on working with the individual. MI arose as a response to a disease model of 'addiction' and as such it offers a more progressive and client-centred approach. However, it does not engage with the complex social causes of substance misuse problems.

Thus, for instance, the failure of MI to help pregnant women who smoke may in part be because MI failed to address the social context of deprivation that the women live in. In this respect, social work needs to have a critical engagement with MI rather than simply using MI as practised in other settings. We think a more positive approach would be for social work as a profession to enter into a dialogue with MI. Such a dialogue has the potential to enrich social work through the use of a powerful evidence-based intervention, but equally it has the potential to inform MI by consideration of how it can be used in ways that consider broader structures of oppression and discrimination and how these might be addressed in work with individuals. Thus, we would argue that while the theoretical challenges identified are real, they are best addressed by careful and reflective use of MI in practice.

The practical challenges to using MI in child welfare settings are perhaps more significant. It appears clear that it is not easy to become skilled in MI. Brief training needs to be followed up with extensive supervision of direct practice. This is not surprising: becoming skilled in working with people is rather like becoming skilled at any other activity, it requires practice and feedback. Thus, learning netball or the piano requires constant practice and benefits from feedback from those who have previously mastered the skill. In the only published research on the impact of training child welfare social workers in MI, Forrester *et al.* (2008b) found that a two-day training course had a significant impact on practice, but that it did not lead to skilled practice. Furthermore, practitioners did not make use of follow-up supervision and consultation. The main reason they gave was finding it difficult to find the time. In addition, they received little attention to their skills or ways of working in their normal supervision.

This is a massive challenge for social work as currently practised for it seems clear that social work courses do not tend to teach social work methods in a manner that allows students to become skilled, that those who supervise students rarely focus on developing their ability to use evidence-based approaches (indeed, their direct observation of practice is usually limited) and that once they have qualified, social workers receive little supervision or training that focuses on their direct work skills. It is hard to underestimate how dire the situation is. White (2008) suggests that 80% of social worker time is spent completing forms on computers. This leaves little time for direct practice and virtually none for the development of practice skills, for this process requires skilled supervision and feedback, and in itself takes time. Furthermore, even if Government were to acknowledge the errors of the policies of the past, the systematic failure to attend to social work skills means that a vicious circle has been created, for few of the managers or practitioners currently working in social work are able to deliver evidence-based approaches skilfully. It is therefore difficult to know who would develop the skills of the next generation of practitioners. There are few social work academics, managers or practitioners currently able to deliver evidence-based interventions. In part this is because the career structure of social work has never supported the development of such skills. Thus, there is very limited career progression for those who want to become highly skilled practitioners. Beyond senior social worker positions there tend only to be management positions, which take individuals away from direct practice. Social work does not generally have 'consultant' social workers who still practise, in the way medicine, psychology, speech therapy, nursing and many other professions do. These are the people who should provide the reservoirs of skill, knowledge and experience which the profession should be replenished from; in social work these reservoirs have been systematically drained. This leaves those coming into the profession all too often deprived of the input they need from experienced and skilled supervisors. In sum, social work does not concentrate on developing highly skilled practitioners and this makes putting MI into place extremely challenging in practice.

Yet, this should not be a counsel of despair. On the contrary, there are many examples of areas which have systematically changed in order to create change for the better. Indeed, the progress of MI itself may be seen as an example of this. Bill Miller first introduced MI into the substance misuse field when disease models that often focused on confrontation were dominant. Now MI is the most common approach in this field. This has been achieved in a variety of ways, but at the centre of the change has been the combination of systematic research indicating MI's effectiveness and the enjoyment that individual practitioners experienced in seeing themselves become more skilled and effective.

This offers a hopeful example for child welfare and child protection. It suggests that MI offers an opportunity to radically transform Children's Services. For in learning how to deliver this evidence-based intervention, or indeed any other, it is necessary to re-imagine Children's Services. The focus needs to be on skill development through effective supervision. This in itself requires a new career structure for social workers, a focus on the quality of the service as delivered to clients and a massive reduction in the bureaucracy that has come to bedevil the service. As such, moving towards delivering evidence-based practice entails a commitment to a new vision of social work.

MI is exceptionally well placed to provide the approach at the heart of this. However, it should not be thought to be the sole approach that workers or services should use. Rather it provides a foundational way of understanding and communicating with people around problem behaviours that is compatible with a range of other interventions. In the next chapter we turn to consider some services designed for working with families affected by parental substance misuse. Most use MI and some appear to have used it with considerable success in families where there are serious child protection concerns. There are therefore important lessons to be learnt from these projects.

DISCUSSION AND CONCLUSIONS

In this chapter it has been argued that MI provides a helpful description of basic skills that could and should be used in child welfare and child protection work. This approach is now being tried in three pioneer areas with a view to a roll-out across Wales (Forrester, 2010). However, good practice based on MI does not preclude the need for specialist services designed to intervene more intensively with families who require such input. In the next chapter we describe and evaluate such interventions in the UK.

10 Family Interventions with Parental Substance Misuse

Previous chapters have considered the literature on substance misuse treatment in general and the lessons that can be learnt from it. It was concluded that Motivational Interviewing provided a promising communication style which might be of particular usefulness in child welfare settings. In this chapter we turn to family-based interventions and parental substance misuse. The research literature in this area is very limited. There are no randomized controlled trials, few make use of quasi-experimental designs, the samples are often small and indeed few studies even provide robust measures of welfare before and after the interventions This does not mean that the interventions or services do not work, simply that we do not have strong evidence about whether they work or not. In these circumstances, there are important indications of what works with parental substance misuse but caution needs to be taken in applying the findings. The focus of this chapter is on describing the key features of the most promising current approaches. It concludes with a discussion of the lessons for good practice that can be learnt from the various examples discussed.

This chapter can therefore be seen as providing case studies of interventions that have been evaluated with encouraging findings. However, before discussing these further it is worth highlighting what is not covered. It does not consider interventions at a general level of 'prevention'. There are, for instance, many services aimed at helping families in general or families considered to be at some level of increased risk (for instance, because they are in areas of deprivation). These include services such as SureStart or Homestart, parenting programmes like *Families and Schools Together* (FAST) or the *Strengthening Families Programme* (Wilding and Barton, 2004). Such supportive interventions are interesting and important, and some have produced positive outcomes in relation to both parental drinking and behaviours in children that might be linked to later problematic drinking or drug-taking. Yet while important and worthy in their own right, these are not the focus of this

Parents Who Misuse Drugs and Alcohol. Effective Interventions in Social Work and Child Protection, 1st edition. By Donald Forrester and Judith Harwin.
© 2011 John Wiley & Sons, Ltd.

chapter. Rather, the focus is on serious parental substance misuse, that is parental substance misuse at the level where it is leading to the statutory involvement of Children's Services. There are particular challenges in such work, including engaging individuals who often have very serious drug or alcohol problems, working with people who are often (indeed usually) not voluntary clients and trying to work for change when there is a high risk of a negative outcome for children when change is not achieved or not sustained. These are different concerns from those one encounters in more general preventative programmes, and it is the nature of effective work with these concerns that is the focus of this book.

At the time of writing there is a very limited amount of published material on interventions of this type in the UK context. This chapter considers all the published literature, which relates to three case studies. The first is the Family Alcohol Service (FAS) in North London. The second is the range of services known as 'Intensive Family Preservation Services' (IFPS). This is a model of working imported (with significant adaptations) from the USA and used with some indications of success in services such as 'Option 2' in Wales and 'Families First' in Middlesbrough. These services work explicitly with families at risk of the child entering care. The final example is a pilot Family Drug and Alcohol Court (FDAC) at the Inner London Family Proceedings Court. The Family Drug and Alcohol Court is only for families subject to care proceedings when parental substance misuse is one of the key reasons for the application (Harwin and Ryan, 2007). As with Option 2, FDAC is based on a model widely used in the USA and has been adapted to comply with English law and services following a feasibility study (Ryan et al., 2006). The pilot is being independently evaluated (Harwin and Ryan, 2007) and if the results prove encouraging and affordable, the Government has stated its intention to roll out FDAC nationally.

Towards the end of the chapter we attempt to identify the key lessons across the different types of service. We suggest that successful services for families affected by serious parental substance misuse tend to have some common features and we try to identify the nature of these features.

FAMILY ALCOHOL SERVICE

FAS was the result of a joint initiative between Alcohol Recovery Project and the NSPCC in Camden, London. The project was set up in 2002 as a pilot scheme in response to increasing concern about the number of children presenting to Children's Services and/or on the Child Protection Register (CPR) as a result of parental alcohol problems. FAS delivers its services through an integrated interdisciplinary team. It includes both alcohol and child and family specialist workers. The model of intervention incorporates work with families, couples and individuals using strengths-based and solution-focused models of working, underpinned by MI techniques and a family systems approach (see Robinson and Dunne, 1999; University of Bath, 2003).

FAS intervention has two stages. The first usually consists of five sessions, generally with two workers and seeing some family members individually. Information is gathered from the family about all aspects of their life, with an emphasis on what the family feel that they do well. This positive 'reframing' is a common approach in solution-focused and motivational approaches (see Hamer, 2005; Miller and Rollnick, 2002; Robinson and Dunne, 1999). It is considered to help families to become motivated to change by looking at what is important to them as a family (their family values), and then focusing on what they are already doing well (their strengths). The FAS team have developed a number of approaches to help them in achieving these aims. They have written a book for children about parental drinking, and also work with parents to explain problem drinking to children (see Robinson and Dunne, 1999). They use cards with pictures representing important values to help family members talk together about their values. This is important for the family in identifying their key shared values, and also often starts the process of creating a perceived difference between the values and aspirations of family members and family life as affected by alcohol misuse. A further session uses cards to identify the strengths of different family members. After sessions using these approaches the family meet with the workers and the referrer and the work undertaken is discussed and future work is considered.

The second stage of the intervention appears very varied. The nature of the work continues to be based on MI skills and techniques, with solution-focused and systemic insights, however the specifics of the package of work are tailored to the needs of the particular family. They may include sessions with the whole family, with the parents alone or together, or with the children alone. Throughout, the focus is not on the drinking as such, but on improving the quality of family life through changes in the behaviour of family members. This can sometimes require an explicit focus on drinking, but sometimes the focus is on other issues, though these may be closely related to drinking patterns.

An independent evaluation of FAS was published in 2002 (Velleman et al., 2003). The evaluation attempted to explore changes in child welfare, parental drinking and parental welfare over time and to combine these with a qualitative exploration of the experiences of families known to the service. Unfortunately, the evaluation encountered serious difficulties in getting staff to ensure that clients completed the questionnaires and instruments that were meant to be integral to the research. Instead, the evaluation became heavily dependent on qualitative interviews with a relatively small number of individuals who had experienced the service (11 children, 17 problem drinkers and six parents who were not problem drinkers) and more widely with those delivering the service and other professionals. This failure to engage the staff in the intended rigorous evaluation seriously compromises the findings – something the evaluation team acknowledged. However, the evaluation is important as the first one focusing on work with very serious parental substance misuse and child welfare concerns.

A number of features of the service stood out. First, the families that FAS was working with had complicated and serious problems. Children had relatively severe difficulties at the time they came to the service, and levels of drinking by parents were combined with a large number of other problems. There were indications that families appreciated the service and felt positive about the work undertaken. Only a very small number of children or adults had measures before and after the intervention, and therefore great caution is needed in interpreting findings, as it is possible that those who found the service helpful were more likely to complete the measures, however for these individuals the indications were that the service was making a positive difference.

A major issue identified in the evaluation was engaging families, with both the service and the evaluation. This was particularly difficult for families referred by social services. The challenge of engaging families had a major impact on the service. Of the 74 families referred to the service only 39 attended FAS on even one occasion and only 17 had 'sustained engagement'. Taylor *et al.* (2008) explored this issue in depth. They found that the families had a complex array of problems that made engaging with the service problematic. The profound and overlapping difficulties that the families had also contributed to the difficulties in engaging them in the evaluation. This was exactly what we found in the research described in Chapter 2. In light of these difficulties, the apparent success of the next service to be discussed – Option 2 – in engaging 'hard to reach' families appears particularly interesting.

INTENSIVE FAMILY PRESERVATION SERVICES AND OPTION 2

Intensive, in-home family interventions to reduce placements in public care were first developed in the USA in the mid-1970s. Homebuilders was the first such intervention, and remains the most widely used and the most thoroughly evaluated. Key elements of the Homebuilders model include:

- *Intervention at the crisis point.* Families are considered to be 'in crisis' – with this crisis generally being linked to the possibility of their child entering public care. The response is informed by crisis intervention theory and focuses on immediate, intensive and short-lived intervention. Services are concentrated in a brief period (4–6 weeks), intensive (usually 40–50 hours) and provided in the client's home.
- *Low caseloads.* Therapists carry at most 2–3 cases at a time, and often just one.

- *Flexibility.* Therapists provide a wide range of services, from helping clients meet the basic needs of food, clothing and shelter, to therapeutic techniques. (Institute for Family Development, 2007).

Homebuilders attracted considerable attention when initial evaluations suggested that up to 90% of children 'at risk' of entering public care avoided doing so following the intervention. However, more rigorous evaluations that randomly allocated children to 'receive the service' or 'service as normal' found that Homebuilders had little or no impact on the rates at which children come into care or other measures of child welfare (see Forrester *et al.*, 2008a for a review of this literature). The reasons are complex and include issues about whether the intervention was being delivered appropriately (there was wide variability in what Homebuilders was in different settings), whether the appropriate type of families were being referred to the service (many were not genuinely at risk of coming into care) and whether crisis intervention was the right response to what were often chronic and long-term problems. The findings highlight the importance of evaluations of services including a valid comparison group.

The Option 2 service in Wales (and related IFPS services in the UK) are based on the Homebuilders model, but they differ from it in important ways. Most obviously:

- All the families have substance misuse problems.
- The intervention is based on MI and solution-focused approaches (Homebuilders does not specify the therapeutic approach to be used, only the crisis intervention framework).
- The British context is different from the American context. For instance, Britain has a stronger welfare state and significantly fewer children per head of population are taken into public care.

It is worth noting that substance misuse problems were associated with IFPS being less successful in the USA (Forrester *et al.*, 2008a). It is possible that an intervention found to be effective in the USA might not be effective in the UK, perhaps because our general welfare provision is of a higher standard.

WHAT IS THE OPTION 2 SERVICE?

Option 2 is run by a manager experienced in MI and with knowledge of substance misuse and child welfare issues. Workers with relevant experience are drawn from social work or psychology backgrounds. All receive extensive training and supervision devoted to the development of skills in delivering the Option 2 intervention. The service has also been unusually successful in retaining staff, with comparatively low turnover and a strong commitment to the values and worth of Option 2. The service operates on two sites in south Wales.

Hamer (2005) sets out in some detail the ways in which Option 2 works. There are noteworthy similarities to the FAS model of working. MI provides the basic set of communication skills. This is augmented by elements of a solution-focused approach. Some structured sessions are used, and these use cards as prompts for discussion of values. However, there are differences in the services. The most striking is that Option 2 operates very flexibly with staff allocated to one family but available 24 hours a day during the brief period of involvement.

An evaluation of Option 2 was carried out for the Welsh Assembly Government in 2007 (Forrester *et al.*, 2008c, d). The study used mixed methods. A quasi-experimental element compared data solely relating to care entry (e.g. how long children spent in care and its cost) collected from local authority records for 279 children whose family had received the Option 2 service and a comparison group of 89 children who were referred but not provided with the service because it was full (and does not run a waiting list). The follow-up period was on average 3.5 years after referral. The study found that about 40 per cent of children in both groups entered care, however Option 2 children took longer to enter, spent less time in care and were more likely to be at home at follow-up. As a result, Option 2 produced significant cost savings. A small-scale qualitative element of the study involved interviews with 11 parents and seven children in eight families. Parents reported that they very much appreciated Option 2 and thought it was a very professional service. For some families it achieved what appeared to be long-lasting or perhaps permanent positive change. For others, particularly those with complex and long-standing problems, significant positive changes were not sustained. An interesting feature of the evaluation was that Option 2 succeeded in meeting with every family referred to the service, and a high proportion of these were engaged with the work of Option 2. This is unlikely to have been primarily because of the nature of the families or the level of concern from social services, as the families appear to be in rather similar situations to those within FAS. Rather, it seems related to the ability of workers from the service to visit families repeatedly, often outside normal working hours, in an attempt to engage them.

The evaluation of Option 2 offers intriguing findings. It suggests that Option 2 has some success in reducing the use of public care and this may generate cost savings, and the qualitative interviews suggest a professional service that is much appreciated. However, there are significant limitations in this evaluation. The most important is that it reports solely on outcomes related to care entry. Child welfare and parental drinking issues were not measured directly. (These are the subject of a further evaluation by the same team.) This is an important limitation, because children's welfare often improves after coming into care. A service that delays or reduces the use of care may therefore not always have a positive impact on children in the long term. There were some concerning indications in the qualitative data that Option 2 was highly effective for some families in which the problems were less severe but that the impact might be less long-lasting for families with entrenched and complex difficulties. This is an issue that is considered relatively little in the British literature about preventing care, however it is potentially of concern because family support services may inadvertently be bad for children if they prevent or delay care entry rather than preventing the need for care entry. On the other hand, it perhaps points to the importance of longer-term support and intervention for some families. A strange anomaly within our system of Children's Services is that we are prepared to make permanent interventions in children's lives by removing them from home, but it is rare for us to be prepared to provide permanent family support services (Forrester, 2008). The findings from the more in-depth evaluation are therefore likely to be of considerable significance.

An adaptation of the Option 2 model, 'Families First', was set up in Middlesbrough in 2006 (see Woolfall *et al.*, 2008). Unusually, this was jointly funded by adult and children's social services and the team involved members from both. While modelled on Option 2, there were some important differences. Like Option 2 it is an intensive family intervention service that offers advice and support for adults and families affected by substance use, using brief solution-focused therapy as its key method alongside parenting skills and alcohol and drug interventions. It comprises staff seconded from regional Primary Care Trusts or workers specifically funded for the service. Unlike Option 2 the team includes six social workers who have statutory responsibilities that enable them to remove children from the family home if necessary as well as family workers. Families First works with families in their homes where children are registered, or are at risk of registration, due to child protection concerns. For most families it is the last resort before alternative care arrangements are made for their child or a source of support during a temporary period of care for their child. It does not operate a 24-hour service but offers out-of-hours support if needed. Support is provided for kinship carers too and work will continue with the parent where the child is already in care, or subsequently taken into care, during the intervention to maximize the chances of a safe and early return to the family home.

The initial intensive intervention lasts up to eight weeks with additional 'low-key' services for up to four months, after which the case is transferred to mainstream services along with a maintenance plan or decisions about permanency. During this time the staff member with case responsibility works intensively with the whole family on their strengths and values, using motivational techniques and focusing on solutions and agreed goals. Additional support is given in other areas if required (e.g. resolution of housing and benefit problems).

A recent evaluation of the service was carried out by researchers from Liverpool John Moore's University in order to 'to identify the processes involved in service delivery, including intervention approach, the implementation and integrity of Families First and local context, including interagency working, as well as the outcomes of the intervention for participating families'

(Woolfall *et al.*, 2008, p. 13). It used a variety of questionnaires and interviews to collect data over a 12-month period from 11 parents and carers, 15 professionals and five other 'key stakeholders'. As most of the children were very young they were not included. Data were collected at baseline, six months and 12 months, from the start of the intervention. Three measures focusing on adults were used and one that seeks to establish quality of life for children based on reports from parents and children (who were old enough).

The evaluation produced interesting findings, though the very small numbers involved and the lack of a control group and the small number of families involved in the evaluation are serious limitations. However, positive results included what was believed to be a reduction in the need for care placements in that staff and families felt there was less use of care, and minimizing the time spent in care for some children. Illicit drug use but not alcohol use by parents was reduced and stabilized during the 12-month period. Parental reports showed that levels of anxiety among children reduced, but there were no differences in other physical or emotional problems (Woolfall *et al.*, 2008, p. 4). Importantly, parents did not think their health was a concern and none felt it affected their parenting or daily activities. No change was seen in levels of depression, although qualitative reports suggest some parents described improved self-esteem from being able to talk to Families First staff. Some parents described family conflict improving once additional family support was available to them. No changes were seen in employment or education, although some parents suggested housing changes were helpful in supporting their reduction in drug use and having children returned to their care.

The parents felt positively about the Families First intervention and particularly valued the 'truthful relationship' established with the social worker, as well as the importance of other factors such as the timing of the intervention, housing support, taking personal responsibility for changes and the solution-focused approach. The evaluation also highlighted the need to review the timeframe of the support allocated to families as some needed longer-term support.

Given the limitations of the study in terms of size and lack of control group, further research is necessary to determine whether other outcomes that suggested no improvement or change can be addressed within the programme, for example, parental mental health or child emotional health, and whether the positive indications found here are replicated across a larger group and attributable to the intervention. However, what appears to be particularly important is the process of working with people in a strengths-focused, honest and open way, an apparently novel approach from the experience of some parents' contact with social services previously. There are positive indications about reducing the need for, and time spent in, care for the children concerned. This suggests some cautious optimism, but the lack of other child welfare outcomes suggests this needs to be explored further, particularly as the outcomes reported in this study were based on parents' reports and the parents might not wish to suggest their child's health or well-being had deteriorated due to their own fears of the child being removed from their care.

THE FAMILY DRUG AND ALCOHOL COURT INTERVENTION – RATIONALE

The final example of an intervention targeted at families with serious problems is the FDAC. This intervention is being piloted by Camden, Islington and Westminster Children's Social Care services and the Inner London Family Proceedings Court. Three main reasons lie behind its development. First is the high incidence of parental substance misuse in care proceedings. Research in the three pilot Central London authorities identified parental substance misuse as a key factor in over 60% of cases. Second is the evidence from the USA suggesting that this model can help achieve better outcomes for children and often for their parents. Finally, all 57 respondents in the feasibility study (from legal, adult and child social care, health and specialist substance misuse services as well as parents) were in favour of the proposed family drug and alcohol treatment court. They saw the court as a good basis for trying to promote reunification, but were just as positive about its potential to secure permanent new homes for the children more rapidly than at present if the treatment did not work (Ryan *et al.*, 2006).

WHAT IS THE FAMILY DRUG AND ALCOHOL COURT INTERVENTION?

The Family Drug and Alcohol Court (FDAC) is a specialist court within care proceedings. Its purpose is to help parents address their substance misuse and associated difficulties at this very crucial time when they face the possibility of losing their child/ren. It is available for all parents except those with active florid psychosis, extremely severe current domestic violence or a history of severe sexual or physical abuse of the children.

Parents decide for themselves whether or not to take up the offer of the FDAC court and if they accept, they commit themselves to an intensive programme of assessment, structured support and monitoring. If parents make good progress with their substance misuse and other problems and are also able to demonstrate safe and satisfactory parenting, they remain within FDAC throughout the care proceedings and any subsequent order. If, however, they are unable to engage with the interventions, then they leave the FDAC court and the case reverts to standard care proceedings. It is made clear to parents at the outset that accepting the FDAC programme is no guarantee of reunification or that their child will remain at home. But it is made equally clear that the programme seeks to actively support parents and help motivate them to engage with services. The whole process can take 9–12 months, but may be shorter depending on progress made.

The FDAC differs from traditional care proceedings in several important ways. First, the judge plays a highly innovative dual role. She or he manages both the care proceedings and the specialist FDAC programme, working actively to engage the parent in relevant substance misuse services and to ensure that any assessments needed are carried out in a timely and coordinated way. The same judge deals with the case throughout to promote parental engagement. The case is brought back to court for fortnightly review hearings – another radical difference from standard care proceedings. These reviews are used to provide encouragement, review progress, review the intervention plan, problem-solve any difficulties that arise and make decisions in order to reach permanency as quickly as possible and to prevent problems from building up. The whole ethos of these reviews is entirely different from standard care proceedings. They are very informal and the judge engages directly with the parent. Lawyers only attend review hearings if there is a specific legal issue to be resolved.

The second novel feature is the specialist FDAC multidisciplinary team which is attached to the court, advises the judge and coordinates the process and the intervention plan as long as parents stay engaged with FDAC. The FDAC team includes a service manager, nurse, drugs worker, an adult and children's social worker and sessional work from a child and adolescent psychiatrist, adult psychiatrist and family therapist. Finally, the team has named links in the Housing and Domestic Violence Teams within the local authority as substance misuse is typically only one of many parental difficulties which need timely and often simultaneous assistance. The FDAC team will assess these problems and draw up a treatment plan and work closely with the judge to review parental progress and to advise on continuation in the programme. This team is an entirely new structure, designed to prevent parties to the proceedings requesting time-consuming and expensive expert assessments, to ensure active case management and rapid access to a wide range of local services.

The final important innovation is the provision of parent mentors, who have personal or family histories of substance misuse. The mentors provide flexible support to all parents, help mediate the court experience, act as positive role models and liaise closely with the FDAC team. In the longer term the intention is to recruit parent mentors who have lost children in care proceedings because of substance misuse but have overcome their problems and gone on to parent successfully.

THEORETICAL UNDERPINNINGS AND THE US EVIDENCE BASE

The FDAC is rooted in the model of American problem-solving courts. These courts are very widespread in the USA and family treatment drug courts, as they are known, are the fastest growing type of problem-solving court. By 2006 there were over 183 such courts in 43 states with many more under development. All have sprung up in the last 12 years and deal with alcohol as well as illegal drugs. Parental progress is a key issue in the decision as to whether a parent can continue to parent or needs to have their parental rights terminated with a view to finding a new home for the child. Common to all the problem-solving courts are a number of key features. They include:

- Increased judicial oversight;
- A supportive environment;
- Individualized care plans;
- An integrated drug court team which provides support and wraparound services;
- More coordinated service delivery;
- Accessible, appropriate treatment resources;
- Relapse support.

All these features are thought to help motivate the parents and to increase the likelihood of successful engagement in treatment and change in behaviour. Some of the features outlined above are shared with other interventions described in this chapter, as is the emphasis on motivating parents and focusing on strengths as well as being honest about difficulties. Beyond a commitment to motivational approaches, the American model is eclectic and does not ally itself with any specific theoretical framework.

What, however, is distinctive in the FDAC model is the role and approach of the judge, which is very different from that common in adversarial systems:

> Judges go from being a detached, neutral arbiter to the central figure in the team … the judge is both a cheerleader and stern parent, encouraging and rewarding compliance, as well as attending to lapses.
>
> (Chase and Fulton Hora, 2000)

Research into problem-solving courts in other countries, including the FTDCs in the USA, suggests that this involved and proactive judicial role is more effective in getting people to engage with services and maintain that engagement (Burton, 2006; Edwards and Ray, 2005; Green *et al.*, 2007; Petrucci, 2002; Worcel *et al.*, 2008). What is less clear is why. One of the founding fathers of the FDTCS, Judge Len Edwards, suggests that it is a combination of the judge exercising judicial authority and behaving in a completely non-traditional way that may have a therapeutic component. In his words:

> Judges have learned that there are a number of 'tools' available to them including persuasion, support, and motivation can add greatly to the traditional judicial tools of warnings and coercion.
>
> (Edwards, launch of FDAC, 28 November 2008)

It has not been determined which components of the model are the active ingredients. Ultimately, this kind of information is very important because it helps establish which components of the model should be replicated and which are less important. However, although less fine-grained, by comparing standard court process and services with the specialist family drug treatment courts, the US national evaluation was able to show that the model delivers encouraging results (Green *et al.*, 2007a and b). More children were reunited with their parents, fewer cases ended in termination of parental rights and more children were placed faster in permanent homes when reunification was not possible. These child welfare outcomes were also associated with cost savings, particularly on foster care services. Parents were more likely to enter and complete substance misuse treatment than comparison parents and, if they relapsed, were more likely to resume treatment. They were also more likely to access treatment faster.

Some confidence can be attached to the results because they were based on a large sample of cases (1,220) carried out by independent evaluators. Moreover, although no RCT was used, the design involved a comparison sample of matched cases in US states that do not have FDTCs as well as untreated but eligible mothers in the FDTCS sites. (These parents were not provided with the FDTC service because of capacity issues.) Sampling took place over a four-year period and all cases were followed up for two years. Additionally, there was a small retrospective study. All data were collected from administrative records. At the time of writing, an application has been made to carry out a further follow-up of the sample which would generate a minimum window post-court hearing of five years. This is exactly the kind of longer-term monitoring that is needed. The sheer scale of the study also permitted comparison of results within the family drug treatment courts in different states as the models do vary. This was particularly interesting because it suggested that outcomes were poorer in the sites that required more long-term family support work in the community before the judicial process could begin. As has been shown so many times in this book, in the UK context the timing of care proceedings is a critical issue, and policy and legal guidance, as well as practice, play a crucial role in this matter. What counts as constructive or destructive delay is one of the most contentious matters affecting child well-being.

THE ENGLISH EVALUATION OF THE FAMILY DRUG AND TREATMENT COURT

The results from the USA are promising but they cannot simply be transposed to our own system for several reasons. The FDAC model has been adapted to the English context and, unlike the FDTCS, it is not exclusively abstinence-based and does not use explicit rewards and sanctions. The legal framework differs as do some services and, to a lesser extent, drug problems. In the USA methamphetamine use is frequent whilst heroin and crack cocaine use is less common, although alcohol misuse is found in both settings. Finally, the costings and cost benefits cannot be extrapolated from the USA to England. For all these reasons an independent evaluation of the FDAC pilot was always planned as an integral element of the FDAC programme.

The Interim Evaluation Report (Harwin *et al.*, 2009) provided some encouraging early indications of the FDAC model. It showed that it is possible to set up and implement an entirely different model of court to deal with care proceedings when parental substance misuse is a key issue in the case. In line with FDAC objectives, parents were getting immediate access to substance misuse services and benefiting from the court's assistance in addressing other issues affecting their ability to parent, such as housing, domestic violence and financial hardship. Judicial and FDAC team continuity helped give parents confidence in the process, with three-quarters of parents attending at least 75% of their hearings. Swift decisions were made if parents were unable to take advantage of FDAC, thereby enhancing the prospects of achieving permanent alternative homes for these very vulnerable children. Based on the first year of FDAC cases these were all encouraging results.

The full evaluation, which is funded by the Nuffield Foundation and Home Office, has four main aims. It will:

- Compare FDAC with standard court process and service delivery;
- Compare costs;
- Compare child and parental interim outcomes between FDAC and standard court and services;
- Identify set-up and implementation lessons.

All these questions are ambitious and challenging and make use of comparison of local authorities to generate similarities and differences. If the early results from this first-stage descriptive study are promising, a second-stage outcome study will need to be undertaken with longer timeframes to follow up the parents and children. But the study is important because it uses the court setting as the basis for trying to bring about change. All too often the court is seen as a last resort by practitioners and policy-makers alike and, as shown in earlier chapters, the consequences for children can be very damaging. The FDAC evaluation, along with other studies, will help increase our understanding of the determinants and limits of motivation and the impact of intensive, medium-term support in changing behaviour and parenting and safeguarding child well-being. FDAC gives parents a chance, but for the sake of the child, the chance is time-limited.

DISCUSSION

The interventions all have promising indications that they may work, though none has robust evidence that it makes a significant positive difference in a UK context. Furthermore, it needs to be understood that even if such evidence existed, it would only indicate that the service makes a difference for a proportion of the families it works with. Interventions are often talked about as if they worked for everyone, but this is never true, and with this group achieving positive outcomes may be particularly difficult.

While these are important caveats it is striking that the services share a number of key features in the way in which they work with families affected by serious parental substance misuse. First, all of them pay considerable attention to skilful communication. MI appears to have been particularly influential here, but even the communication of the judge in the FDAC shares many of the principles of MI. All the projects are sensitive to the situation that parents find themselves in and there is a focus on effectively engaging parents in such situations.

Second, the interventions are structured. Innovative ways of doing this (such as values card games) and adaptations from other settings (such as solution-focused approaches) are useful in this respect. All of them help the practitioners to identify strengths in families where it is much easier to see the many problems, and to explore what the family members want their family to be like.

Third, all the services aim for time-limited interventions. In some instances, such as Option 2, the period of work is very brief, but even in the FDAC there is an attempt to ensure a comparatively brief period of work is undertaken. This element of the interventions is perhaps problematic, not because significant change cannot be achieved in a relatively short time, but because for some families there are issues about whether change can be sustained and whether there may be lapses or relapses. The focus on brief, time-limited work may be as much a function of the system's requirements and resource constraints as it is the needs of the families. What happens to the families in the longer term remains an important question for all these services. As noted above, Children's Services appears to be prepared to work over long term with children who are removed, but it is rare for there to be an equivalent commitment to working long-term with families who need support.

Fourth, the content and structure of the interventions is not the only thing they have in common. All the services are led by highly committed managers and considerable time is spent in training and supervising staff to deliver skilful interventions. Indeed, most of the projects have a charismatic and committed individual who champions the changes they believe are needed. These common issues are not immediately obvious in reading the evaluations, but they are likely to be as important as the form of the service as described on paper.

What is most striking about these findings is the commonalities they have with the key elements of good practice identified in previous chapters. The focus on skilled communication around difficult issues relates closely to our findings from Chapter 7. The key place that MI may play in addressing these issues echoes our conclusion in Chapters 8 and 9. The broader issues about working with the whole family and holding in mind the needs of the parents and those of the children resonate with those identified in Chapters 2 and 6. Finally, the significant attention paid to ensuring that workers have the skills and support necessary to deliver services effectively is similar to the conclusions of Chapter 8. Taken together, these begin to portray a comparatively consistent picture of the nature of good practice with serious parental substance misuse. The problem is that this appears rarely to be achieved. As we have noted, we consider this to be a systemic problem And as such requires a systemic response. In the final chapter we therefore turn to consider the broader policy context and how it can support the delivery of effective services for families affected by serious parental substance misuse.

Conclusion

The book is divided into three parts. In Part 1, we considered the nature of substance misuse and its impact on children and their welfare. We argued that both substance misuse and, by extension, the impact of parental substance misuse were complex and multifaceted phenomena. In particular, we highlighted that they were not helpfully understood as an individual 'addiction' but rather as a psycho-social issue. This included an understanding of some of the difficulties involved in defining the terms that are used and an awareness that the area is as saturated with value issues as it is with empirical facts. As such, it seems particularly appropriate that social workers should deal with this complex psycho-social problem.

Part 2 considered how social workers deal with such issues. It did this primarily by reporting our research study which followed up 185 children allocated a social worker over two years. The findings from this study were profoundly concerning. Around half of the children were removed from their parents and those who stayed at home tended to have significantly poorer outcomes than those removed. This was perhaps not surprising, for when we interviewed the social workers they presented a picture of being poorly prepared for work with substance misuse and feeling 'stuck'. This made the process of assessing risk and engaging parents problematic. All too often workers were anxiously monitoring until something went wrong.

Given these disturbing findings, Part 3 turned to consider what might usefully be learnt from the broader literature. The chapter on assessment attempted to provide a clearer and more coherent structure for undertaking risk assessment. There then followed three chapters that looked at the evidence base for how social workers might most helpfully work with parents who misused drugs or alcohol. A number of lessons were drawn from this review. The first chapter considered further research we were involved in, this time exploring the communication skills of social workers. It was concluded that at present social workers often use rather confrontational and unskilled listening styles. The following chapters identified Motivational Interviewing as a promising approach for social workers to use in working with PSM, and

Parents Who Misuse Drugs and Alcohol. Effective Interventions in Social Work and Child Protection, 1st edition. By Donald Forrester and Judith Harwin.
© 2011 John Wiley & Sons, Ltd.

indeed a range of other challenging issues. The final chapter looked at a range of additional interventions that might be used to complement a basic MI approach. In particular the limited literature on what works with families affected by serious concerns about PSM was reviewed.

However, the review of the evidence base indicated that using evidence-based practice in reality was more complex and challenging than might have been expected. These issues were considered in Chapter 8. Here a specific formulation of EBP was argued for – one in which a specified intervention had been supported through rigorous experimental research. However, a careful reading of the research literature identified that delivering evidence-based interventions is not a straightforward approach. On the contrary, research that evaluates interventions tends to pay great attention to ensuring that practitioners are able to deliver the specified interventions and that they are actually delivering them in practice. After all, there is no point evaluating an intervention if one cannot be sure that the intervention is actually being delivered!

An unexpected outcome from this examination of the literature was that it has profound implications for the ways in which services are currently structured and delivered. In earlier chapters we indicated our deep concerns and anxiety about the current social work system. Here we analyse in greater depth the reasons for the structure of the current system so that we can propose an alternative, one based on *professional excellence in delivering evidence-based interventions*. The next section attempts such an analysis. It is followed by one that links issues around parental substance misuse with those across the field of child welfare and child protection.

POLICY AND PRACTICE

We have stated at various points our concerns about the current system, however it is worth reiterating them at this point. We believe that the following tend to be true of social work at the moment:

- Social work education does not prepare social workers with skills for direct practice.
- Once qualified, social workers do not receive systematic attention to developing their skills. In particular, there is little focus on the development of skilled practice through supervision.
- Virtually no field social workers use any particular method or approach.
- The career structure of social workers does not support individuals to remain in practice and develop high levels of skill, or to support others in developing skill to deliver evidence-based interventions.
- The reforms over the last 10 years have led to a massive increase in bureaucracy and a consequent reduction in the attention paid to skills development.

This is a catalogue of serious concerns. However, in order to understand how and why services developed in such a way it is necessary to step back from the concerns of everyday practice and to think like a policy-maker. Imagine, if you will, that you are the senior civil servant or Government minister responsible for social services. In such a position you are faced with two key questions: 'What should social workers be doing?' And, 'How can we make them do it?'

If we consider these two questions it becomes clear that the current mess is not the result of deliberate policies intended to make social services worse, but rather reflects the difficulty involved in answering these key questions and the consequences of pursuing the wrong answers. In this regard, it is not just – or even primarily – the politicians who have been misguided, it as much the fault of social work as a profession which has failed to address the foundational empirical questions: 'What do social workers do?' And, 'Does it make a difference?'

In order to better understand the policy-making process it is helpful to consider the theories of Le Grand (2006; 2007). We therefore briefly outline Le Grand's discussion of approaches to policy-making; and then illustrate the unintended negative consequences of a particular approach – central control through targets – with the example of the Looked After Children materials, Assessment Framework, Common Assessment Framework and ICIS.

Le Grand is a particularly important figure in recent policy-making. Not only has he been a senior social policy researcher and theorist, but for most of Tony Blair's premiership he was the Government's senior policy adviser. His continuing influence can be seen in the pursuit of the idea of social work practices operating in quasi-markets.

Le Grand helpfully identifies a problem that many practitioners may not have considered, namely how does one create change in public services? and proposes there are four main ways to achieve this:

1. *Trust* in professionals;
2. Giving users of services a *voice*;
3. Central control, for instance through *targets* and inspection;
4. Creating *markets* or quasi-markets in which there is competition to provide a service.

Le Grand concedes that there is a place for all four approaches in a pluralist society, but his review is highly critical of the first two, somewhat critical of the third and he sees markets as creating unique advantages. However, he does not dwell on their limitations. (His books were written before the collapse of the global financial markets.) It is worth considering the criticisms that Le Grand makes in some depth, not only because they are reasonable but also because they are the considerations that explain the Government's distrust of professionals and service users in delivering policy reform.

Le Grand's central criticism of trusting professionals is that professionals do not always act in the interest of clients. If a professional group has control over a service, they tend to run it in their own interests. At the very least, most groups are a mixture of what Le Grand terms 'Knights' (i.e. those with the interests of others at heart) and 'Knaves' (those who put their own interests first). The problem with trusting professionals is that there is no curb on the behaviour of Knaves. Thus, for instance, in summer 2009 one of us attended a GP's surgery. It was a sweltering hot day and the patients in the waiting room were visibly sweating. There was one fan but it was on the receptionist's desk pointing toward her and away from the patients. This is an illustration of the way that, if left to their own devices, public services can become more concerned about the welfare of those delivering than those receiving services. Unlike the private sector, in which individuals can choose to go to a different shop if they receive poor service, patients tend to feel that they have little choice. This illustration is merely one manifestation of a wider phenomenon. Le Grand quite rightly suggests that if left to their own devices, professionals will tend to create services that are run as much in their own interests as they are run in the interests of clients.

A second way to run services is to place the voice of the client as more central. This can range from simply having complaints procedures, through consultation with users of services to full-blown service user control of services. Le Grand is equally dismissive of service user 'voice'. In particular, he argues that where services are controlled by their users this tends to favour more educated and better resourced groups. There are other difficulties with service user control of services in the field of child welfare and child protection. The most important is that service users are only one interest group within the complex area of child protection. Society as a whole funds and mandates the service. It would not be feasible or appropriate for those allocated the service to run it. In the area of child protection there are also difficult issues about who the users of services are. Is anyone who has been investigated a service user? What of someone whose child was removed but who is no longer allocated a social worker? Most importantly, to what degree are parents the users of services and to what degree is it children?

These are not trivial issues. The increasing emphasis on the importance of involving users in running services has enormously enriched social services in recent years. The process of exploring how service users should be involved in different settings has been and is an important humanizing influence in service delivery. In this respect, Le Grand's views seem rather dismissive. However, in the area of child protection (unlike some others) Le Grand appears to be substantially correct. Obtaining the views of service users is a vital element in delivering services, but the area of child protection does not seem to be one where service users can control the delivery of the service.

Le Grand then turns to the third way in which services can be run, namely central control through setting and monitoring of targets. Le Grand presents a robust defence of targets as a way of running services. He gives the example of similar hospitals in Wales and England. The English ones were given targets and services improved, while in Wales there was no change. His conclusion is that targets provide a strong way of focusing a service on a particular outcome. However, he discusses at length their limitations. Most importantly, creation of a specific target can lead to manipulation of figures and can result in services becoming inappropriately focused on a particular target. It is, in short, an unsubtle – though sometimes effective – tool for achieving public policy goals.

The final approach, the creation of markets, is the one the Le Grand clearly favours. Where pure markets cannot be created, Le Grand argues for the establishment of 'quasi-markets'. Quasi-markets are public sector structures designed to reap the supposed efficiency gains of free markets without losing the equity benefits of traditional systems of public administration. So, for instance, within the NHS the purchaser/provider split was intended to increase efficiency through competition, without requiring individuals to pay for NHS services.

Le Grand is passionate in his advocacy of market-based solutions to welfare and public policy issues. He argues that there are a number of advantages, the most important of which is that a market creates a constant impetus towards better services because markets reward success and punish failure. Thus, in a market successful schools will have more pupils, good hospitals will have the potential to expand, and so on. Provided resources follow people this would lead to success being rewarded and failure resulting in negative consequences. To take the example of the receptionist who directed the fan towards herself. In a market-based system of welfare it is argued that this would be less likely to happen because GP practices would be competing for custom. As a result, they would be set up in the interests of those who use them rather than those who work within them. Under a market system perhaps fans would be turned towards patients. (Indeed, in the long-term Le Grand might argue that under a market system air conditioning or more fans would be purchased if this was considered to be important in retaining the custom of patients.) Of course, this may not be true; poor service is certainly not confined to the public sector. But it does seem true that simply leaving professionals to deliver services can lead to services becoming focused on the needs of the professionals.

However, Le Grand is not only interested in the creation of the incentives and punishments that a market-based system creates. He also argues vigorously that issues of social justice can best be addressed through market-based reforms. This is a complex argument and one that we do not need to consider in depth as it does not seem likely to apply to child welfare work. In brief, Le Grand argues that creating incentives to address inequality is likely to be the best way of ensuring the best services for those with the least in society. For instance, having a voucher system to pay for education and then ensuring that children from deprived sections of society have larger vouchers than other children would systematically tilt the market towards those with the greatest need.

Given the limited applicability of market-based solutions within child welfare work it is not necessary to explore the limitations in Le Grand's analysis in great depth. However, it is worth noting that Le Grand's thinking is behind the introduction of social work practices to provide services for looked after children. The idea is that social workers in practices akin to GP surgeries would contract to provide services for a number of looked after children. This arrangement would, it is argued, provide the greater professionalism and consistency which are currently lacking within social work.

There are myriad problems with such an argument. Indeed, Le Grand's passionate belief in markets seems less convincing in light of the widespread failure of the financial markets. For these failures illustrate the limitations of markets in many areas. Several are worth noting. The first is that for markets to work there needs to be the possibility of business units going bust. The impact of this on children and families needs to be considered. Second, markets need to be regulated. This can create considerable additional costs, particularly where the market is effectively trading child welfare. Third, those using markets should have a say in which service they use. Fourth, markets do not operate well in situations where there are limited choices or where purchasers have limited information. In such situations quasi-monopolies are created. These are likely to prove very expensive ways of providing services.

While Le Grand's arguments for market-based solutions seem of limited applicability for child welfare and child protection work, his outline of the different approaches to public policy-making provides a useful conceptual schema for thinking about how senior policy-makers put ideas into practice. Over the last 10 years targets have been the dominant approach within social services. It is worth considering the largely unintended and generally harmful consequences of a focus on a target-based management system before outlining an alternative. We do this by considering a brave but ultimately misguided attempt to relate research findings more closely to practice.

THE LAC MATERIALS, THE ASSESSMENT FRAMEWORK FORMS AND BUREAUCRACY OUT OF CONTROL

For many years there has been a recognition that social workers do not record information well (and a suspicion that this is because they do not collect important information). This has contributed to an inability on the part of local authorities to collate and present even the most basic information. Thus, until recently local authorities could often not provide accurate data on the numbers of children looked after, let alone their age, gender or reason for being in care for these children. This is clearly unacceptable.

In the early 1990s a group of key researchers with close links to the Department of Health carried out an exciting series of studies to address this problem (see Ward, 1995). They tried to identify from parents in the community the key areas that they would expect their child to progress in. These were used as the basis for a series of forms – and accompanying training – known as the Looked After Children (LAC) materials. They included forms for when a child came into care, detailed information for any child in care and related forms for the meetings set down in guidance, such as reviews of looked after children.

As a senior social worker with an interest in bringing research and practice into closer alignment these developments were greeted with excitement by one of us (DF). I presented them to my team with enthusiasm and we welcomed the Government putting them into use. However, the actual implementation of the LAC materials proved worse than a disappointment. It actually made practice worse. There were a number of reasons for this.

First, in their enthusiasm for creating a better system researchers and policy-makers created an extensive array of very long forms. It was difficult for social workers to fill these in and all too often social workers would simply fill in the first page and leave the rest for later. Second, in an attempt to make the forms comprehensive the creators infantilized them. There were tick-boxes for important information and small boxes for complex plans. There was a strange misunderstanding of the complex realities of real children in forms which reduced children to pages of information, much of which appeared meaningless. The forms were laborious for social workers to complete and fairly rapidly they became despised by the children and young people themselves.

However, worse was to follow. Having addressed the problem of data collection and collation in the LAC system the researchers/policy-makers turned to children in need. The Assessment Framework was a thoughtful and helpful attempt to synthesize best practice and research in assessing the needs of children. As such it made a major contribution to improving the practice of social workers. However, the assessment forms that accompanied it were a disaster. They were extremely long, with a profusion of tick-boxes and no space to recognize the needs of children or families holistically. They also increased inordinately the amount of time that social workers spent in completing forms. For instance, in one of the local authorities that we studied a child in need assessment for a family with four children in 1999 might involve four or five typed pages of description with an analysis and recommendation. By the end of 2000 the equivalent assessment required a social worker to complete 128 pages of forms.

There are many problems with this attempt to resolve a problem in professional practice through a bureaucratic solution. First, the burden of paperwork leads to many forms not being completed, and even if they are (and the new computerized systems make it more difficult for workers not to complete them), they are unlikely to be read. This is a major problem for any attempt to improve recording of information. Second, the conceptualization of assessment as the gathering of discrete items of information is simply a misunderstanding of the nature of assessment. As we saw in Chapter 6, assessment is only in part about the collection of information. Processes of understanding and analysing data, putting meaning to information and interrogating one's own assumptions are the core elements of assessment. Yet the focus on forms and information-gathering has profoundly shaped the nature of the social work task. Third, the information collected is largely of little merit. For instance, there are tick-boxes relating to substance misuse. What does a tick indicate? Do different social workers tick for the same reasons? To what degree is there consistency? And if there is no consistency, then how useful is the information?

Unaware of or undeterred by the view of practitioners on the ground the Government and researchers (who were increasingly difficult to differentiate) rolled out computerized versions of the forms. These included the Integrated Children's System (ICS). Completion of forms was also a key way in which local authorities were judged. Performance Indicators required forms to be completed in particular timescales and government inspections concentrated on whether forms were completed without in general meeting the people that the forms related to.

It is only in recent years that the enormous harm that these well-intentioned but fundamentally misguided reforms created is becoming clear. The Government delayed publication of the independent evaluation of the ICS, perhaps in part because it was critical of the ways in which the system was undermining professional judgement (Bell *et al.*, 2007; Shaw *et al.*, 2009). White and colleagues undertook detailed research into the current state of social work practice. Her work described a de-professionalizing and infantilizing system that effectively tied social workers to a computer rather than allowing them to go out and do social work. She estimates that social workers currently spend around 80% of their time in front of a computer screen (White, 2008).

This state of affairs is a profoundly troubling one for the profession of social work. However, it is in its implications for the children and families that social workers engage with that the harmful effects are most likely to be seen. In recent years the high-profile deaths of children such as 'Baby P' have pushed Children's Services into public focus. What emerges is a system that is fundamentally not working. Workers are demoralized, undervalued and – it is said time and again – burdened with paperwork. They are not able to pursue the reason that they came into the profession, namely to help some of the most vulnerable children and families in society. It is little wonder that as a result they do not hang around for long. Turnover – particularly in inner city areas with high levels of deprivation – is at extremely high levels.

These appalling consequences are a result of government policies that were intended to do good. However, they produced the opposite because they relied on a form of 'target'-based central management that undermined and distrusted professional autonomy and attempted to replace it through forms, PIs and inspection. This left social workers tied up by bureaucracy with little room for autonomy and a lack of support for the development of skilled and creative practice. In short, the target culture has been a disaster for Children's Services. Yet is there any alternative?

CRITICAL TRUST AND EVIDENCE-BASED PRACTICE

The findings of earlier chapters point to a different way of managing Children's Services. Here we try to bring them together into a different vision for how Children's Services should be run. It is an approach that focuses on developing and delivering evidence-based interventions. It takes cognizance of Le Grand's critique of professional trust and tries to put in place a more critical form of trust in professional excellence. Central to this vision is research and evaluation of services, not as a luxury or helpful addition but as crucial to ensuring that the highest standards of professional excellence are being achieved and delivered. It is in effect research that provides the critical element that allows us to trust professionals.

It is worth bringing together the findings of previous chapters as a starting point for considering our approach to developing 'critical trust' in professionals. We believe that our review of the evidence – particularly in Part 3 – has suggested that in general professionals who deliver evidence-based approaches will produce better outcomes than those who carry out service as usual, particularly when service as usual is characterized by a primarily bureaucratic and target-driven approach.

Second, evidence-based approaches have many features in common, but in particular they tend to involve good communication skills and a structured approach to facilitating change.

Third, it is hard for practitioners to become skilled in delivering evidence-based interventions. Ensuring that individuals are able to develop the requisite skills requires good training in the interventions as well as regular and in-depth supervision using direct observation of tapes of practice. This should be the norm for all social work students and social workers.

Taken together these suggest a very different direction for improving Children's Services. It emphasizes professional excellence in delivering evidence-based interventions. For social workers to be able to work in evidence-based ways we need to profoundly reform current services. Four changes are particularly important.

First, in order to ensure a supply of social workers able to help others deliver such interventions it is necessary to review the career structure of social work, with a particular focus on retaining and rewarding excellent practitioners through career progression to the level of consultant social worker. Consultant social workers are necessary to ensure we deliver excellent services and also to develop newer and less skilled workers. However, it is crucial that professional progression is tied to clear sets of skills. There has been a tendency for social work to rely on rather vague 'competences'. Evidence-based approaches provide far clearer and more operationalizable definitions of key skills.

Second, research and evaluation should be a fundamental and ongoing element of all practice. This can be carried out by individual social workers to monitor their impact on children and families, but it also needs a substantial element of independent research. For instance, all social workers could use specific standardized instruments with families at point of allocation and at three-monthly intervals. Unlike the forms accompanying the Assessment Framework, such information would have external validity as a measure of changes in child and parent welfare over time.

Third, in order to free social worker time to develop skills there would need to be a major review and cull of current forms and PIs, with only the few essential ones retained. This is likely to be harder to achieve than it might seem. Almost every form or requirement has been developed for a good reason. The problem is that what does not seem to be taken into account is the collective 'opportunity cost' of the time spent completing forms. Thus, while there may be good reasons for a particular form to be completed, there is an overall loss from so much time spent in bureaucracy. Put another way, if White *et al.* (2008) are correct that 80% of social work time is spent in front of a computer, then if this was halved social workers would have three times as much time to do other things. This would be the equivalent of doubling the number of social workers.

Finally, we cannot achieve an evidence-based profession if we do not invest in developing an evidence base. At present each person working in the NHS has about £1,600 spent annually on research and evaluation to support them in delivering the best possible health services. In social care the figure is £25 (Marsh and Fisher, 2005). Unless we invest in finding out what works we will not be able to move away from bureaucratic and managerial approaches.

These reforms would essentially serve to reprofessionalize social work in an effort to allow social workers to deliver evidence-based interventions. The impact of such changes could be monitored to ensure that they were achieving positive outcomes for parents, children and other family members.

We are not alone – or the first – to make recommendations such as these. Indeed, there seems to be a widespread and consistent belief that the current system is fundamentally flawed and a hunger for new and different ways of working. In some trailblazing areas there have been attempts to make reforms based on these ideas. One example is Hackney. Hackney has fundamentally reconfigured its services, so that consultant social workers lead small teams of professionals in delivering evidence-based interventions. Initial indications from the evaluation of the Hackney initiative are very promising (Munro *et al.*, forthcoming). However, Hackney struggles with introducing system change within a wider structure that does not support the delivery of such services. For instance, most of the recruits to consultant social worker positions qualified abroad and at the time of writing it has not been possible to fill all the positions despite a high number of applicants. This suggests a significant skills deficit in social work within the UK, and this requires a fundamental restructuring of the profession to make it more attractive and social work education to make it more rigorous and evidence-based.

A further exciting set of changes are being proposed within Wales. The Welsh Assembly Government is proposing to move towards professionals delivering evidence-based approaches, with specialist teams (Intensive Family Support Services) to act as engines for this change. These teams will initially focus on parental substance misuse, but will use this as a base for creating broader changes towards a more evidence-based approach (Forrester, 2010). This is to be accompanied by a reform of the career structure of social work, with progression up to consultant level being tied to the ability to deliver evidence-based interventions.

These are, then, in some ways exciting times. The current system has become so dysfunctional that there is widespread recognition that it must change. The final report of the Social Work Taskforce (2009) makes some suggestions that are broadly pointing in the right direction. Its 15 recommendations address aspects of the profession from initial recruitment, to the creation of a single, nationally recognized career structure, an overhaul of social work education, new training programmes for front-line management and the creation of a National College of Social Work. The clear statement that the profession needs to concentrate on 'outcomes for service users and quality of service' rather than focusing 'narrowly on tasks and processes, and on meeting indicators' is precisely what social work should be about. The Taskforce report and the National College it is proposing provide an important opportunity for social work to outline a new vision of what social work can and should be. However, sadly lacking from the Taskforce recommendations is a commitment to developing and using evidence-based ways of working. We would argue that at the heart of any vision for social work must be *professional excellence in delivering evidence-based interventions.*

How will this be achieved? The Taskforce lays down some of the basic drivers, such as the calibre of social work entrants and their ability to demonstrate analytical skills, the quality of the social work curriculum and the extent to which employers prioritize evidence-based practice and promote ready access to research findings and collaborations with researchers. Yet it does not go far enough in arguing for the development and use of evidence-based ways of working. A particular gap is the systematic lack of investment in developing an evidence base in social work. The disparity between what the Government and major charities spend on research for each person working in social care and for each person in the NHS (Fisher and Marsh, 2005) is unsupportable. This is a gross and unacceptable level of underfunding, not because it is not 'fair' on social care but because as a result we do not have a strong evidence base for the effectiveness – or cost implications – of much that we currently do. There are strong economic arguments that, even during times of public spending cuts, there should be investment in this area, because without strong research on what works it is likely that we are using a range of interventions that do not work, some of which are likely to be very expensive.

Yet developing a better evidence base is not enough. We also need leadership and systems that are prepared to support the development of evidence-based ways of working. There are indications (for instance, in current developments in Wales and in the Hackney model) that there is an appetite for such approaches. Currently they seem the most exciting attempts to re-imagine and reinvigorate the profession.

We are aware that in a book focusing on a discrete area – namely PSM – we have come to conclusions that appear to go far wider. Indeed, we are explicitly outlining a vision for a fundamentally different structure in Children's Services. Is this warranted, given our substantive focus on substance misuse?

IS SUBSTANCE MISUSE A DISCRETE ISSUE?

In reviewing the findings and recommendations of the book – at both the practice and policy levels – we are struck by the fact that almost all of our recommendations have a broader applicability across Children's Services. For instance, the central dilemma practitioners wrestled with in assessing risk was that the future in unpredictable. This may be particularly pronounced in relation to substance misuse, particularly where individuals may be abstaining but are at risk of relapse, but it is not an issue that is confined to substance misuse. Indeed, in broad terms the problem of the predictability of the future, and our suggestions for managing this by making explicit a range of outcomes, apply to any social work assessment. Similarly, we were struck by the issue of client resistance and effective ways of working with this. In this regard the ability to combine a focus on the parent and simultaneously on the child, and to be both clear about concerns and empathic, were central elements of effective practice. Yet once again these do not seem to be issues that are likely to be confined to substance misuse. On the contrary, these appear likely to be issues that apply across all of social work, with far wider applicability than substance misuse. The same seems to be true in relation to evidence-based practice. There are variations in relation to what works with different issues. However, it is worth noting that in general interventions that work with one issue have a tendency to work with a range of problems. Thus CBT was developed as a treatment for depression, but it appears effective with a wide range of issues. Similarly, MI works in helping those with alcohol problems but there are indications of its effectiveness with a far wider range of problems. Yet across different evidence-based interventions the requirements for effective training and supervision appear fairly consistent. Once again the issues around what works for substance misuse do not appear to be confined to substance misuse.

In broad terms we have tended to conclude that good practice with parental substance misuse is pretty much good practice full stop. There are some specific issues that need to be understood, such as the nature of dependency and the impact of particular substances. However, beyond this, substance misuse is a problem behaviour that is very similar to a range of other problem behaviours. There are obvious parallels, for instance, in relation to working with domestic violence, neglect or challenging teenagers. If this is the case, then the education, training and organizational structures required to deliver effective services for working with parental substance misuse are essentially the same as those required to deliver good practice in any other area.

As such, our concerning findings about the lack of preparation and support for social workers, and the ways in which this hindered them in carrying out their roles effectively, should not be seen to apply solely to substance misuse. They appear likely to be much broader systemic failures in supporting the delivery of effective services. Yet, on a more positive note, in reviewing the literature on what works in the substance misuse field we identified key elements of effective policy and practice that are likely to be applicable across Children's Services. Putting these in place does not just require individual practitioners to read a book such as this and try to improve their practice (though this we hope might be helpful). It also requires each of us to take responsibility for creating services that put good practice and outcomes for children and their parents at the heart of everything they do.

It is because these types of considerations are at the heart of evidence-based interventions that we consider evidence-based practice to be superior to the bureaucratic or managerial approaches tried and found wanting over recent decades. Target-based approaches tend to focus on bureaucratic processes. At the heart of all evidence-based interventions is a focus on what happens when a professional meets a parent or a child. Evidence-based approaches are all about practice: what good practice is, what difference it makes and what is needed to ensure that professionals can deliver it. That is why, despite the fact that they are difficult to deliver effectively and require the highest levels of professionalism, they offer the most promising alternative to the current bureaucratic system. They take the best elements of trusting in professionals, but by emphasizing the role of research and ongoing evaluation they add a crucial critical element. It is this that avoids the danger of complacent practice and services focused on the needs of the professionals rather than clients. As such we have argued for professional excellence in delivering evidence-based interventions as a crucial alternative to the current system. We believe that it is the least that the children and parents described in this book deserve.

References

Advisory Council on the Misuse of Drugs (2003) *Hidden Harm: Responding to the Needs of Children of Problem Drug Users*. Report of an inquiry by the Advisory Council on the Misuse of Drugs, London: Home Office.

Alcohol Concern (2004) *Women and Alcohol*, Factsheet 2, London: Alcohol Concern.

Alcohol Concern (2006) *Parental Alcohol Misuse and the Common Assessment Framework*. www.alcoholconcern.org.uk/files/20060912_130927_CAF.pdf. Accessed 12 March 2008.

Arendt, R. E., Minnes, S. and Singer, L. T. (1996) Fetal cocaine exposure: neurologic effects and sensory-motor delays. *Physical & Occupational Therapy in Pediatrics*, *16*(1–2): 129–44 (doi:10.1080/J006v16n01_09).

Arkowitz, H., Westra, H. A., Miller, W. R. and Rollnick, S. (Eds) (2007) *Motivational Interviewing in the Treatment of Psychological Problems*. New York: Guilford.

Armhein, P. C., Miller, William, R., Yahne, C. E., Palmer, M. and Fulcher, L. (2003) Client commitment language during motivational interviewing predicts drug use outcomes. *Journal of Consulting and Clinical Psychology*, *71*(5): 862–78.

Asay, T. P. and Lambert, M. J. (1999) Therapist relational variables. In D. J. Cain and J. Seeman (Eds.), *Humanistic Psychotherapies: Handbook of Theory and Practice* (pp. 531–57). Washington, DC: American Psychological Association.

Babor, T. F., Caetano, R., Casswell, S., Edwards, G., Giesbrecht, N., Graham, K., Grube, J., Gruenewald, P., Hill, L., Holder, H., Homel, R., Österberg, E., Rehm, J., Room, R. and Rossow, I. (2003) *Alcohol: No Ordinary Commodity – Research and Public Policy*. Oxford and London: Oxford University Press.

Babor, T. F., Higgins-Biddle, J. C., Saunders, J. B. and Monteiro, M. G. (2001) *The Alcohol Use Disorders Identification Test, Guidelines for Use in Primary Care* (second edition). Geneva: World Health Organization. whqlibdoc.who.int/hq/2001/WHO_MSD MSB_01.6a.pdf. Accessed 20 February 2009.

Baird, C. and Wagner, D. (2000) The relative validity of actuarial- or consensus-based risk assessment systems. *Children and Youth Services Review*, *22*(11/12): 839–71.

Bancroft, A., Wilson, S., Cunningham-Burley, S., Backett-Milburn, K. and Masters, H. (2004) *Parental Drug and Alcohol Misuse: Resilience and Transition among Young People*. York: Joseph Rowntree Foundation.

Barnard, M. (2007) *Drug Addiction and Families*. London: Jessica Kingsley.

Barr, A. (1998) *Drink: A Social History*. London: Pimlico.

Bates, T., Buchanan, J., Corby, B. and Young, L. (1999) *Drug Use, Parenting and Child Protection: Towards an Effective Interagency Response*. Liverpool: University of Central Lancashire.

Baumann, D. J., Law, R. J., Sheets, J., Reid, G. and Graham, J. C. (2005) Evaluating the effectiveness of actuarial risk assessment models. *Children and Youth Services Review*, 27: 465–90.

Bell, M., Shaw, I., Sinclair, I., Sloper, P. and Rafferty, J. (2007) *The Integrated Children's System: An Evaluation of the Practice, Process, and Consequences of the ICS in Councils with Social Services Responsibilities*. London: Department for Education.

Berridge, V. (2005) *Temperance: Its History and Impact on Current and Future Alcohol Policy*. York: Joseph Rowntree Foundation.

Bohman, M., Sigvardsson, S. and Cloninger, C. R. (1981) Maternal inheritance of alcohol abuse: cross-fostering analysis of adopted women. *Archives of General Psychiatry*, 38: 965–9.

Brent (1985) *A Child in Trust: The Report of the Inquiry into the Circumstances Surrounding the Death of Jasmine Beckford*. Harrow: London Borough of Brent/ The Kingswood Press.

Brisby, T., Baker, S. and Hedderwick, T. (1997) *Under the Influence: Coping with Parents Who Drink Too Much. A Report on the Needs of the Children of Problem Drinkers*. London: Alcohol Concern.

Brown, J., Cohen, P., Johnson, J. G. and Salzinger, S. (1998) A longitudinal analysis of risk factors for child maltreatment: findings of a 17-year prospective study of officially recorded and self-reported child abuse and neglect. *Child Abuse and Neglect*, 22(11): 1065–78.

Burton, M. (2006) Judicial monitoring of compliance: introducing 'problem solving' approaches to domestic violence courts in England and Wales'. *International Journal of Law, Policy and the Family*, 20: 366–78.

Buster, M. A. and Rodger, J. L. (2000) Genetic and environmental influences on alcohol use: DF analysis of NLSY kinship data. *Journal of Biosocial Science*, 32: 177–89.

Calder, M. C. (2007) The Assessment Framework: a critique and reformulation. In M. C. Calder and S. Hackett, *Assessment in Child Care: Using and Developing Frameworks for Practice*. Plymouth: Russell House.

Camasso, M. and Jagannathan, R. (1995) Prediction accuracy of the Washington and Illinois risk assessment instruments: an application of receiver operating characteristic curve analysis. *Social Work Research*, 19: 174–83.

Carkhuff, R. K. (1969) *Helping and Human Relations*. New York: Human Learning Resource Development.

Chaffin, M., Kelleher, K. and Hollenberg, H (1996) Onset of physical abuse and neglect: psychiatric, substance abuse and social risk factors from prospective community data. *Child Abuse and Neglect*, 20(3): 191–203.

Chase, D. and Fulton Hora, P. (2000) The implications of therapeutic jurisprudence for judicial satisfaction. *Court Review*, Spring: 12–20.

Cleaver, H. and Freeman, P. (1995) *Parental Perspectives in Cases of Suspected Child Abuse*. London: HMSO.

Cleaver, H., Nicholson, D., Tarr S. and Cleaver, D (2007) *Child Protection, Domestic Violence and Parental Substance Misuse*. London: Jessica Kingsley.

Cleaver, H., Unell, I. and Aldgate, J. (1999) *Children's Needs – Parenting Capacity. The Impact of Parental Mental Illness, Problem Alcohol and Drug Use and Domestic Violence on Children's Development*. London: The Stationery Office.

Cleaver, H. and Walker, S. with Meadows, P. (2004) *Assessing Children's Needs and Circumstances. The Impact of the Assessment Framework*, London: Jessica Kingsley

Cloninger, C. R., Bohman, M. and Sigvardsson, S. (1981) Inheritance of alcohol abuse: cross-fostering analysis of adopted men. *Archives of General Psychiatry, 36*: 861–8.

Copello, A., Templeton, L., Orford, J., Velleman, R., Patel, A., Moore, L., MacLeod, J. and Godfrey, C. (2008) The relative efficacy of two levels of a primary care intervention for family members affected by the addiction problem of a close relative: a randomized trial, *Addiction, 104*(1): 49–58.

Coulshed, V. and Orme, J. (1998) *Social Work Practice: An Introduction* (third edition). London: Palgrave Macmillan.

Davies, M. (1994) *The Essential Social Worker: An Introduction to Professional Practice in the 1990s* (second edition). London: Arena.

Department for Children, Schools and Families (2010) *Working Together to Safeguard Children. A Guide to Inter-Agency Working to Safeguard and Promote the Welfare of Children*. London: HM Government, March 2010, publications.dcsf.gov.uk/eOrderingDownload/00305-2010DOM-EN.PDF. Accessed 12 June 2010.

Department of Health (1988) *Protecting Children: A Guide for Social Workers Undertaking a Comprehensive Assessment*. London: HMSO.

Department of Health (1991) *Child Abuse: A Study of Inquiry Reports 1980–1989*. London: HMSO.

Department of Health (2000a) *Assessing Children in Need and their Families: Practice Guidance*. London: Stationery Office.

Department of Health (2000b) *Framework for the Assessment of Children in Need and their Families, Guidance Notes and Glossary for: Referral and Initial Information Record, Initial Assessment Record and Core Assessment Record*. London: The Stationery Office.

Department of Health (2001) *Studies Informing the Framework for the Assessment of Children in Need and their Families*. The Stationery Office; London.

Department of Health, Home Office and Department for Education and Skills (1999) *Working Together to Safeguard Children: A Guide to Inter-Agency Working to Safeguard and Promote the Welfare of Children*. London: HMSO.

Department of Health, Welsh Office and Home Office (1991) *Working Together under the Children Act 1989: A Guide to Arrangements for Inter-Agency Co-operation for the Protection of Children from Abuse*. London: HMSO.

Deren, S. (1986) Children of substance abusers: a review of the literature. *Journal of Substance Abuse Treatment, 3*: 77–94.

Devaney, J. (2009) Chronic child abuse: the characteristics and careers of children caught in the child protection system. *British Journal of Social Work, 39*(1): 24–45; doi:10.1093/bjsw/bcm089.

Dingwall, R., Eekelaar, J. and Murray, T. (1995) *The Protection of Children: State Intervention and Family Life* (second edition). Oxford: Basil Blackwell.

Dion, K. K. and Berscheid, E. (1974) Physical attractiveness and peer perception among children. *Sociometry, 37*(1): 1–12, doi:10.2307/2786463.

Drugscope (2009) Drugscope website: http://www.drugscope.org.uk/.

Edwards, L. P. and Ray, J. A. (2005) Judicial perspectives on family drug treatment courts. *Juvenile and Family Court Journal* (Summer): 1–27.

Elliot, E. and Watson, A. (1998) Responsible carers, problem drug-takers or both? in M. Murphy and N. Harbin (Eds.), *Substance Misuse and Child Care: How to Understand, Assist and Intervene when Drugs Affect Parenting*. Lyme Regis: Russell House.

European Monitoring Centre for Drugs and Drug Addiction (2005) *United Kingdom: New Developments, Trends and In-Depth Information on Selected Issues*. National Report to the EMCDDA by the Reitox National Focal Point, www.drugscope.org. uk/goodpractice/availabilityhome.asp. Accessed 6 September 2006.

FAST (2008) website: http://familiesandschools.org/.

Ferguson, H. (2004) *Protecting Children in Time. Child Abuse, Child Protection and the Consequences of Modernity*. Basingstoke: Palgrave Macmillan.

Forrester, D. (2000) Parental substance misuse and child protection in a British sample. *Child Abuse Review*, 9: 235–46.

Forrester, D. (2001) Prevalence of parental substance misuse in Britain'. *Children Law UK Newsletter*, pp. 4–5.

Forrester, D. (2004) Social work assessments when parents misuse drugs or alcohol (pp. 163–80). In Phillips, R. (Ed.) *Children Exposed to Parental Substance Misuse: Implications for Family Placement*. London: BAAF.

Forrester, D. (2008) Is the care system failing children? *Political Quarterly*, 79(2): 206–11.

Forrester, D. (2010) *Evidence Based Approaches to Working with Families Affected by Parental Substance Misuse*. Report Prepared for the Welsh Assembly Government.

Forrester, D., Cocker, C., Goodman, K., Binnie, C. and Jensch, G. (2009) What is the impact of public care on children's welfare? A review of research findings and their policy implications. *Journal of Social Policy*, 38(3): 439–56.

Forrester, D and Harwin, J. (2004) Social work and parental substance misuse, in R. Phillips (Ed.), *Children Exposed to Parental Substance Misuse: Implications for Family Placement*. London: BAAF.

Forrester, D. and Harwin, J. (2006) Parental substance misuse and child care social work: findings from the first stage of a study of 100 families. *Child and Family Social Work*, 11(4): 325–35.

Forrester, D., Kershaw, S., Moss, H. and Hughes, L. (2008a) Communication skills in child protection: how do social workers talk to parents? *Child and Family Social Work*, 13(1): 41–51.

Forrester, D, McCambridge, J., Waissbein, C., Emlyn-Jones, R. and Rollnick, S. (2008b) Child risk and parental resistance: the impact of training social workers motivational interviewing. *British Journal of Social Work*, 38: 1302–19 (October).

Forrester, D. and Pitcairn, R. (2008) *Evidence Based Practice: A User's Guide*. Community Care Inform website, www.ccinform.articles.

Forrester, D., Pokhrel, S., McDonald, L., Copello, A. and Waissbein, C. (2008c) How to help parents who misuse drugs or alcohol: findings from the evaluation of an Intensive Family Preservation Service, *Child Abuse Review*, 17(6): 410–26.

Forrester, D., Pokhrel, S., McDonald, L., Giannou, D., Waissbein, C., Binnie, C., Jensch, G. and Copello, A. (2008d) *Final Report on the Evaluation of 'Option 2'*. Cardiff: Welsh Assembly Government.

Fransen, G. A. J., Hiddink, G. J., Koelen, M. A., Van Dis, S. J., Drenthen, A. J. M., Van Binsbergen, J. J. and Van Woerkum, C. M. J. (2008) The development of a minimal intervention strategy to address overweight and obesity in adult primary care patients in the Netherlands. *Family Practice*, 25: 1112–15.

Freud, S. ([1894] 1959) The defense neuro-psychoses. In E. Jones (Ed.) *Collected Papers*, J. Riviere (Trans.) (Vol. 1, pp. 59–75). New York: Basic Books.

Galvani, S. (2006) Alcohol and domestic violence: women's views. *Violence against Women*, 12(7): 641–62.

Garrett, K., Heimendinger, J., Barnes, D., and Klushman, B. (2008) Healthy options and personal exploration (hope): results of a telephone counselling study using Motivational Interviewing and print material to address the informational and healthy lifestyle concerns of breast cancer survivors. *Psycho-Oncology*, 17(3): S21.

Gifford, E. and Humphreys, K. (2007) The psychological science of addiction. *Addiction*, 102(3): 352–61 (March), doi: 10.1111/j.1360-0443.2006.01706.x.

Gossop, M. (2006) *Treating Drug Misuse Problems: Evidence of Effectiveness*. National Treatment Agency, www.nta.nhs.uk/uploads/nta_treat_drug_misuse_evidence_effectiveness_2006_rb5.pdf.

Greaves, C. J., Middlebrooke, A., O'Loughlin, L., Holland, S., Piper, J., Steele, A., Gale, T., Hammerton, F. and Daly, M. (2008) Motivational Interviewing for modifying diabetes risk: a randomised controlled trial. *British Journal of General Practice*, 58(553): 535–40.

Green, B. L., Furrer, C. J., Worcel, S. D., Burrus, S. W. M. and Finigan, M. W. (2007a) How effective are family treatment drug courts? results from a four-site national study. *Child Maltreatment*, 12(1): 43–59.

Green, B. L., Rockhill, A. and Furrer, C. J. (2007b) Does substance abuse treatment make a difference for child welfare case outcomes? *Children and Youth Services Review*, 29(4): 460–73.

Greenwich (1987) *A Child in Mind: Protection of Children in a Responsible Society: The Report of the Commission of Inquiry into the Circumstances Surrounding the Death of Kimberley Carlile*. Presented to the London Borough of Greenwich and the Greenwich Health Authority by members of the Commission of Inquiry, Greenwich, London Borough of Greenwich.

Groeneveld, I. F., Proper, K. I., Van Der Beek, A. J., Van Duivenbooden, C. and Van Mechelen, W. (2008) Design of a RCT evaluating the (cost-) effectiveness of a life-style intervention for male construction workers at risk for cardiovascular disease: the health under construction study. *BMC Public Health*, 8

Grove, W. and Meehl, P. (1996) Comparative efficiency of informal (subjective, impressionistic) and formal (mechanical, algorithmic) prediction procedures: the clinical-statistical controversy. *Psychology, Public Policy and Law*, 2(2): 293–323.

Grove, W., Zald, D., Lebow, B., Snitz, B. and Nelson, C. (2000) Clinical versus mechanical prediction: a meta-analysis. *Psychological Assessment*, 12(3): 19–30.

Hall, C., Slembrouck, S. and Saranagi, S. (2006) *Language Practices in Social Work: Categorisation and Accountability in Child Welfare*. Abingdon: Routledge.

Hamer, M. (2005) *Preventing Breakdown: A Manual for Those Working with Families and the Individuals within Them*. Plymouth: Russell House.

Hamilton, C. and Browne, K. (1999) Recurrent maltreatment during childhood: a survey of referrals to police child protection units in England. *Child Maltreatment*, 4(4): 275–86.

Hammersley, R., Finnigan, F. and Millar, K. (1992) Alcohol placebos: you can only fool some of the people all of the time. *Addiction*, *87*(10): 1477–80 (October).

Harbin, F. and Murphy, M. (Eds.) (1998) *Substance Misuse and Child Care: How to Understand, Assist and Intervene When Drugs Affect Parenting*. Lyme Regis: Russell House.

Harford, T. C., Parker, D. A. and Grant, B. F. (1992) Family history, alcohol use and dependence symptoms among young adults in the United States. *Alcoholism: Clinical and Experimental Research*, *16*, 1042–6.

Hart, D. and Powell, J. (2006) *Adult Drug Problems, Children's Needs. Assessing the Impact of Parental Drug Use: A Toolkit for Practitioners*. London: National Children's Bureau.

Harwin, J. *et al.* (2009) *Family Drug and Alcohol Court Evaluation Project: Interim report to the Nuffield Foundation and Home Office*. London: Nuffield Foundation.

Harwin, J. and Ryan, M. (2007) The role of the court in cases concerning parental substance misuse and children at risk of harm. *Journal of Social Welfare and Family Law*, *29*: 277–92.

Hayden, C. (2004) Parental substance misuse and child care social work: research in a city social work department in England. *Child Abuse Review*, *13*(1): 18–30.

Hepburn, M. (2007) Drug use in pregnancy. In I. A. Greer, C. Nelson-Piercy and B. Walters (Eds.), *Maternal Medicine: Medical Problems in Pregnancy*. Philadelphia: Elsevier Health Sciences.

Hetherington, R., Cooper, A., Smith, P. and Wilford, G. (1997) *Protecting Children: Messages from Europe*. Lyme Regis: Russell House Publishing.

Hettema, J., Steele, J. and Miller, W.R. (2005) Motivational Interviewing. *Annual Review of Clinical Psychology*, *1*: 91–111.

Holland, S. (2004) *Child and Family Assessment in Social Work Practice*. London: Sage.

Institute for Family Development (2007) *Key Elements of the Homebuilders Programme*. http://www.institutefamily.org/. Accessed 3 March 2007.

Jacob, T., Waterman, B., Heath, A., True, W., Bucholz, K. K., Haber, R. and Scherrer, J. (2003) New insights using an offspring-of-twins design. *Archives of General Psychiatry*, *60*: 1265–72.

Jellinek, E. M. (1960) *The Disease Concept of Alcoholism*. New Haven, CT: Hillhouse.

Kearney, P., Levin, E. and Rosen, G. (2003) *Alcohol, Drug and Mental Health Problems: Working with Families*. Research Report No. 2. London: SCIE.

Kelleher, K., Chaffin, M., Hollenberg, J. and Fischer, E. (1994) alcohol and drug disorders among physically abusive and neglectful parents in a community based. sample. *American Journal of Public Health*, *84*: 1586–90.

Kempe, R. and Kempe, H. (1978) *Child Abuse*. Cambridge, MA: Harvard University Press.

Kendler, K. S., Heath, A. C., Neale, M. C., Kessler, R. C. and Eaves, L. J. (1992) A population-based twin study of alcoholism in women. *Journal of the American Medical Association*, *268*(14) (14 October).

Kratochwill, T. R., McDonald, L., Levin, J. R, Bear-Tibbetts, H.Y. and Demaray, M. K. (2004) Families and schools together: an experimental analysis of a parent-mediated multi-family group program for American Indian children. *Journal of School Psychology*, *42*(5): 359–83 (September–October).

Kroll, B. and Taylor, A. (2003) *Parental Substance Misuse and Child Welfare*. Chichester: Jessica Kingsley.

Laming, H. (2003) *The Victoria Climbié Inquiry*. London: Department of Health.

Le Grand, J. (2006) *Motivation, Agency, and Public Policy: Of Knights and Knaves, Pawns and Queens*. Oxford: Oxford University Press.

Le Grand, J. (2007) *The Other Invisible Hand: Delivering Public Services Through Choice and Competition*. Princeton, NJ: Princeton University Press.

Lishman, J. (1988) Social work interviews: how effective are they? *Research, Policy and Planning, 5*(2): 1–5.

Luthar, S. S. (Ed.) (2003) *Resilience and Vulnerability adaptation in the Context of Childhood Adversities*. Cambridge: Cambridge University Press.

MacDonald, G. and Sheldon, B. (1998) Changing one's mind: the final frontier? *Issues in Social Work Education, 18*(1): 3–25.

Manning, V., Best, D. W., Faulkner, N. and Titherington, E. (2009) New estimates of the number of children living with substance misusing parents: results from UK national household surveys. *BMC Public Health, 9*: 377 doi:10.1186/1471-2458-9-377.

Marsh, P. and Doel, M. (2005) *The Task-Centred Book*. Routledge and Community Care: Abingdon.

Marsh, P. and Fisher, M. (2005) *Developing the Evidence Base for Social Work and Social Care Practice*. London: Social Care Institute for Excellence. www.SCIE.org. uk.

Mayer, J. and Timms, N. (1970) *The Client Speaks*. London: Routledge & Kegan Paul.

Miller, W. R. and Rollnick, S. (2002) *Motivational Interviewing: Preparing People for Change* (2nd edition). New York: Guilford Press.

Miller, W. R. and Wilbourne, P. L. (2002) Mesa Grande: a methodological analysis of clinical trials of treatments for alcohol use disorders. *Addiction, 97*(3): 265–77 (March).

Miller, W. R., Yahne, C. E., Moyers, T. B., Martinez, J., and Pirratano, M. (2004) A randomized trial of methods to help clinicians learn motivational interviewing. *Journal of Consulting and Clinical Psychology, 72*, 1050–62.

Morse, R. M. and Flavin, D. K. (1992) The definition of alcoholism. The Joint Committee of the National Council on Alcoholism and Drug Dependence and the American Society of Addiction Medicine to Study the Definition and Criteria for the Diagnosis of Alcoholism. *JAMA: The Journal of the American Medical Association, 268*(8): 1012–14, doi:10.1001/jama.268.8.1012. PMID 1501306.

Munro, E. (2002) *Effective Child Protection*. London: Sage.

Munro, E. and others (forthcoming) *Evaluation of Hackney Reclaiming Social Work Reforms*. Hackney: Children's Services.

Murphy, M. and Harbin, N. (Eds.) (2000) *Substance Misuse and Child Care: How to Understand, Assist and Intervene When Drugs Affect Parenting*. Lyme Regis: Russell House.

Nijnatten, C., Hoogsteder, M. and Suurmond, J. (2001) Communication in care and coercion: institutional interactions between family supervisors and parents. *British Journal of Social Work, 31*: 705–20.

Nutt, D., King, L. A., Saulsbury, W. and Blakemore, C. (2007) Development of a rational scale to assess the harm of drugs of potential misuse. *Lancet, 369*: 1047–53.

Olds, D. (2006) The nurse–family partnership: an evidence-based preventive intervention. *Infant Mental Health Journal*, Special Issue: Early Preventive Intervention and Home Visiting *27*(1): 5–25.

Orford, J. (2001) *Excessive Appetites A Psychological View of Addictions* (2nd edition). Chichester: Wiley.

Orford, J., Hodgson, R., Copello, A., John, B., Smith, M., Black, R., Fryer, K., Handforth, L., Alwyn, T., Kerr, C., Thistlethwaite, G. and Slegg, G. for the UKATT Research Team (2006) The clients' perspective on change during treatment for an alcohol problem: qualitative analysis of follow-up interviews in the UK Alcohol Treatment Trial. *Addiction, 101*: 60–8.

Orford, J. (2008) Asking the right questions in the right way: the need for a shift in research on psychological treatments for addiction. *Addiction, 103*(6): 875–85.

Partanen, J., Bruun, K. and Markkanen, T. (1966) *Inheritance of Drinking Behavior.* Helsinki: Finnish Foundation for Alcohol Studies.

Parton, N. (1985) *The Politics of Child Abuse.* London: Macmillan.

Parton, N. (1991) *Governing the Family: Child Care, Child Protection and the State.* London: Macmillan Education.

Parton, N., Thorpe, D. H. and Wattam, C. (1997) *Child Protection: Risk and the Moral Order.* Basingstoke: Macmillan.

Pawson, R. and Tilley, N. (1997) *Realist Evaluation.* London: Sage.

Payne, M. (1997) *Modern Social Work Theory.* Chicago: Lyceum Books.

Pearson, G. (1987a) *The New Heroin Users.* Oxford: Blackwell.

Pearson, G. (1987b) Social deprivation, unemployment and patterns of heroin misuse. In N. Dorn and N. South (Eds.), *A Land Fit For Heroin? Drug Policies, Prevention and Practice.* Basingstoke: Macmillan.

Peters, R. and Barlow, J. (2003) Systematic review of instruments designed to predict child maltreatment during the antenatal and postnatal periods. *Child Abuse Review, 12*: 416–39.

Petrucci, C. (2002) Respect as a component in the judge–defendant interaction in a specialised domestic violence court that utilises therapeutic jurisprudence. *Criminal Law Bulletin, 38*(2): 263–95.

Platt, D. (2006a) Investigation or initial assessment of child concerns? The impact of the refocusing initiative on social work practice. *British Journal of Social Work, 36*(1): 267–81.

Platt, D. (2006b) Threshold decisions: how social workers prioritize referrals of child concern. *Child Abuse Review, 15*(1): 4–18.

Platt, D. (2007) Congruence and cooperation in social workers' assessments of children in need. *Child and Family Social Work, 12*(4): 326–35.

Platt, D. (2008) Care or control? The effects of investigations and initial assessments on the social worker-parent relationship. *Journal of Social Work, 22*(3): 301–15.

Prescott, C. A. and Kendler, K. S. (1999) Genetic and environmental contributions to alcohol abuse and dependence in a population-based sample of male twins. *American Journal of Psychiatry, 156*: 34–40 (January).

Prime Minister's Strategy Unit (2004) *Alcohol Harm Reduction Strategy for England.* London: Cabinet Office; www.strategy.gov.uk/downloads/su.

Quinton, D. and Rutter, M. (1985) Parenting behaviour of mothers raised in care. (pp. 157–201). In A. R. Nicol (Ed.), *Longitudinal Studies in Child Psychology and Psychiatry.* Chichester: Wiley.

Reder, P. and Duncan, S. (1999) *Lost Innocents. A Follow-up Study of Fatal Child Abuse.* London: Routledge.

Reder, P., Duncan, S. and Gray, M (1993) *Beyond Blame: Child Abuse Tragedies Revisited.* London: Routledge.

Robinson, W. and Dunne, M. (1999) *Alcohol, Child Care and Parenting: A Handbook for Practitioners*. London: NSPCC.

Rosenthal, R. (1994) Interpersonal expectancy effects: a 30-year perspective. *Current Directions in Psychological Science*, *3*(6): 176–9.

Royal College of Psychiatrists (2000) *Drugs: Dilemmas and Choices*. London: Gaskell.

Rutter, M. (2003) Genetic influences on risk and protection: implications for understanding resilience. In S. S. Luthar (Ed.), *Resilience and Vulnerability Adaptation in the Context of Childhood Adversities*. Cambridge: Cambridge University Press.

Ryan, M., Harwin, J. and Chamberlain, C. (2006) *Report on the Feasibility of Establishing a Family Drug and Alcohol Court at Wells St Family Proceedings Court*, prepared for LB Islington, Westminster, CAFCASS, Wells St Inner London FPC and Brunel University.

Secretary of State for Social Services (1974) *Report of the Committee of Inquiry into the Care and Supervision Provided in Relation to Maria Colwell*. London: HMSO.

Seden, J. (1997) *Counselling Skills in Social Work Practice*. London: Open University Press.

Sennett, R. (2003) *Respect in a World of Inequality*. London: W. W. Norton.

Shaw, I., Bell, M., Sinclair, I., Sloper, P., Mitchell, W., Dyson, P., Clayden, J. and Rafferty, J (2009) An exemplary scheme? An evaluation of the integrated children's system. *British Journal of Social Work*, doi:10.1093/bjsw/bcp040.

Shlonsky, A. and Wagner, D. (2005) The next step: integrating actuarial risk assessment and clinical judgement into an evidence-based practice framework in CPS case management. *Child and Youth Services Review*, *27*: 409–27.

Social Work Taskforce (2009) *Building a Safe, Confident Future – The Final Report of the Social Work Task Force*. London: Department for Education. http://publications. education.gov.uk/default.aspx.

Stainton Rogers, W., Hevey, D. and Ash, E. (Eds.) (1989) *Child Abuse and Neglect. Facing the Challenge*. London: Open University.

Statham, J., Candappa, M., Simon, A. and Owen, C. (2002) *Trends in Care: Exploring Reasons for the Increase in Children Looked After by Local Authorities*. Understanding Children's Social Care, Number 2, Thomas Coram Research Unit: Institute of Education; London.

Strauss, A. & Corbin, J. (1989) *Basics of qualitative research: Grounded Theory Procedures and Techniques*. London: Sage.

Tappin, D. M., Lumsden, M. A., Gilmour, W. H., Crawford, F., McIntyre, D., Stone, D. H., Webber, R., MacIndoe, S. and Mohammed, E. (2005) Randomised controlled trial of home based motivational interviewing by midwives to help pregnant smokers quit or cut down. *British Medical Journal*, *331* (13 August): 373–7, doi:10.1136/ bmj.331.7513.373.

Taylor, S. (1989) How prevalent is it? In W. Stainton Rogers, D. Hevey, J. Roche, and E. Ash (Eds.), *Child Abuse and Neglect. Facing the Challenge*. London: Open University.

Taylor, A., Toner, P., Templeton, L. and Velleman, R. (2008) Parental alcohol misuse in complex families: the implications for engagement. *British Journal of Social Work*, *38*(5): 843–64.

Thoburn, J., Chand, A. and Procter, J. (2004) *Child Welfare Services for Minority Ethnic Families: The Research Reviewed*. London: Jessica Kingsley.

Thorpe, D. H. (1994). *Evaluating Child Protection*. Buckingham: Open University Press.

Tober, G. (2007) Motivational enhancement therapy in the UK Alcohol Treatment Trial. In G. Tober and D. Raistrick (Eds.), *Motivational Dialogue*. London: Routledge.

Trevithick, P. (2000) *Social Work Skills A Practice Handbook*. Buckingham: Open University Press.

Trotter, C. (1999) *Working with Involuntary Clients A Guide to Practice*. London: Sage.

Turnell, A. and Edwards, S. (1999) *Signs of Safety: A Solution and Safety-oriented Approach to Child Protection Casework*. New York: W. W. Norton.

University of Bath (2003) *Final Report on the Evaluation of the Family Alcohol Service*. Mental Health Research and Development Unit, University of Bath for NSPCC/ARC.

Velleman, R. and Orford, J. (1999) *Risk and Resilience. Adults Who Were the Children of Problem Drinkers*. Amsterdam: OPA.

Velleman, R., Templeton, L., Taylor, A. and Toner, P. (2003) *The Family Alcohol Service: Evaluation of a Pilot*. London: NSPCC www.nspcc.org.uk/Inform/publications/Downloads/familyalcoholservicesummary_wdf48197.pdf.

Ward, H. (Ed.) (1995) *Looking after Children: Research into Practice*, The Second Report to the Department of Health on Assessing Outcomes in Child Care. Norwich: HMSO.

White, S. (2008) JSWEC conference presentation.

Wilding, J. and Barton, M. (2004) *Evaluation of the Strengthening Families, Strengthening Communities Programme 2004/5*. Race Equality Foundation and SCIE, www.parentingacrosscultures.com/research/images/6REF.pdf.

Woolfall, K., Sumnall, H. and McVeigh, J. (2008) *Addressing the Needs of Children of Substance Using Parents: An Evaluation of Families First's Intensive Intervention, Final Report*. Liverpool: John Moores University for Department of Health.

Worcel, S. D., Furrer, C. J., Green, B. L., Burrus, S. W. M. and Finigan, M. W. (2008) Effects of family treatment drug courts on substance abuse and child welfare outcomes. *Child Abuse Review*. Special Issue: *Parental and Young People's Substance Misuse*, 17: 427–43.

World Health Organization (2007a) *Lexicon of Drug and Alcohol Terms*. www.who.int/substance_abuse/terminology/who_lexicon/en. Accessed 8 August 2007.

World Health Organization (2007b) *International Statistical Classification of Diseases and Related Health Problems*, 10th revision. www.who.int/classifications/apps/icd/icd10online. Accessed 8 August 2007.

Zlotnik, J. L. *et al.* (2005) *Factors Influencing Retention of Child Welfare Staff: A Systematic Review of Research*. A Report from the Institute for the Advancement of Social Work Research, in collaboration with University of Maryland.

Index

AA *see* Alcoholics Anonymous
Aboriginals 54–6
actuarial models 87–9
'addiction' 10–12
    definition 10
ADP approaches *see*
    anti-discriminatory approaches
advice 160–1
aggression 79
aims of social work intervention
    154–63
    gathering information 154–7
    obtaining information 157–9
    success in achieving aims 159–63
aims of social worker interviews
    70–86
Alcohol Concern 138
Alcohol Recovery Project 202
Alcohol Use Disorders Identification
    Test 175
Alcoholics Anonymous 13, 133–4,
    160–3, 179–80
alcoholism 9–28
Alice's Adventures in Wonderland 181
allocation of social worker re parental
    substance misuse 60
alternative care arrangements 96–8,
    103–7
    families that changed 103–7
AMA *see* American Medical
    Association
ambivalence 24–7, 193–4, 197
American Medical Association 10–11

analysis in assessment 128–34
    giving meaning to information
        132–4
    specifying range of outcomes
        128–31
    testing capacity for change 131–2
anti-discriminatory approaches 173,
    192–3
anti-oppressive theory 192–3
anti-racism 145
appearance of resilience 109–10
appetitive behaviour *see* 'excessive
    appetites' model
approach to analysis 93–101
    differences in child welfare
        post-referral 98–9
    predicting welfare outcome 99–101
    remaining at home/moving to
        alternative care 96–8
    where children were living
        post-referral 94–6
approaches to understanding resistance
    146–50
appropriateness of MI as an approach
    190–7
arguments in favour of risk assessment
    126–7
asking for parent perspective 156–7
assessing parental substance misuse
    74–5
assessment of child welfare 71–3
assessment framework forms 33, 59,
    132–41, 221–4

Parents Who Misuse Drugs and Alcohol. Effective Interventions in Social Work and Child Protection, 1st edition.   By Donald Forrester and Judith Harwin.
© 2011 John Wiley & Sons, Ltd.

assessment of risk in misuse cases
     127–42
AUDIT *see* Alcohol Use Disorders
     Identification Test

'babies at risk of harm' 94–7, 107
'Baby P' 148, 187–8, 223
background to current study 58–9
Barr, Andrew 11, 19
basic information-gathering 155
battered baby syndrome 53–4
Beckford, Jasmine 123
'being on the wagon' 12
bereavement 20–1
Bill W. 13
binge behaviour 39, 139
binge-eating 11, 17
Blair, Tony 218
buffering 48
bureaucracy out of control 221–4

CAF *see* Common Assessment
     Framework
capacity for change 88–9, 131–2,
     140–1
carer remains same post-referral 103–7
     families change 103–7
Carkhuff's levels of empathy 153
case predictions 89–92
case studies
     Amy 30–1, 34
     Blackburn family 112–15
     Charlie 155–8, 161–6
     Dylan 139–40
     Frame family 108–9
     James family 103–6
     Jenny 29–30, 40, 48
     Jez 29–30
     Lang family 76–8
     Lydia 109–10
     McDonald family 106–7
     Natalie 83
     Patel family 104
     Robin family 110
     Sam 42
     Staccy 83–4
case study analysis 101–2
CBT *see* cognitive behavioural therapy

central tenet of MI 192
     see also understanding client
          resistance; working with
          resistance
challenges for MI in child/family social
     work 197–9
challenges to assessment 84–6
characteristics of effective intervention
     182–3
Child Assessment Framework 33, 59,
     87–9, 120, 132, 221–4
child factors in parental misuse families
     63
child protection 152–4
     research on 152–4
Child Protection Register 54, 57, 60, 63,
     68, 72, 113, 202
child resilience in face of family
     disruption 45–7
child welfare 29–50
     assessment of 71–3
     and impact of parental substance
          misuse 29–50
child-focused assessment 138–9
Children Act 1989 100, 120
'children in need' 103
children's evidence 83–4
Children's Services 53–69
     background to study 58–9
     conclusion 68–9
     how they work with other agencies
          66–8
     introduction 53–7
     nature of research 58
     recent research on social work 57–8
     results of study 60–6
child's remaining at home 96–8
choosing EBP 185
Churchill, Winston 23–4
client minimization 75–9, 144–52
     see also denial; resistance
client relationship with social worker
     81–2
client resistance 146–50
     and family resistance 147–8
client-identified goals 162–3
The Client Speaks 151
Climbié, Victoria 4, 148

Clinton, Bill 41
cognitive behavioural therapy 172, 179, 191–4, 197
collecting information for assessment 134–41
Colwell, Maria 4
'coming down' 36, 147
Common Assessment Framework 121, 135
commonalities and differences in good outcomes 102–11
commonly misused substances 64
communication 151–4
    effective 152–4
comparison groups 175–7
concrete information 139–40
conflict 24–7
confrontation 84–5, 149–50, 195
congruence 149
consequences of child evidence on assessment 83–4
constructive co-working 67–8
Conversation Analysis 152
cooperation creation 92, 163–6
coping mechanisms 32, 133
Core Assessment 135
Counselling Skills in Social Work Practice 145–6
CPR see Child Protection Register
'crack babies' 35, 65–6
crack cocaine 64–8, 94, 104, 107, 111, 212
crack and heroin cases at point of allocation 66
creating cooperation in parents 92, 163–6
criminal conviction 62–3
crisis point 204
critical trust 224–7
'cure' for alcoholism 13
current policy and practice 217–21
current situation in social work 216–28
    critical trust 224–7
    LAC materials 221–4
    policy and practice 217–21
    substance misuse as discrete issue 227–8
current social work theories 144–52
cystic fibrosis 71

decisional matrix 24–6
defence of evidence-based practice 172–4
definitions
    addiction 10–12, 17
    drug misuse 9–10
    drug use 9
    problem drinking/drug-taking 10
    'substance misuse' 9–28
delivery of services 172–4, 217
demonstrating understanding 163–6
denial 75–9, 143–4
    see also resistance
dependence syndrome 11
    see also alcoholism; drug addiction
depressants 38
detox 77, 91
developing heavy use of drugs or alcohol 19–21
development of 'addiction' 21–4
development of physical dependence 23
deviance 55
differences in child welfare post-referral 98–9
differences in statutory basis for allocation 63–4
direct effects of misuse on the child 33
direct harm from parental substance misuse 34–40
    harm in utero 34–5
    prioritization of substance use over child needs 39–40
    result of parent behaviour 36–9
directive approaches 196
disadvantage 62
discussing child with good welfare outcome 110–11
disease model of addiction 12, 197–8
The Disease Concept of Addiction 12
Dodo effect 181–4
    see also understanding the Dodo
doing the assessment 119–42
    arguments in favour of risk assessment 126–7
    assessing risk and need in misuse cases 127–42
    conclusion 142
    history and theory of assessment 121–2

doing the assessment (*cont'd*)
  introduction 119
  poverty of theory 119–21
  research on risk assessment 122–6
doubt 129–31
Dr Bob 13
Drink: A Social History 19
'drinker's check-up' 190
drug addiction 9–28
drug/alcohol misuse: definition 9–10
drug/alcohol use: definition 9
Drugscope 37
duty of care 5

early-onset drinking 15
EBP *see* evidence-based social work
effect of being in a study 183–4
effective communication 152–4
  research on 152–4
effective work with misusing parents
    189–200
effectiveness of MI 190–3
  anti-oppressive theory 192–3
  specific intervention or general
      communication style 193
  understanding/working with client
      resistance is central 192
EIP *see* evidence-informed practice
emotional abuse 39–40, 63, 70, 140
empathy 153–4, 195–6
engaging misusing parents 143–67
English evaluation of Family Drug and
    Alcohol Court 212–13
environmental factors in parental
    misuse families 62
ethics 4
ethnicity 61–2, 66, 94, 192
evaluating work undertaken 187–8
everyday family life 140
evidence in EBP 175–7
  key outcomes 175
  using a comparison group 175–7
evidence-based practice (EBP) *see*
    evidence-based social work
evidence-based social work 168–88,
    225–7
  choosing 185
  critical trust 225–7

defence of 172–4
what counts as evidence in 175–7
what it is 170–2
evidence-informed practice 171
  see also evidence-based social work
Excessive Appetites 12
'excessive appetites' model 6, 17–27
expectations two years after referral
    89–92
extent of the problem 3–8

factors influencing outcomes for
      children 40–50
  child resilience and family disruption
      45–7
  nature of 'welfare outcomes' 41–3
  preventing childhood difficulties
      becoming adulthood
      difficulties 48–50
  risk and resilience factors 43–4
  social situations promoting resilience
      47–8
  substance misuse and family
      disruption 44–5
factors predicting welfare outcome
    99–101
factors preventing childhood difficulties
    becoming adult difficulties 48–50
factors within client 182
false consciousness 55
Families First 202, 207–8
Families and Schools Together 173, 201
families that changed 103–7
Family Alcohol Service 202–4
family disruption 44–7
  child resilience factors 45–7
  protective factors 44–5
Family Drug and Alcohol Court 202,
    209–13
  rationale behind 209
  theoretical underpinnings and US
      evidence base 210–12
  UK evaluation of 212–13
  what it is 209–10
family interventions in misuse cases
    201–15
  conclusion 213–15
  Family Alcohol Service 202–4

intensive family preservation services
    204–13
introduction 201–2
Option 2 204–13
family resistance 147–8
FAS *see* Family Alcohol Service
FAST *see* Families and Schools
    Together
FAT *see* Foetal Alcohol Tendency
FDAC *see* Family Drug and Alcohol
    Court
features of parental substance misuse
    families 60–4
    child factors 63
    differences in statutory basis for
        allocation 63–4
    parental factors 62–3
    similarities with other families 60–1
    social and environmental factors 62
    summary 64
feminism 145
flexible intervention 193
    see also motivational interviewing
focus on child not problem 138–9
focus on quality of intervention 186–7
Foetal Alcohol Syndrome (FAS)
    34, 38
Foetal Alcohol Tendency 34, 38
'forbidden' foods 20
foster care 84, 95
Freud, Sigmund 147–8
fulfilment 49
full assessment 76–8
future behaviour predicated on past
    behaviour 140–1
future of children and parents
        post-referral 93–116
    approach to analysis 93–101
    case study analysis 101–2
    conclusion 115–16
    good welfare outcomes 102–11
    introduction 93
    'mixed' or 'poor' welfare outcomes
        111–15

GA *see* Gamblers Anonymous
Gamblers Anonymous 13
gambling 17, 20, 23

gathering information 154–7
    asking for parent perspective
        156–7
    basic information-gathering 155
    raising concerns 155–6
    specific 139–40
general communication style 193
    see also motivational interviewing
genetic predisposition 13–16, 21, 31
getting 'out of it' 36
giving meaning to information
    132–4
good welfare outcomes 102–11
    child moved 107–11
    same carer 103–7
government assessment frameworks
    87–9
gripe water 19
Grounded Theory 154
guidelines for risk assessment 136–7
    accommodation and home
        environment 136
    family social network 137
    health risks 137
    parental drug use 136
    parents' perception 137
    procurement of drugs 136–7
    provision of basic needs 136
    see also Standing Conference on
        Drug Abuse

harm from substance misuse 34–40
harm *in utero* 34–5
harm prevention 108–9
heavy smoking 34–5
heavy-end allocation 57, 63, 68
helping overcome harm 108–9
helping people with alcohol problems
    177
history of 'addiction' 12–17
history of assessment 121–2
Homebuilders 204–5
Homestart 201
honesty 81–3, 151
    open-mindedness about harm
        82–3
'hopes and fears' approach 90–2,
    128–9

how Children's Services work with
    other agencies 66–8
how parental substance misuse impacts
    on child welfare 32–3
how to gather information 154–7

ICD–10 10–11
ICS *see* Integrated Children's System
IFPS *see* intensive family preservation
    services
impact of misuse on parental behaviour
    36–9
impact of parental substance misuse on
    child welfare 29–50
  conclusion 50
  direct harm from substance misuse
      34–40
  factors influencing outcomes for
      children 40–50
  how substance misuse impacts on
      child welfare 32–3
  introduction 29–32
implications for policy and practice
    184–8
  choosing EBP 185
  evaluate work being done 187–8
  focus on quality of intervention
      186–7
importance of method vs. therapist
    skills 181–2
importance of therapist skills over
    method 181–2
in utero harm 34–5
incorporating doubt 129–31
indirect effects of misuse on the child
    33
influencing outcomes for children
    40–50
information and meaning 132–4
Integrated Children's System 121, 135,
    223
intelligence 45–7
intensive family preservation services
    204–13, 226
  FDAC intervention 209
  theoretical underpinnings and US
      evidence base 210–12

UK evaluation of Family Drug and
    Treatment Court 212–13
what the FDAC intervention is
    209–10
what is Option 2? 205–9
inter-generational links 16
interaction between social worker and
    client 149–50
  see also understanding client
      resistance
Interim Evaluation Report 213
internet use 11, 17
intervention of Family Drug and
    Alcohol Court 209–10
intimidation 79
'involuntary' clients 146

Jellinek, Elvin Morton 12, 23

key definitions of substance misuse
    9–10
key elements of anti-oppressive theory
    192–3
  see also motivational interviewing
key issues in engaging parent 166–7
key outcomes pre- and post-
    intervention 175
kinship placements 107
'Knights and Knaves' 219
knowledge of social worker 79–81

LAC materials 120, 218, 221–4
Le Grand, Julian 218–21, 224
limited assessments 75
'looked after children materials' *see*
    LAC materials
low self-esteem 20–1, 41, 46

Marx, Karl 50
Marxism 145
'Master Craftsmenship' 186
MATCH project 179–80, 183–7
measuring key outcomes pre- and
    post-intervention 175
medical model of addiction 20
mental illness 56, 61, 65, 94
Mesa Grande project 178–85

MET *see* Motivational Enhancement
  Therapy
methods in social worker interviews
  70–86
  assessing parental substance misuse
    74–5
  assessment of child welfare 71–3
  children's evidence and consequences
    for assessment 83–4
  client minimization and denial 75–9
  intimidation 79
  limited assessments 75
  open-mindedness 82–3
  social worker roles and knowledge
    79–81
  social worker–client relationship 81–2
  strategies to deal with challenges
    84–6
methods of working with resistance
  144–52
MI *see* motivational interviewing
Michigan Risk Assessment Model 123
'miracle question' 196–7
miscarriage 34
'mixed' or 'poor' welfare outcomes
  111–15
  child with main same carer 112–15
Motivational Enhancement Therapy
  179–80, 183, 190
motivational interviewing 179, 184,
  189–200
  challenges for MI in child and family
    social work 197–9
  conclusion 200
  introduction 189–90
  reasons why MI is appropriate
    approach 190–7
moving away from main carer 95–6,
  107–11
  appearance of resilience 109–10
  discussion of child with good welfare
    outcome 110–11
  swift action to prevent harm 108–9

NA *see* Narcotics Anonymous
Narcotics Anonymous 13
narrowing of drinking repertoire 22–3

National Children's Bureau 138
National College of Social Work 226
National Health Service 34, 220, 225–6
nature of research 58
nature of 'welfare outcomes' 41–3
needs assessment in misuse cases
  127–42
  analysis in assessment 128–34
  type of information to collect 134–41
  where information should be
    collected from 141–2
negative stereotyping 149
neglect 4, 16, 22, 39–40, 54–5, 63, 140
neonatal abstinence syndrome 34
Neuro-Linguistic Programming 185
The New Heroin Users 14
NHS *see* National Health Service
NLP *see* Neuro-Linguistic Programming
Nobel prize 23
non-cooperation 92, 143–6, 149, 192–4
  see also denial; resistance
non-judgement 13
Nonconformism 12
NSPCC 202
Nuffield Foundation 5, 213

open-mindedness about harm 82–3
opiates 37
opium 19
optimism 78, 129
Option 2 204–13
  what it is 205–9
  see also intensive family preservation
    services
The Orange Book 87, 120
Orford, Jim 6, 11–12, 17–27, 180–2
Orford's model of 'excessive appetites'
  17–27
  conflict and ambivalence 24–7
  developing 'addiction' 21–4
  developing heavy use of drugs or
    alcohol 19–21
  trying out alcohol or drugs 18–19
outcomes for children 40–50
outcomes expected two years after
  referral 89–92
overeating 11, 17

paranoia 150
parental drug use 136
parental factors in parental misuse
    families 62–3
parent–social worker relationship 74,
    194
partnership 81–2
past behaviour as predictor of future
    behaviour 140–1
patterns of consumption 38
patterns of misuse in parental misuse
    sample 64–6
    similarities and differences
            between parental substance
            misuse 65–6
    substances misused 64
    who misused substances 64–5
people who commonly misused
    substances 64–5
personality types 13
persuasion 160–1
pessimism 81
physical dependence 23
post-referral expectations 89–92
post-referral living arrangements 94–6
poverty 35, 48, 170–1
poverty of theory 119–21
predicting welfare outcome 99–101
predictions from assessments 89–92
    expectations two years after referral
    89–92
pregnancy 31, 34–5, 49
prematurity 31, 34
preventing childhood difficulties
    becoming adulthood difficulties
    48–50
preventing harm 108–9
prioritization of substance use over
    child need 32, 39–40
problem behaviour as reward 11, 20
problem drinking/drug-taking:
    definition 10
problem-solving courts 210–12
process of moving away from main
    carer 95–6
procurement of drugs 136–7
producing change 175
    see also evidence-based social work

professional assessment in Children's
    Services 119–21
Project MATCH 179–80, 183–7
protective factors against family
    disruption 44–5
Protestantism 12
provision of basic needs 136
PSM 216–17, 227

quality of intervention 186–7
quasi-experimental trial 175–7, 201,
    206

raising concerns 155–6
raising consequences 161–2
randomized controlled trial 175–7,
    191
range of outcomes 128–31
rationale behind Family Drug and
    Alcohol Court 209
RCT see randomized controlled trial
Reagan, Ronald 41
reasons why MI is appropriate
    approach 190–7
    effectiveness of MI 190–3
    MI in theory and practice 193–7
recent research on social work 57–8
referral 66–8, 89–92, 96–8
regression analysis 94
relapse 14
remaining with same main carer 96–8,
    112–15
    'mixed' or 'poor' welfare outcome
    112–15
research on child protection 152–4
research on risk assessment 122–6
research on social work communication
    151–2
resilience 43–8, 109–10
    child resilience in face of family
            disruption 45–7
    and risk factors 43–4
    social situations that promote
            resilience 47–8
resistance 144–52, 194–5
    and communication 150–1
response to social work intervention
    148–9

results from current study 60–6
    allocation of social worker re
        substance misuse 60
    features of parental misuse families
        60–4
    patterns of misuse in parental misuse
        sample 64–6
review of EBP research findings 177–81
risk 43–4, 53–4
    see also resilience
risk assessment 122–6
risk assessment checklist 125
risks in assessments 89–92
    case predictions 89–92
Rogers, Carl 196
roles of social worker 79–81
'rule of optimism' 78

SBNT *see* Social and Behavioural
    Network Therapy
school as sanctuary 46
SCODA *see* Standing Conference on
    Drug Abuse
'scoring' 32
secrecy 143
self-help 179
self-medication 21
self-worth 46–9
sex 11, 17
sexual abuse 4, 40, 63–4, 67, 109,
    112–13
Shakespeare, William 56
shoplifting 40
similarities between substance misuse
    and other families 60–1
similarities and differences between
    crack and heroin cases 66
similarities and differences between
    parental substance misuse 65–6
similarities in therapist across
    conditions 184
skilful communication 151–4
'slow trudge' of addiction 22–3
Social and Behavioural Network
    Therapy 180, 185, 191
social control 54
social factors in parental misuse
    families 62

social situations promoting resilience
    47–8
Social Work Taskforce 226
social worker aims 154–63
social worker assessments 70–92
    conclusion 92
    interview aims and methods 70–86
    introduction 70
    using information from interviews
        86–92
social worker–client relationship 81–2
Solution Focused Counselling 185
source of information for collection
    141–2
specific information 139–40
specifying a range of outcomes 128–31
Standing Conference on Drug Abuse
    135–7
    guidelines 136–7
Starsky and Hutch 22
strategies to deal with challenges 84–6
Strengthening Families Programme 201
strengths of assessments 89–92
    case predictions 89–92
substance misuse: what it is 9–28
substance misuse as discrete issue 227–8
substance misuse and family disruption
    44–5
substance misuse and impact on parent
    behaviour 36–9
substance misuse treatment 168–88
success in achieving social work aims
    159–63
    advice and persuasion 160–1
    raising consequences/threats 161–2
    support for client-identified goals
        162–3
suicide 71
supervision 86, 134
support for client-identified goals 162–3
SureStart 201
sustained engagement 204
sustained information-gathering 157–9
swift action to prevent harm 108–9

task-centred working 173–4, 197
temperance movement 12–13
testing capacity for change 131–2

Thatcher, Margaret 14
theoretical underpinnings of Family
Drug and Alcohol Court 210–12
theory 87–9
theory of assessment 121–2
theory and practice of MI 193–7
therapist skills 181–2
threatening behaviour 161–2
treatment of substance misuse
168–88
conclusion 188
in defence of EBP 172–4
evidence-based practice (EBP)
169–70
helping people with alcohol problems
177
introduction 168–9
review of research findings 177–81
understanding the Dodo 181–8
what counts as evidence in EBP?
174–7
what is EBP? 170–2
trust 218, 224–7
trying out alcohol or drugs 18–19
12 Steps Programme 13, 179–80
twin studies 15–16
types of drug and effects 37–8
types of information to assess 134–41
focus on child not problem 138–9
past behaviour as predictor of future
behaviour 140–1
specific and concrete information
139–40
understanding everyday family life
140

UKATT project 179–80, 183–7
underfunding 226–7
understanding client resistance 146–50,
192
as central tenet in MI 192
resistance as product of interaction
between social worker and
client 149–50
resistance as response to social work
intervention 148–9
resistance within client or family
147–8

understanding the Dodo 181–8
characteristics of effective
interventions 182–3
client factors 182
effect of being in a study 183–4
implications for policy and practice
184–8
similarities in therapist across both
conditions 184
therapist and skills more important
than methods 181–2
understanding everyday family life
140
unfettered bureaucracy 221–4
unpredictable behaviour 39
unwanted pregnancy 49
US evidence base of FDAC 210–12
use of theory 87–9
using comparison groups 175–7
using information from assessments
86–92
strengths, risk, predictions 89–92
use of theory 87–9

Vietnam War 14
violence 4, 31–2, 35–6, 44–5, 53, 56,
60–4, 71, 96–100

WA see Workaholics Anonymous
'web of disadvantage' 32
welfare outcome prediction 99–101
'welfare outcomes' 41–3
what EBP is 170–2
what 'substance misuse' is 9–28
conclusion 27–8
history of addiction 12–17
introduction 9–10
Orford's model of 'excessive
appetites' 17–27
what addiction is 10–12
what works in engaging misusing
parents 143–67
conclusion 166–7
creating cooperation in parents
163–6
current social work theories
144–52
introduction 143–4

research on effective communication
152–4
social worker aims 154–63
where child lives post-referral 94–6
moving away from main carer 95–6
where information should be collected
from 141–2
Who's Who (Iceland) 41
withdrawal symptoms 23, 26, 37–8
women and drinking levels 18–19

Workaholics Anonymous 13
working with other agencies 66–8
working with resistance 144–52, 192
approaches to understanding client
resistance 146–50
as central tenet in MI 192
discussion 150–1
research on social work
communication 151–2
Working Together 120